P9-EDB-818

The Cooking of the Caribbean Islands

LIFE WORLD LIBRARY
LIFE NATURE LIBRARY
TIME READING PROGRAM
THE LIFE HISTORY OF THE UNITED STATES
LIFE SCIENCE LIBRARY
GREAT AGES OF MAN
TIME-LIFE LIBRARY OF ART
TIME-LIFE LIBRARY OF AMERICA
FOODS OF THE WORLD
THIS FABULOUS CENTURY

Foods of the World

The Cooking of the Caribbean Islands

by

Linda Wolfe

and the Editors of

TIME-LIFE BOOKS

photographed by Richard Meek

TIME-LIFE BOOKS, NEW YORK

THE AUTHOR: Linda Wolfe is the author of *The Literary Gourmet,* published in 1963, a cookbook that investigates the fascination food has always held for fiction writers. Her own fiction has appeared in various literary publications and she has written articles on food for *Gourmet* magazine. Mrs. Wolfe now works for Time Inc. Her daughter Jessica, who appears in this photograph, has often accompanied her on her extensive Caribbean travels.

THE PHOTOGRAPHER: Richard Meek, a member of the original SPORTS ILLUSTRATED photographic staff, is now a freelance photographer who has covered subjects as varied as the America's Cup races, Shaker furniture and the wildlife of the Canadian Rockies. His first major assignment in food photography was *The Cooking of Scandinavia* in the FOODS OF THE WORLD library.

THE CONSULTING EDITOR: Michael Field, who supervised the adapting and writing of recipes for this book, is one of America's leading culinary experts. His books include *Michael Field's Cooking School, Michael Field's Culinary Classics and Improvisations* and *All Manner of Food* (1970).

THE CONSULTANT: Elisabeth Lambert Ortiz lived in Jamaica as a girl and has traveled frequently in the Caribbean. An expert on the cooking of Mexico and South America as well as on that of the islands, she served as principal consultant for *Latin American Cooking* of the FOODS OF THE WORLD library. She contributes articles to *Gourmet* magazine, *House and Garden* and other publications and wrote *The Complete Book of Mexican Cooking.*

THE COVER: Enticing fruits—mangoes, papayas, guavas and the more familiar pineapple, watermelon, bananas and citrus fruits—play an essential role in the cooking of the Caribbean islands.

TIME-LIFE BOOKS

EDITOR: Maitland A. Edey
Executive Editor: Jerry Korn
Text Director: Martin Mann
Art Director: Sheldon Cotler
Chief of Research: Beatrice T. Dobie
Picture Editor: Robert G. Mason
Assistant Text Directors: Ogden Tanner, Diana Hirsh
Assistant Art Director: Arnold C. Holeywell
Assistant Chief of Research: Martha T. Goolrick
Assistant Picture Editor: Melvin L. Scott

PUBLISHER: Walter C. Rohrer
General Manager: John D. McSweeney
Business Manager: John Steven Maxwell
Production Manager: Louis Bronzo

Sales Director: Joan D. Manley
Promotion Director: Beatrice K. Tolleris
Managing Director, International: John A. Millington

FOODS OF THE WORLD

SERIES EDITOR: Richard L. Williams
Series Chief Researcher: Helen Fennell
EDITORIAL STAFF FOR THE COOKING OF THE CARIBBEAN ISLANDS:
Associate Editor: Harvey B. Loomis
Picture Editor: Grace Brynolson
Designer: Albert Sherman
Assistant to Designer: Elise Hilpert
Staff Writer: Gerry Schremp
Chief Researcher: Sarah B. Brash
Researchers: Malabar Brodeur, Marjorie Chester, Patricia Turbes
Test Kitchen Chef: John W. Clancy
Test Kitchen Staff: Fifi Bergman, Sally Darr, Leola Spencer

EDITORIAL PRODUCTION
Color Director: Robert L. Young
Assistant: James J. Cox
Copy Staff: Rosalind Stubenberg, Eleanore W. Karsten, Florence Keith
Picture Department: Dolores A. Littles, Joan Lynch
Traffic: Arthur A. Goldberger

©1970 Time Inc. All rights reserved.
Published simultaneously in Canada.
Library of Congress catalogue card number 75-108615.

The text for this book was written by Linda Wolfe, the recipe instructions by Michael Field, and the picture essays and appendix material by members of the staff. Valuable assistance was provided by the following individuals and departments of Time Inc.: Editorial Production, Robert W. Boyd Jr., Margaret T. Fischer; Editorial Reference, Peter Draz; Picture Collection, Doris O'Neil; Photographic Laboratory, George Karas; TIME-LIFE News Service, Murray J. Gart; Correspondents Maria Vincenza Aloisi (Paris), John Bradley (Jamaica), Nat Carnes (Puerto Rico), Margot Hapgood (London), George Hunte (Barbados), and Johnston Ince (Trinidad).

Contents

The Recipe Booklet that accompanies this volume has been designed for use in the kitchen. It contains all of the 85 recipes in this book plus 58 more. It also has a wipe-clean cover and a spiral binding so that it can either stand up or lie flat when open.

The Island Cuisines Are Finally Coming into Their Own

On a July morning in 1929 I saw for the first time the majestic mountains of Martinique. I was traveling to Tahiti via Panama aboard an intermediate class French steamer; we had been 17 days at sea, and I was anxious to feel firm soil beneath my feet. But I was even more anxious to sample a change of food. The menus on board had been well enough, but you weary of any cuisine after a week, and this particular ship did not pretend to be first rate. The birthplace of the Empress Josephine should surely be able to supply an antidote.

Soon after the ship docked in Fort-de-France I found a café on the main square; the sky was blue, the sun was shining, and the northeast trade wind tempered the midsummer heat. I ordered a rum punch. A waitress set before me a bottle of rum, an earthenware water jug, a small bottle containing some kind of sauce, and a couple of limes. I was invited to help myself. I had, naturally, no idea of how to employ this do-it-yourself kit, and explained this to the waitress. She emitted a high-pitched cackle and gave me my first lesson in concocting the Caribbean's chief potation. First she sliced a lime and squeezed a few drops of its juice into my glass. She then added a minute contribution from the small bottle. It contained cane syrup, I discovered. The rum came next, a two-finger measure. Finally the water.

That is the classic formula for rum punch: one of sour, two of sweet, three of strong and four of weak. The method of making punch varies in the different islands because the flavor of the rum is different everywhere; fruit and other flavors can be added. But I prefer the Martinican method. It is the simplest and the purest and you get the direct flavor of the spirit. On French liners I always order it. And as I sip it, I recall that morning when I first tasted it in Fort-de-France, looking across the *savane* to the white statue of Josephine with its circlet of sentinel palms. Peace descended on my spirit then, and I repeated the punch ritual to make sure I had learned my lesson. I clearly had. My euphoria deepened. "And now," I thought, "for lunch."

Lunch, however, was a very different matter. There was fried fish that was rescued from tastelessness only by the lime juice that I squirted over it; then came two slices of dry overcooked beef that were accompanied by a dish of starchy, flavorless yams and breadfruit. The meal was rounded off by two bananas. It was no better and very little different from the meals that had been served to me on board ship; nor was the wine any better than the *vin compris* Côte de Bourg that had been supplied there. I enjoyed myself because of the setting, because it was a gay and crowded scene, and my spirit was at peace after those two punches. But there was no denying that it had been a very ordinary meal.

That first lunch was to prove typical of many of the meals that I ate in the Caribbean during the next three decades. In the following year I made a five-month tour of the whole area. In 1938 I visited most of the islands that I had missed on that first trip. After World War II, between 1948 and 1958, I went again most years, and I stayed in every kind of hotel and guesthouse; I visited with friends. I always asked for "the special local dish." I always looked forward to my meals; and it is true that I usually enjoyed them. How could I not have in such a setting, either on a shaded porch or high on a veranda, overhung with bougainvillea, looking out "over the bright blue meadow of a bay," my spirits soothed with rum.

And indeed there were many admirable foods to enjoy—particularly the fruits and vegetables. The mango is in a class by itself. Out of the soursop can be made a delicious cool drink—it is almost a soup—with which to begin a lunch. Guava jelly takes the place of marmalade. A cook I had in Martinique greatly enhanced her coffee with a thick white cream she squeezed out of the pulp of the coconut. In St. Lucia I had some excellent wild woodcock. Barbados had its flying fish, Trinidad its pepper pot, a pungent stew that is handed down from one generation to another. Dominica has a bullfrog —called "mountain chicken" in case delicate susceptibilities might be affronted by exact definition—that has a most delicate flavor.

Nevertheless, almost everywhere I went in those days I was reminded of that first, disappointing meal in Fort-de-France. There was an uninspired sameness in most of the food served me, and a lack of distinction in the cooking. I always felt it should have been better somehow, in view of the rich soil and the congenial climate.

The author of this book, Linda Wolfe, formed the same opinion when she first went to the islands in 1958, and in the opening pages she gives the historical reasons for the mediocrity of the cuisine. The greater part of the book, however, is devoted to the changes for the better that have taken place during the 1960s. Partly in response to the tourist boom that has struck the area like a hurricane, and partly out of rising national pride, the West Indians—citizens, restaurateurs and government people alike—have set themselves the task of fostering a cuisine based on the materials available in and peculiar to the islands. They are, Mrs. Wolfe says, achieving remarkable success.

I was fascinated by her account. It is some years since I have been in the islands, and she told me a great deal I did not know. Her book will be invaluable to the tourist. It will tell him what to look for, explain to him what he is being served. It will also encourage local chefs to experiment further.

I have often wondered during recent years whether I should ever go down to the West Indies again. So many of my old friends have vanished, so many familiar beaches have been appropriated by hotels. But now thanks to Mrs. Wolfe I have a powerful inducement to return. With her book in hand, I propose to make a thorough tour of the islands, sampling and savoring the dishes that so long eluded me. It should be one of the most rewarding trips that I have ever made in the Caribbean and I do not propose to hurry it. I am very grateful to Mrs. Wolfe.   —*Alec Waugh*
Mr. Waugh, author of "Island in the Sun," "A Family of Islands" and other books and magazine articles about the West Indies, wrote the volume on "Wines and Spirits" for the Foods of the World Library.

I

A Lively Cuisine in the Making

The first time I traveled the Caribbean was in 1958. My husband and I spent ten days in Puerto Rico and the Virgin Islands, staying at hotels whose dining rooms flaunted plastic greenery embellished with fake tropical fruits—we dubbed them the ReaLemon trees—and whose bedrooms were furnished with teak chairs from Sweden and inexpensive prints of French Impressionist paintings. In the evening we listened to American girl singers in strapless gowns chant pop tunes. And we never once were served, anywhere, a breadfruit, a mango or a papaya.

One evening we decided to escape from hotel living. We drove to the outskirts of San Juan and stopped at an outdoor restaurant where entire families, babies and all, were eating at long tables beneath colored lanterns. In the enclosed courtyard we examined the fare, which turned out to be exclusively land crabs. Caged in large wire-netted pens, the dark clawing creatures looked grotesque but, we reasoned, no more so than the costly sea crabs in our New York fish market. We questioned the restaurant owner and learned that land crabs, which are scavengers, must be purged before they can be eaten. This was accomplished by putting the crabs on a strict three-day diet. The first day of their captivity they were fed coconut, the second day corn and water, and the third corn alone. This coarse, bland food both fattened the crabs and cleansed their innards. Everyone at the restaurant looked happy and hale, so we decided to have our dinner there. The land crabs that were served to us were boiled, removed from their shells, cut into small pieces, and mixed with a sauce that contained garlic, olive oil, coriander leaves and tomatoes. It was an exhilarating new taste to me, the crab meat soft-

Opposite: Framed by palm fronds, a laden Grenadian woman walks along a sun-blanched beach. Her large baskets are filled with smaller baskets in turn full of local spices—allspice, nutmeg, cinnamon and other seasonings closely identified with the Caribbean cuisine. She sells the smaller spice baskets to tourists as souvenirs.

er and more chewy than that of the crab and the sauce glitteringly spicy.

A woman from a nearby table stopped to chat with us and regaled us with a story about Sir Francis Drake, one of the early explorers of the Caribbean. Once Drake and his men lay in ambush on Hispaniola, hoping to attack the Spanish, when they were frightened from their hiding place by the terrifying sound of a cavalry onslaught. They ran back to their boats in alarm only to realize that the sound they had heard was the noisy scuttling of an army of land crabs through the bushes.

We enjoyed that dinner far more than the glazed baked ham, the beef Stroganov and sirloin steaks spawned in our hotel's kitchen, although I admit it wasn't the crabs, or *jueyes,* alone that delighted us. We were also beguiled by the chance to use our bookish Spanish and listen to the silvery sounds of laughing children and guitar-playing fathers.

For me that evening was the beginning of an enduring interest in both the people and the cooking of the Caribbean. At that time it was very difficult to obtain authentic Caribbean food either in the United States or in the Caribbean itself. I knew of one restaurant in New York City operated by a transplanted Trinidadian. It was a tiny, dark, herb-redolent place that was actually the living room of the owner's apartment, a room crowded with students who, like me, enjoyed the inexpensive, filling rice dishes and peppery sauces that were perfect for our budgets.

In the islands themselves there were only a few restaurants that specialized in local food. Hotel dining rooms tended to serve a cuisine billed as Continental, an often unsatisfying version of French cooking based on frozen ingredients from the United States. Although there are hundreds of Caribbean dishes that could have been prepared from fresh ingredients, most hoteliers ignored these and often denigrated native Caribbean food. Indeed, on the night my husband and I returned from our land crab dinner, we mentioned it to the hotel manager, an American, who frowned and said, "You shouldn't have gone there. There's no telling how clean those crabs are."

"Then where," we asked, "is a good place to sample Puerto Rican food?"

"No place," he said. "Because there is none. No decent Puerto Rican food anyway. Except, perhaps, the slice of lime we put in the rum punch."

All of this is different today. At sophisticated new resorts the furniture is made by local craftsmen out of native hardwoods such as *gommier* and *boistibaume,* and on the walls hang island-made patchwork tapestries or intricate hand-woven straw mats. Calypso singers, steel bands and limbo dancers perform nightly at all the bastions of tourism. Throughout the islands those who cater to the needs of the tourist have come to recognize that he *wants* to experience Caribbean culture, that there *is* a culture in the Caribbean worth experiencing, and that one of the most exciting aspects of that culture is its cuisine.

It is a cuisine based on the treasures of the region's rich tropical soil—guava, mango, papaya, pineapple, coconut, okra, cassava, breadfruit, plantain and a host of other exotic fruits and vegetables. It is a cuisine that is at its most successful when dealing with the fruits of the tropical sea, the local spiny lobster, conch, shrimp and endless varieties of fish. Two foods that Europeans did not know about before Columbus explored the Caribbean—tomatoes and hot peppers—give island cooking its most important flavorings. And spiciness and heartiness are the cuisine's most dominant characteristics.

A term often used in relation to Caribbean cooking is "Creole," though it is a word with many meanings. Originally, both in the United States and in the islands, Creole meant a person of pure French or Spanish descent born in the New World. Today in much of the United States and throughout the Caribbean the meaning has been turned around to identify a person of mixed Negro and white descent. Sometimes in the Caribbean it is defined as "all mixed up and born in the islands." That description applies as well to much of the cuisine. Except for delicacies right off a tree or just out of the sea that are served with utter simplicity, the best Caribbean dishes are spicy mixtures of island flavors, blended often with tomatoes, usually with hot peppers and always with imagination.

It would be foolish to claim that the Caribbean cuisine is on a par with the great European cuisines or that it is as well developed as some of the long-established cuisines of the Orient. At the time of their discovery by Columbus in 1492 the islands of the Caribbean were peopled by primitive Indians. Sizable colonies did not exist until some hundred years after that. For the next two centuries wars and piracy and poverty ravaged the islands, inhibiting the development of such graces as an intricate cuisine. Furthermore, what indigenous cooking did exist was buried by colonialist contempt for anything "native"—a derogatory opinion of the local food that to some extent was shared by the natives themselves. Today, with many of the islands newly independent and with more stable economies developing, Caribbean cuisine is beginning to flower. It is a cuisine in the making—enticing, exotic and above all experimental.

For all their proximity to the United States, the Caribbean islands are still a mystery to most Americans, even to those who have visited them. There are more than 7,000 islands in all in the area, some little more than rocks in the sea, some of considerable size. Cuba, the largest, is almost as big as Pennsylvania. Hispaniola, the name for the island that comprises both Haiti and the Dominican Republic, is next biggest, followed by Jamaica and Puerto Rico. These four islands and some 25 other relatively large ones make up most of the land area of the Caribbean; they are known collectively as the West Indies or, sometimes, the Antilles, a name 14th Century Europeans used to describe a group of imaginary islands in the Atlantic.

The West Indies form a grand arc that curves east and south from Cuba, just below Florida, to Trinidad, just off the coast of Venezuela, and that encloses the Caribbean Sea in its mountainous embrace. Though the sea itself covers an area of 750,000 square miles, all the islands would fit easily into an area the size of Wyoming. Geologists say that during the last Ice Age the islands were part of an unbroken isthmus, a land bridge that spanned the distance between Florida and Venezuela. This land bridge was submerged in later times by a cataclysmic series of earthquakes, hurricanes and volcanic eruptions—three furies that still bedevil the region—and only the tops of mountains remained above sea level to form the islands we know today.

The first impression they give, of course, is one of unsurpassing beauty. Columbus, the Caribbean's first foreign intruder, was astonished by the natural splendors of the area and his admiration has been echoed by every traveler since. I myself am overwhelmed every time I go there. First of all, the water

Continued on page 14

GULF OF MEXICO

FLORIDA

Miami ⊙

BAHAMA ISLAND

Havana ⊙

Cardenas ⊙

C

U

B

A

ISLA de PINOS

Manzanillo ⊙

Guantanamo ⊙

Santiago de Cuba ⊙

HIS

ILE de la TORTU

JARDINES de la REINA

G

R

E

A

T

E

R

LITTLE CAYMAN

CAYMAN BRAC

GRAND CAYMAN

HAITI

Montego Bay ⊙

Ocho Rios ⊙

Port Antonio

JAMAICA

Kingston ⊙

Port-au-Prince ⊙

A

N

T

HONDURAS

C

A

R

I

B

B

E

A

N

NICARAGUA

0   100   200   300 miles

COSTA RICA

Cartegena ⊙

PACIFIC

PANAMA CANAL

PANAMA

COLOMBIA

A Garland of Islands Flung across a Tropic Sea

Sailing into the 2,600-mile chain of islands that stretches from Florida to Venezuela to enclose the Caribbean, Columbus thought he had found the Garden of Eden. "Always the land was of the same beauty," he wrote, "and the fields very green and full of an infinity of fruits, as red as scarlet, and everywhere there was the perfume of flowers and the singing of birds, very sweet." Once discovered, nothing that lovely could remain undespoiled. As the pawns of various great powers for nearly five centuries, the islands have become a political patchwork. But their beauty and fruitfulness endure, and the climate that nourishes their rich tropical crops also draws an ever-growing crop of sun seekers.

ATLANTIC OCEAN

ST. THOMAS (U.S.) ST. JOHN (U.S.)

ANEGADA (U.K.)

ANGUILLA (U.K.)

TORTOLA (U.K.) ST. MARTIN (NETH.) (FR.)

San Juan

ST. BARTHELEMY (FR.)

DOMINICAN REPUBLIC

Caguas

Santo Domingo

PUERTO RICO

VIRGIN ISLANDS

BARBUDA (U.K.)

ISLA MONA

Ponce

VIEQUES

SABA (NETH.)

ST. CROIX (U.S.)

ST. EUSTATIUS (NETH.)

St. John's

ANTIGUA (U.K.)

ST. KITTS (U.K.)

NEVIS (U.K.)

MONTSERRAT (U.K.)

GUADELOUPE (FR.)

Pointe-a-Pitre

Basse Terre

MARIE GALANTE (FR.)

AVES (VEN.)

DOMINICA (U.K.)

Roseau

MARTINIQUE (FR.)

Fort de France

Castries

ST. LUCIA (U.K.)

Vieux Fort

ST. VINCENT (U.K.)

BARBADOS

Kingstown

Bridgetown

GRENADINES (U.K.)

ARUBA (NETH.)

CURACAO (NETH.)

St. George's GRENADA (U.K.)

Willemstad

ISLAS los ROQUES

ISLA la BLANQUILLA

BONAIRE (NETH.)

LOS TESTIGOS

Scarborough

TOBAGO

ISLA de MARGARITA

ISLA la TORTUGA

Port of Spain

TRINIDAD

Caracas

VENEZUELA

Crystalline water, smooth beaches, wooded hills plunging into the sea, and the sight of other islands—these are some of the enchantments of the Caribbean. This hawk's-eye view shows Turtle Bay on St. John in the Virgin Islands. The houses are part of the Caneel Bay Plantation, a resort developed by the Rockefeller family.

of the Caribbean is soft and caressing, buoyant and never cold. It is so radiant with sunlight that its color is constantly changing from crystal to aqua to sapphire to emerald—a perpetual rainbow of white, blue and green. Along the water's edge are the beaches that have made the region a tourist mecca. Some are rocky, with great cliffs that thrust down fiercely into the water and make even the experienced swimmer uneasy. Others are long, gentle miles of uninterrupted sand either gleaming white or intense lava black.

The islands' beauty is not just skin deep. Their interiors are lovely too. Some are arid and pricked with cactus; others are gently fertile, with orderly banana groves and fields of waving sugar cane. Still others are crazily overgrown with tumbling vegetation, ferns and palms, flowers and fruits and creepers all entangled. Even more dramatic are the mountains, seemingly too high and weighty for the floating earth that bears them. They rise skyward like cathedrals, and on their slopes are dark chapels of rain forests, mysterious with bird and insect chants.

But perhaps the most breathtaking sight on a Caribbean island is the view of another island. The first time I looked across from one island to another was on Trinidad, where we had been driving in the rain along a scary narrow road. The sea was cloudy and churning all around us. I felt more as if I were

on a ship than on land. Then suddenly the clouds parted and there, quite close, was a great looming shape—the island of Tobago. It startled me, and I have never quite grown used to such sudden ghostly appearances. When I left Martinique by boat, I was sad at leaving its beaches and mountains and one of the few really romantic towns in the Caribbean, Fort-de-France, with its secretive old houses and wrought-iron balconies. But no sooner had Martinique disappeared behind us than there on the horizon was fortresslike Dominica, and my spirits leaped at once at the thought of exploring its forests, its waterfalls and hundreds of streams. From Dominica I could see Guadeloupe, from Guadeloupe the Îles des Saintes. One is really never out of sight of land in the Caribbean and never able to quell one's wanderlust. This is the most compelling of all its qualities, as Columbus himself discovered. Like a tourist confronted with too many travel folders, he wrote, "I saw so many islands that I could not decide to which I would go first." Each island he visited impressed him more than the last with its fertility, its soft breezes, its looming mountains; and time after time he concluded of one island after another, "It is the loveliest thing that I have seen," or, "It is the fairest island that eyes have beheld."

What makes the islands so fair, besides their beauty, is their glorious climate. They bask in the tropic sun, caressed by the boisterous Atlantic Ocean on one side and the gentler Caribbean on the other. They are alternately buffeted and soothed by the trade winds that blow off the ocean, and their tropical heat is often subdued by torrential rains. Though the weather can change dramatically from one minute to the next, climatic conditions in the course of a year are remarkably constant and, with some exceptions, are much the same from island to island. It is a climate in which a man can grow lazy but in which plants grow with abandon. This means that a great variety of trees and plants—including those basic to the cuisine, such as coconut, mango and breadfruit trees, peppers, plantains, sugar cane—grow naturally and profusely from one end of the Caribbean to the other.

The political history of the area has been much less equable than its climate. Today a good many of the islands are self-governing countries. But independence has come to them only in the past few decades. For most of the past four and a half centuries the islands have been under the continuous domination of various European powers. Sometimes a single island successively belonged to several owners. Jamaica was Spanish for 146 years, then English for 307 years; Guadeloupe was Spanish, then English, then French; St. Lucia changed hands six times in 20 years. Not only Spain, England and France, the major colonial powers, but also Holland, Denmark and the United States have owned Caribbean islands.

Because of this pattern of history it has long been customary to view the islands not as a cultural entity but rather as appendages of their European owners. Before I began seeing them for myself I shared this view, particularly as it related to food. I expected that if an island was owned by France or Holland or Spain or England not only the hotel but the local fare would be French or Dutch or Spanish or English.

Then I began traveling among the islands and paying close attention to what I was eating. Sometimes my husband went with me, sometimes I took our daughter Jessica, sometimes I went with friends. I went whenever possible to those islands most famed for their cuisine or for their cultural contribution to the area as a whole—to Jamaica, Trinidad, Barbados, Dominica, Guadeloupe, Martinique, Puerto Rico, the Dominican Republic and Curaçao—though I have not been to two other places that have importantly influenced the region's cooking: I was unable to make arrangements to visit Cuba and unwilling to visit inhospitable Haiti. To understand the cooking on these two islands I have had to content myself with book learning, and eating and talking with Cubans and Haitians living in other parts of the Caribbean and in the United States.

I survived dozens of airports, and—coping haltingly with the various languages of the Caribbean—enjoyed hundreds of meals with friends and new acquaintances and ate in restaurants great and small; and I came to a very surprising conclusion. There *is* a cuisine common to all the islands, whatever their colonial past. It is not accurate, I decided, to discuss the West Indies' cuisine strictly in terms of "Spanish islands," "French islands," "English islands" and so on. Most of us were taught history as the history of nations rather than of peoples, but the fact is that a Martinican does not bear a closer cultural resemblance to a Frenchman than he does to a Jamaican, nor a Curaçaoan a closer resemblance to a Dutchman than to a Puerto Rican.

Caribbean culture and Caribbean cuisine are based not on the various European nations that have ruled there for lengths of time but on four waves of influence shared by all the islands: what might be called intercontinental rather than international waves.

To start with, there were the native inhabitants of the region—Carib and Arawak Indians originally from South America, who had pushed off from what is now Venezuela and the Guianas and spread northward through the islands. They were displaced and dispersed by the settlers who followed upon Columbus' voyages—Spanish soldiers, English pirates, Dutch merchants, Irishmen, Scotsmen, Frenchmen, fortune seekers from everywhere in Europe. After the Europeans came Africans from the Congo, Guinea and the Gold Coast, enslaved and brought in to work the sugar-cane fields the Europeans planted. The blacks were followed by Orientals, indentured servants from China and India. Not all but most islands in the Caribbean have experienced these four waves of settlement, as their mixed populations testify.

You quickly become aware in the Caribbean of how much the races have mixed and, more than that, of how beneficial the results have been for island society. This is a matter of pride for many islanders, whatever their color. I was first struck by this fact one morning some years ago during a visit to Jamaica. I was traveling with a friend, a blue-eyed golden-haired girl. I myself am dark-haired and dark-eyed. The policeman in front of our hotel, trim in his red-striped uniform, greeted us with characteristic Jamaican courtesy. "Good morning," he said as I came out, trailed at some distance by my friend. "It's a lovely morning, isn't it? And you're looking lovely this morning to match it." Then, seeing my companion, he added, "and your sister is too." Priscilla and I laughed. "Sisters?" I asked. "How can we be sisters with her so fair and me so dark?" He laughed and said, "Why not? Jamaica does that all the time to families."

He was exaggerating, but the islanders are indeed ethnically mixed. And so too is their cuisine. The same amalgam of races that created the population created Caribbean cooking.

The first influence was a primitive one. Some of the Indians were farmers of sorts, raising starchy roots like cassava—from which they made bread—sweet potatoes and arrowroot; others were hunters and gatherers of game and fish, of guava and cashew fruit and pineapple. The Europeans had never seen many of these, and they learned the dangers and the delights of native Caribbean foods from the Indians.

But the Indians' foods were not sufficient to sustain the large numbers of European colonists who followed the discoverers. Columbus, charged by the Spanish monarchs with colonial responsibility, learned this quickly, and he soon began demanding that Spain send flour and meat, oil, vinegar and wine. The Spanish priest Las Casas, who came to settle on Hispaniola just eight years after it was discovered, wrote that only the finding of gold—a rare occurrence—brought as much happiness to the colonists there as the arrival of food from Spain. But it was risky to rely on such shipments and so the settlers were forced to experiment with new crops that might take hold in the hospitable climate. Thus they initiated the area's second culinary wave. Many of the foods we now consider virtually synonymous with the word Caribbean, including breadfruit, oranges, limes, mangoes, rice, coffee and even

Overleaf: A typical scene in the Caribbean can be bustling as well as languid. Clustered in the early morning sunlight, farmers and their customers fill noisy Market Square in the town of St. George's, on Grenada. Everybody's Store, which fronts the square, has not even opened for business yet; but the fruit and vegetable sellers—who rose long before dawn to pack up and travel to town in trucks and aboard jitney buses with names like *Show Time* and *St. Andrew's Pride*—are already briskly vending such staples as bananas, plantains, breadfruit, tomatoes, yams and peppers.

sugar cane, were introduced to the West Indies by European colonists.

The next great influence in Caribbean cooking was the result of the influx of African slaves. Fifteen million slaves were imported into the Americas between 1518 and 1865. Exactly how many of these were taken to which islands is not certain, but it is known that during one century at the height of the slave trade two million Africans went to the British West Indies alone. Besides bringing certain foods with them—plants like okra and callaloo, taro and akee—the Africans developed a style of cooking that is basic to Caribbean food today. Because they were so often fed with foods their masters rejected or that were cheap to raise and had little taste, they learned how to flavor their food cleverly. Pungent seasoning and spicing were essential to make poor foods palatable.

Today, no stew on the English-speaking islands starts without the cook's first buying "a bunch of sive," and the "sive," which is scallion, comes tied in a bouquet with parsley or coriander leaves and thyme. On the Spanish-speaking islands dozens of recipes are launched from a similar herb base; dish after dish begins with *sofrito*, a sauce made from annatto seeds, coriander leaves, tiny green peppers, onions, garlic and tomatoes. On all the islands meat and fish are likely to be marinated and seasoned with herbs before anything else is done to them. Ginger, nutmeg, cloves and allspice are heavily used. So is cinnamon; in fact, if you ask simply for "spice" in

Fine French cooking is rare in most of the Caribbean but easy to find on Martinique, where there are several restaurants that could hold their own in Paris. Le Foyal, on the harbor front of Fort-de-France, is one of the best. The waitress is dressed in the old Martinican way, with a traditional "madwas" on her head.

the islands, cinnamon is what you will get. But the most important element in Caribbean seasoning is the hot pepper—which in the United States is more often called the chili pepper. To a palate unfamiliar with them, one hot pepper is indistinguishable from another except to the degree it burns the mouth. But to an islander each variety of hot pepper has a quality and flavor of its own; Jamaicans, for instance, will argue endlessly over the relative virtues of the Scotch bonnet and the country pepper. Good island cooks recognize, however, that even their favorite peppers must be handled with discretion if they are to enhance, not annihilate, other flavors. There is a French Creole story that makes this point, mocking a foolish woman who found that she had no ingredients but hot peppers in her kitchen and who thought that because they were so tasty she could make a palatable soup of them for the family's dinner. Her children took one swallow of the soup, ran to the river to cool their mouths, and drank and drank until they drowned.

The fourth intercontinental wave reached the Caribbean only in the last century. In the early 1800s agitation against the slave system began to be heard in Europe, particularly in England, and pressure was gradually applied to the colonialists to free their slaves. By 1850 the French and English colonies had grudgingly granted emancipation to their slaves. But though they were then offered wages, working conditions were still brutal and degrading, and many ex-slaves chose to leave the fields entirely. Where this occurred, and also on islands such as Trinidad, where large-scale sugar production did not begin until after emancipation, plantation owners desperately needed a new labor force. Their solution was to import large numbers of indentured servants from the Orient, some from China, most from India. Thus the fourth food influence emerged. While curry may have been eaten in the Caribbean before the 1830s, perhaps prepared in the kitchen of an Englishman who knew Indian cooking, its prevalence throughout the region today comes from the presence of East Indians. On some islands, particularly Hispaniola and Puerto Rico, where there were fewer slaves in the first place, there was no Oriental influx. Elsewhere, however, curry has become as Caribbean a dish as it is Indian. The Dutch islanders call it *kerry* and the French islanders call it *colombo*. All agree that they require curry because it causes them to perspire and thus cools off the body.

Other Oriental influences can be seen in the concern with the proper cooking of rice, in the presence of Chinese vegetables in many of the islands' markets, and in the increasing popularity of Trinidadian *roti*, a flat Indian bread, and of Indian dishes like Jamaica's *katarri*, which one Jamaican defined as "an Indian delicacy of Irish potato, rice, and other else things."

It is the interplay of aboriginal, European, African and Oriental influences that has given Caribbean cuisine its shape—an amalgam that can be found on all the islands. Thus a traveler will find many of the same dishes in a Caribbean meal no matter where he eats. To begin at the beginning, there are a number of interesting foods that we would think of as hors d'oeuvre, readily available on most of the islands whether they were once French or Spanish, English or Dutch. My favorite is a crisp vegetable fritter most commonly made of mashed black-eyed peas or beans, perked up with hot peppers and so finely ground and thoroughly beaten before it is deep-fried that it seems to double in bulk like a yeast cake. These ubiquitous fritters are called *cala*

This is the oldest kitchen in the Americas, re-created in Santo Domingo, capital of the Dominican Republic. In 1509 Columbus' son Diego arrived on the island of Hispaniola as viceroy for the Spanish kingdom of Castile and León. His palace, known as the Alcazar, or fortress, was restored in 1957. The kitchen, despite its single fireplace, furnished food even for state dinners.

on the Dutch islands; French and English islanders call them akkra, a name that comes from the African Yoruba language.

In Puerto Rico one's drink is frequently served with fritters of mashed spicy salt fish, called *bacalaitos* or *hojuelas de bacalao*. These are known as *acrat de morue* or *marinades* on the French islands and by a number of wonderful names on the English islands: sometimes poor-man's fritters, sometimes macadam—because some cooks make them flat and tough as pavement —sometimes John Staggerback, for the same reason. On Jamaica the most popular name for the cakes is stamp and go *(Recipe Index)*, an oddity that reflects the Jamaican's penchant for nautical language. The phrase "stamp and go" was a command given to 17th Century English sailors when they were to perform certain duties—to step out at the capstan, for instance, or to haul on a line. The words struck the people's fancy on Jamaica, came ashore, and were put to a new use.

Crisp, finger-thin fried corn sticks called *surullitos (Recipe Index)* in Puerto Rico are also found under a variety of names on different islands. So are *morcillas*, or blood sausages. Called pudding on the English-speaking islands, blood sausage is inevitably paired with souse, which is the lime-marinated meat of pig's head, tongue and trotters. Pudding and souse can be found on the table at Sunday brunch or at an afternoon gathering almost anywhere on Jamaica or Trinidad or Barbados.

I like best the blood pudding of the French islands, perhaps because there they always mix the blood with bread, while on other islands it is sometimes mixed with sweet potatoes, rice or cassava flour instead. Other islanders sometimes seem ashamed of their fondness for this humble dish, but not the French islanders. It is "dear to the Creole heart," says a French island cookbook writer, Marie-Eugenie Bourgeois, and she adds, "It is the snack of one's dreams."

Stuffed land-crab backs are another inter-island first course specialty. The meat of the land crab, which is superior in flavor to the local sea crab, is boiled, minced and sautéed with hot peppers and herbs, spices and bread crumbs, then stuffed invitingly back into the shells. There are any number of ways to vary the ingredients.

Wherever one goes in the Caribbean one will find these dishes and many more, and the experienced island hopper can tell you which specialty he prefers on which island. Curiously, however, when you talk to an islander, he is very likely to tell you that the akkra or the pudding or the crab back is a particular specialty of his island; he is not aware that it is everybody's specialty. This is so partly because the international rivalry that for so long dominated Caribbean history produced intense isolationism; islands were not encouraged to communicate with one another but only with their European owners. I had this dramatically brought home to me one night at dinner on Bar-

The food for a meal at the Alcazar was carried upstairs from the kitchen to this serving room before being taken to the dining room next door. Most of the great Spanish conquistadors visited the Alcazar, perhaps to eat off china such as the emblazoned plate below. "A Castilla y a Leon Nuevo Mundo Dio Colon," it reads, "To Castile and León, Columbus gave a New World."

bados, during which we ate akkra and blood pudding and sautéed sea eggs. My host, a radical who asserted his ties to Africa, declared that he felt not at all English although he was English-educated. Since I was going on to Guadeloupe, I asked him whether he felt any ties to the people on the French islands. I spoke rhetorically, expecting he would of course say yes, we are all African and have all been exploited in similar ways by Europeans. But surprisingly he said, "No. They are French." I argued that they were African by his own definition. "No," he said, and then, "not like us. Perhaps they are from Algeria. In any case they are not like us." I was not surprised, when I was invited to dinner on Guadeloupe a few days later, to be served akkra and blood sausage and sea eggs. The region and the heritage decreed it. And naturally my host explained to me that these delicacies were Guadeloupe's own specialties.

Certainly there are differences in Caribbean cuisine. There are islands that have special dishes not found elsewhere, sometimes because a certain ingredient cannot be grown or obtained elsewhere. There are differences, too, in cooking methods. One Haitian I know swears he cannot abide eating with Jamaicans because, although they cook virtually the same dishes he makes at home, they use coconut oil for sautéeing while Haitians prefer butter and olive oil, in the French style. More important, there are different attitudes toward food. On Barbados an English-descended Barbadian warned me not to bother tasting callaloo—a thick spicy soup that is a local favorite, made of okra, salt pork, crab meat and a leafy spinachlike vegetable that is also called callaloo. But on Guadeloupe a French-descended islander kissed her fingertips at the mention of callaloo. "The Creole cuisine is superb," she glowed, "and callaloo with crab is the king."

There is even a fifth intercontinental wave now in the process of changing the Caribbean culinary scene. It is, of course, the growing wave of tourism. On many islands the tourist boom has brought a general upgrading of the food and an interest in new dishes that draw upon local ingredients in an imaginative way. A hotelier will wrap bacon around banana and produce a new hors d'oeuvre. Or he will offer papaya and prosciutto, a novel variation on the standard melon and prosciutto. Islanders like hot soups, but tourists prefer something cool to start their meals, so to suit them a rainbow of new cold soups has been devised from local ingredients. Chilled orange soup and chilled avocado soup are among the most successful.

The Caribbean is undergoing dynamic changes. Islands that were colonies are becoming independent; islands that survived for centuries on a one-crop economy are growing greater varieties of foodstuffs; islands that were once remote and isolated are now visited daily by travelers from all over the world. There is an exciting, simmering feeling in the Caribbean these days and it certainly can be sensed in food as well as in politics and economics. The situation reminds me of a classic Caribbean dish, pepper pot, a stew the aboriginal Indians made. Kept going on the fire, with new ingredients added each day over the course of weeks or months—or even, legend says, for generations —pepper pot is enhanced by aging. To me Caribbean cooking is itself a figurative pepper pot with new elements constantly being added and the old ones constantly being mixed, refined and absorbed. The pepper pot is aging and the longer it simmers the better it gets.

Opposite: Pudding and souse are a familiar pair throughout the Caribbean, and a good excuse for an afternoon party in this Jamaican home. The pudding is blood, or "black," sausage; the souse is lime-marinated pork. Conveniently for the hostess, the combination may be served at room temperature. Here they are accompanied by a loaf of banana bread and iced drinks.

To make about 2 cups

Vegetable oil or shortening for deep
frying
1 large green plantain (about 1
pound)
Salt

To serve 6 to 8 as a first course

4 pounds fresh pork hocks
1 large onion, peeled and quartered
4 teaspoons salt
1⅓ cups strained fresh lime juice
1 large cucumber
1 teaspoon finely chopped fresh hot
chilies *(caution: see page 46)*
Watercress or whole fresh hot chilies
for garnish
1 to 1½ pounds commercially made
blood sausage (pudding)

Green Plantain Chips *(Jamaica)*

Fill a deep fryer or large, heavy saucepan with vegetable oil or shortening to a depth of 2 or 3 inches and heat to a temperature of 375° on a deep-frying thermometer.

With a small, sharp knife, trim off the ends of the plantain and cut it in half crosswise. Following the diagram on page 55, cut four evenly spaced slits lengthwise in each half. With your fingers pull the skin away from the white bananalike fruit inside and pull or cut off the fibrous strings. Slice the plantain crosswise into paper-thin rounds.

Deep-fry the plantain slices, a dozen or so at a time, for 3 or 4 minutes, turning them with a slotted spoon until they are golden brown on both sides. As they brown, transfer them to paper towels to drain.

Sprinkle with salt and serve the chips warm or at room temperature.

Pudding and Souse *(Trinidad)*
BLOOD SAUSAGE WITH COLD LIME-MARINATED PORK HOCKS

Wash the pork hocks thoroughly under cold running water, then place them in a 6- to 8-quart casserole or pot and pour in enough cold water to cover them by about 1 inch. Bring to a boil over high heat, meanwhile skimming off the scum and foam that rise to the surface. Add the onion and 3 teaspoons of the salt, and reduce the heat to low. Simmer with the lid partially on for about 2 hours. (Keep the hocks covered with water and add more boiling water to the casserole if necessary.) When they are done, they should show no resistance when pierced with the point of a sharp knife. Transfer the hocks to a plate, strain the cooking liquid through a fine sieve set over a bowl, and put it aside.

While the hocks are still warm, remove and discard the skin and bones. Cut the meat into ½-inch cubes, drop them into a bowl, and add 1 cup of the lime juice and the remaining teaspoon of salt. Turn the meat with a spoon to coat it evenly and marinate it in the refrigerator for at least 12 hours, turning the meat occasionally to keep it well moistened.

Before serving, prepare the sauce in the following fashion: With a small, sharp knife or swivel-bladed vegetable parer, trim and peel the cucumber. Grate enough of the cucumber to fill 1 tablespoon and slice the remaining cucumber crosswise into ¼-inch-thick rounds. Set the slices aside.

Combine the grated cucumber, ½ cup of the reserved cooking liquid, the remaining ⅓ cup of lime juice and the chilies in a serving bowl and stir together until well mixed. Taste the sauce and add salt and freshly ground pepper if desired.

To serve, drain the diced meat thoroughly and discard the marinade. Add the meat and the cucumber slices to the sauce and turn them about with a spoon until the pieces are evenly coated. Garnish the bowl with watercress or whole fresh chilies.

The pudding, or blood sausage, which traditionally is served with souse, may be presented whole or peeled, sliced crosswise into ½-inch-thick rounds, and arranged attractively on a platter.

Combining home-grown foods with imported delicacies is a
popular practice among islanders and often produces
unexpected delights such as this colorful first course of fresh
papaya with prosciutto. The fruit is peeled, seeded and cut
into wedges, the prosciutto is sliced paper thin, and the two
are served with a wedge of lime and a sprinkling of capers,
with a pepper grinder handy. *(See box on page 116.)*

To serve 6

1 quart cold chicken stock, fresh or
    canned
2 envelopes unflavored gelatin
2 egg whites, beaten to a froth
3 cups strained fresh orange juice
Salt
1 unpeeled orange, cut crosswise into
    paper-thin slices

To make about 2 dozen 1½-inch
    cakes

½ pound salt cod
2 tablespoons annatto oil *(page 47)*
1 cup finely chopped onions
1 cup flour
1 teaspoon double-acting baking
    powder
½ teaspoon salt
1 egg, lightly beaten
¾ cup milk
1 tablespoon melted butter
2 teaspoons finely chopped fresh hot
    chilies *(caution: see page 46)*
Vegetable oil

Jellied Orange Consommé (Grenada)

With a large spoon, skim the surface of the chicken stock of all fat. Pour the stock into a deep bowl, sprinkle the gelatin on top, and let it soften for 5 minutes. Then pour the stock into a heavy 3- to 4-quart saucepan and add the beaten egg whites. Over high heat, bring the stock to a boil, stirring constantly with a whisk.

When the stock begins to froth and rise, remove the pan from the heat. Let the mixture rest for 5 minutes, then pour it into a large sieve set over a deep bowl and lined with a double thickness of cheesecloth or a dampened kitchen towel.

Allow the liquid to drain through into the bowl without disturbing it at any point. Then stir in the strained orange juice, taste the soup, and season it with salt if desired.

Refrigerate the consommé for at least 4 to 6 hours, or until it is thoroughly chilled and firm enough to hold its shape lightly in a spoon.

Serve the jellied consommé in chilled soup plates and garnish each portion with slices of orange.

Stamp and Go (Jamaica)
CODFISH CAKES

Starting a day ahead, place the cod in a glass, enameled or stainless-steel pan or bowl, cover it with cold water, and soak for at least 12 hours, changing the water 3 or 4 times.

Drain the cod, rinse under cold running water, place in a saucepan, and add enough fresh water to cover the fish by 1 inch. Bring to a boil over high heat. (Taste the water. If it seems excessively salty, drain, cover with fresh water, and bring to a boil again.) Reduce the heat to low and simmer with the saucepan uncovered for about 20 minutes, or until the fish flakes apart easily when prodded gently with a fork. Drain thoroughly. With a small knife, remove and discard any skin and bones and separate the fish into coarse flakes. Set aside.

In a heavy 8- to 10-inch skillet, heat the annatto oil over moderate heat until a light haze forms above it. Add the onions and, stirring frequently, cook for 5 to 8 minutes, or until they are soft and transparent but not brown. Remove the pan from the heat.

Sift the flour, baking powder and salt into a deep bowl. Make a well in the center of the flour and pour the egg, milk and butter into it. With a large spoon mix together only long enough to blend, then add the onions and their oil, the flaked cod and the chilies, and stir until the ingredients are well mixed and form a fairly smooth batter.

Pour vegetable oil to a depth of about ½ inch into a heavy 10- to 12-inch skillet and heat until it is very hot but not smoking.

Drop the batter a tablespoon or so at a time directly into the hot oil. Do not crowd the cakes; the batter will spread quickly into rounds about 1½ inches in diameter. Fry the cakes for about 3 to 4 minutes, turning them with a slotted spoon or spatula until they are golden brown on both sides. As they brown, transfer the cakes to paper towels to drain.

Stamp and go should be served hot or at room temperature either with drinks or as a first course accompanied by "floats" *(Recipe Index)*.

The vivid orange slices are for effect, but the fruit's fresh-squeezed juice is what gives jellied orange consommé its tangy flavor.

Surullitos *(Puerto Rico)*
CHEESE CORN STICKS

Combine the water and salt in a heavy 2- to 3-quart saucepan and bring to a boil over high heat. Stirring constantly, pour in the cornmeal in a slow, thin stream so the water does not stop boiling; continue to stir for 2 or 3 minutes, until the porridge is smooth and thick. Remove the pan from the heat and beat in the grated cheese with the spoon.

Cool to room temperature, then, moistening your hands from time to time in cold water, shape 2 tablespoons of the mixture at a time into cylinders about 3 inches long and 1 inch in diameter. Covered with plastic wrap or wax paper, the *surullitos* may be kept at room temperature for 2 to 3 hours or in the refrigerator for a day or so.

When you are ready to fry the *surullitos*, preheat the oven to the lowest possible temperature and line a large, shallow baking dish with paper towels. In a heavy 10- to 12-inch skillet, heat the oil over high heat until a light haze forms above it. Fry 4 or 5 *surullitos* at a time, turning them with a slotted spoon or spatula for about 5 minutes, or until they are crisp and golden brown. As the corn sticks brown, transfer them to the lined baking dish and keep them warm in the oven.

Serve the *surullitos* hot or at room temperature either as an accompaniment to drinks or as a hot bread.

To make about 2 dozen sticks

3 cups water
2 teaspoons salt
1½ cups yellow cornmeal
1 cup freshly grated imported Edam
   or Gouda or a mild Cheddar
   cheese
1½ cups vegetable oil

29

Crisp fried *bombas de camarones y papas* make substantial appetizers to serve with drinks or as a first course. Shown before, during and after cooking, the *bombas* are cylindrical cakes made from chopped shrimp (*camarones*) and mashed potatoes (*papas*), flavored with grated cheese and onions, and lightly crusted with egg and bread crumbs. The frying oil is being kept hot over the embers of a clay West Indian coal pot.

To make about 14 two-inch-long cylinders

2 medium-sized baking potatoes (about ½ pound), peeled and quartered
4 tablespoons butter, cut into ½-inch bits, plus 2 tablespoons butter
1 cup freshly grated Munster cheese (4 ounces)
1 egg yolk
¼ cup finely chopped fresh parsley
1½ teaspoons salt
¼ teaspoon white pepper
1 pound raw shrimp in their shells
1 cup finely chopped onions
½ cup flour
1 egg, lightly beaten
1 cup soft fresh crumbs made from homemade-type white bread, pulverized in a blender or finely shredded with a fork
Vegetable oil for deep frying

Bombas de Camarones y Papas (*Dominican Republic*)
SHRIMP AND POTATO CAKES

Drop the potatoes into enough lightly salted boiling water to cover them completely, and cook briskly, uncovered, until they are tender and show no resistance when pierced with the point of a sharp knife. Drain the potatoes in a sieve or colander, return them to the pan and slide the pan back and forth over moderate heat for 10 or 15 seconds, until they are completely dry.

Force the potatoes through a ricer set over a deep bowl, or mash them with a fork or potato masher. Add the 4 tablespoons of butter bits, the cheese, egg yolk, parsley, salt and pepper, and beat vigorously with a large wooden spoon until the mixture is smooth. Cover the bowl tightly with foil or plastic wrap and set it aside.

Shell the shrimp. Devein each by making a shallow incision down the back with a small, sharp knife and lifting out the black or white intestinal vein with the point of the knife. Chop the shrimp coarsely.

In a heavy 8- to 10-inch skillet, melt the remaining 2 tablespoons of butter over moderate heat. When the foam begins to subside, drop in the onions and, stirring constantly, cook for about 5 minutes, until they are soft and transparent but not brown. Add the shrimp and stir for 2 or 3 minutes, until they begin to turn pink. Do not overcook. Add the contents of the skillet to the potato mixture and stir together gently. Taste for seasoning.

To form each shrimp cake, flour your hands lightly, scoop up about 3 tablespoons of the shrimp mixture, and shape it into a cylinder about 2 inches long and ¾ inch in diameter. Roll the cylinder in flour and gently brush or shake off the excess. With a pastry brush, paint the entire surface of the cylinder with beaten egg, then dip it into the bread crumbs. As they are shaped and coated, place the *bombas* side by side on wax paper. Refrigerate them for at least 30 minutes to set the coating.

Fill a deep fryer or large, heavy saucepan with oil to a depth of 3 to 4 inches, and heat it to a temperature of 375° on a deep-frying thermometer.

Fry the *bombas* in the hot oil 4 or 5 at a time, turning them about with a slotted spoon for a minute or two until they are golden brown on all sides. As they brown, transfer them to paper towels to drain.

Serve the *bombas* at once, either as an accompaniment to drinks or as a first course.

Pawpaw and Mango Jam *(Antigua)*

Combine the papaya, mango, sugar and lime juice in a heavy 3- to 4-quart enameled or stainless-steel saucepan. Bring to a boil over moderate heat, stirring constantly. Reduce the heat to the lowest possible point and simmer uncovered for 30 to 40 minutes, or until most of the liquid has cooked away and the mixture is thick enough to hold its shape in a spoon. As it begins to thicken, stir it frequently to prevent the jam from sticking to the bottom and sides of the pan.

Remove the pan from the heat. With a large spoon, ladle the jam immediately into hot sterilized canning jars or jelly glasses. Fill each jar to within ⅛ inch of the top and seal it quickly and tightly with its ring and lid. Fill each glass to within ½ inch of the top, and at once pour a thin layer of hot paraffin over the surface of the jam, making sure it covers the jam completely and touches the glass all the way around. Let the glasses rest until the paraffin cools and hardens; then cover them with metal lids.

To make about 1½ pints

1 small (1 pound) firm ripe fresh papaya *(see box, page 116)*, peeled, seeded and cut into ½-inch cubes (about 3 cups)
1 large (1½ pounds) firm ripe fresh mango, peeled, cut away from the stone, and then cut into ½-inch cubes (about 3 cups)
3 cups sugar
3 tablespoons strained fresh lime juice

Escovitch *(Jamaica)*
PICKLED FISH

Combine the onions, carrots, green peppers, bay leaves, red pepper, salt and a few grindings of black pepper in a 3- to 4-quart enameled or stainless-steel saucepan. Pour in the vinegar, 2 tablespoons of the oil and the water, and bring to a boil over high heat. Reduce the heat to low, cover tightly, and simmer for 20 minutes, or until the vegetables are tender but not falling apart.

Meanwhile, pour the remaining 4 tablespoons of oil into a heavy 10- to 12-inch skillet and heat over moderate heat until a light haze forms above it. Add a few fillets of the fish at a time, and cook them for 2 or 3 minutes on each side, or until delicately brown. As they brown, transfer the fillets to a large, shallow heatproof serving dish.

Pour the hot vinegar mixture over the fish, arranging the vegetables evenly and attractively on top. Serve escovitch immediately or cool to room temperature, cover tightly, and refrigerate until thoroughly chilled.

To serve 4 to 6 as a main course or 8 as a first course

4 medium-sized onions, peeled and cut crosswise into paper-thin slices
2 large carrots, scraped and cut into paper-thin rounds
2 medium-sized green peppers, seeded, deribbed and cut into strips 2 inches long and ¼ inch wide
2 medium-sized bay leaves, crumbled
½ teaspoon crushed hot red pepper
1 tablespoon salt
Freshly ground black pepper
½ cup white wine vinegar
6 tablespoons olive oil
2 cups cold water
2 pounds skinned and filleted red snapper

II

Legacy of the Earliest Islanders

Caribbean islanders, like people in tropical climates everywhere, have a taste for fiery food. The Carib Indians were making hot pepper sauce even before Columbus arrived, and today every island cook has her own version. As this sampling shows, the sauces may be red tomato mixtures or golden turmeric blends; some are chunky and others are puréed. But all have peppers, and all are hot.

The first Europeans in America had to rely heavily upon the Caribbean Indians in learning about the foods of their strange new world. Bizarre plants and animals bewildered the newcomers, who found almost every growing thing to be different from what they knew. The Indians could afford to be generous, both with information about how to survive and with actual offers of food itself, and Columbus himself praised them for this. "Of anything that they possess," he wrote, "they invite you to share it and show as much love as if their hearts went with it." Before long the lot of the Caribbean Indians changed drastically for the worse, but most of the foods they introduced to the Spaniards, as well as some of their primitive ways of cooking, still figure in the islands' cuisine. And the Indians that are left today are still generous, as I discovered when I received an explorer's welcome from some of them on the island of Dominica.

When Columbus sailed into the Caribbean Sea, its islands were inhabited by several hundred thousand Indians, divided into two main groups, the placid Arawaks and the belligerent Caribs; both soon learned the dangers of being hospitable to the invaders. The Arawaks were cruelly exploited and were almost exterminated within a few generations. The Caribs, seasoned by their skirmishes with other tribes, took on the Spanish and later the French and English and fought longer than any other Indian tribe in the New World, including the North American Apaches.

But inexorably they were driven from island to island until finally, harmless in their reduced numbers and tempered disposition, they were allowed to settle in a few scattered groups. One survives on Trinidad, near the town of Arima; the biggest group exists in the mountainous obscurity of the north side of Dominica, the most rugged sizable island of the Caribbean. Fifteen hundred Caribs live there, though probably fewer than one hundred of them are pure blooded, since they have intermarried so much with the island's Negroes. Even so, the Caribs act like a race. They have their elected chief and they deal separately with the island's government.

When my husband and I visited their reserve on Dominica, we were accompanied by a young Carib boy named Faustulus Frederick. He was an artist, as were his two brothers Masclem and John, and we had seen their spare, expressive drawings of the life of their people in a local newspaper. We sought them out, and when Faustulus learned I was interested in Carib cooking he offered to introduce me to his mother, "the best cook I know."

We were on our way to meet her, wandering among the helter-skelter wooden cabins on the Carib reserve, when we passed the home of our guide's uncle. The family was having its one meal of the day. Faustulus' aunt and uncle and two young nieces were squatting on the ground outside their cabin, heels under their haunches, balancing their bowls in their laps. They were eating boiled green bananas topped with a yellow egg sauce. Beside the head of the family was piled the dessert, a mound of green coconuts.

Faustulus introduced me to the family, and immediately they gestured at the coconuts. "They want you to have one," Faustulus explained. "Oh, no," I said. "They have so few." But they repeated the offer, and Faustulus said, "They say you look hot and thirsty. They want you to have one."

We accepted, of course, and this meant that their pile of coconuts disappeared, for they gave one to me, one to my husband, one to our driver and one to Faustulus. We squatted beside them and drank the sweet, cooling coconut water, and smiled and communicated our gratitude without words. When we stood up to leave, Faustulus' uncle got up too and went off into the bush with his machete to gather more coconuts for his family. I was touched, and wondered whether I would have given up the last of the milk in my own house to passing strangers if it meant going to the store during the meal to feed my own family.

The generosity of the Indians centuries ago in sharing their knowledge of the local fruits and plants and wildlife smoothed the way for the European explorers, who thus learned painlessly which foods were poisonous, which were life sustaining, which were delicacies. In some cases the Indians were directly responsible for the survival of the adventurers.

There are many accounts of this. The most touching—a true story immortalized by Richard Steele in the *Spectator Papers*—is about a Carib Indian girl named Yarico who saved the life of a young English colonist, Thomas Inkle. They met in 1647 when the ship in which Inkle had set out to make his fortune in the New World ran into difficulties somewhere along the Spanish Main—the old name for those parts of the Central and South American mainland that touch the Caribbean Sea. Inkle and other members of the ship's company were forced to land, but as they came ashore they were attacked by hostile Indians who killed all except Inkle. Wounded, the young man managed to escape to a remote part of the forest and was lying there, exhausted, when Yarico came upon him. "If the European was highly charmed with the limbs, features and wild graces of the naked American," wrote

Steele, "the American was no less taken with the dress, complexion and shape of a European, covered from head to foot." Yarico fell in love with this covered-up man at first sight and determined to save his life, even from her own people. "She therefore," the story continues, "conveyed him to a cave where she gave him a delicious repast of fruits."

Inkle regained his strength under her careful nursing and eventually the lovers came to understand each other's language. Inkle communicated to his mistress how happy he would be to have her in his country, saying that there she would be clothed in such silks as his waistcoat was made of, and be carried in houses drawn by horses. Yarico agreed to go with him wherever he went and one night succeeded in signaling to a European vessel anchored off the coast. She and Inkle were taken aboard and they set sail for Barbados. But then greed asserted itself in the young fortune seeker. When the ship reached Barbados, Inkle reflected on how his loss of time during his dalliance with Yarico had cost him money, "upon which consideration the prudent and frugal young man sold Yarico to a Barbadian merchant."

This kind of betrayal occurred in one form or another for two centuries until there was no vestige of trust between Indian and European. By then the Europeans had learned to sustain themselves handsomely and they needed no Yarico to help them; they had long since come to value and take advantage of the New World foods the Indians had bestowed on them.

These are the same foods that the present-day Caribbean cuisine still honors as its legacy from the Indians. There are many fruits, for instance, that had never been seen by a European before Columbus' voyage: the avocado, the cashew fruit, the soursop, the mamey, the papaya, the guava and the pineapple. The last named is perhaps the Indians' greatest fruit gift to the world. Gonzalo Fernández de Oviedo, one of the earliest settlers to write about the plants of the New World, recognized its quality immediately and went to great lengths to explain that although the pineapple grew on plants that were like thistles, it was "in taste one of the best fruits in the world. . .for those who are surfeited and do not wish to eat, it is an excellent appetizer."

The pineapple originated in South America and moved along with the Caribs when they migrated to the islands. They esteemed it highly, and like many of their favorite foods it took on a significance beyond its power to nourish. During puberty rites, Carib boys were made to run between rows of spiky pineapple spears to prove their bravery. The fruit itself, when placed on the doors of their huts, served as a symbol of hospitality to strangers. Europeans soon carried the idea back with them to the architects of Spain and England, who made the pineapple a favorite colonial-era motif for decorating gateposts and door lintels. The fruit itself gained a welcome the world around, and was one of the first plants to be carried from America westward across the Pacific. For many people, of course, Hawaii has now become synonymous with pineapple, which, ironically, did not even get to the Polynesian islands until the late 19th Century.

Another delicacy the Indians shared with their invaders has remained a local treasure. This is the mangrove-tree oyster, which grows on the roots of mangrove trees along muddy riverbanks and beaches. Sir Walter Raleigh came upon this phenomenon in Trinidad on a fortune-seeking voyage in 1595 and reported it to Queen Elizabeth on his return to England. He was almost laughed out of court—whoever heard of oysters growing on trees! But

Raised off the ground on wooden pilings and shored up by poles, this Carib Indian house on Dominica reflects the hazards of Caribbean housebuilding. The poles keep it from blowing over in heavy storms; the pilings discourage mongooses as well as the island's voracious termites. John Frederick, 20 years old, drew this sketch of his family's two-room home; its kitchen is in a separate shack a few yards away.

there is no doubting either the oysters' existence or excellence. The method of harvesting them is to cut an underwater root or branch and scrape off the dozens of clustered mollusks growing on it. The oysters are elongated and smaller than most familiar oysters—not more than two inches long. They are extremely tender and refreshing, and it takes a great many to satisfy an aficionado's appetite for them. In Puerto Rico years ago lovers of the *ostione*, as it is locally known, used to ride from San Juan all the way across the island to Bocheron to buy them from harvesters; they would then consume them by the hundreds at a picnic. Now, refrigeration has made it possible for some of San Juan's better seafood restaurants to serve *ostiones*, and they are a specialty well worth the trouble of finding.

The Indian cuisine was too primitive to have contributed many prepared foods to posterity, but one that has survived intact throughout the islands is cassava bread. Cassava, which is called by many names, among them yuca and manioc, is a starchy tuber that was the staple food of most of the Caribbean Indians. It was either boiled and eaten as we eat potatoes, or ground, made into meal, and baked into bread.

Because it was their "staff of life," cassava was revered by the Indians. In a 1554 Spanish history of the Indies, an Indian agricultural ceremony is described in which cassava bread is blessed by Indian priests and pieces of the blessed bread are divided among all the Indians present. Just as some Jews preserve a bit of the Passover matzoh from one year's holiday to the next to ensure their presence at the next year's festivities, so the Indians who received cassava bread at this ceremony preserved it in the belief that a family who did not do so was vulnerable to many dangers throughout the ensuing year.

Their veneration of cassava is understandable: It could not only sustain life but could also take it away. For cassava—there are two kinds, sweet and bitter—contains in its juice varying quantities of prussic acid. This can be removed by cooking or pressing, but the bitter cassava root contains enough acid so that if it is eaten raw it can be fatally poisonous. A common method the Arawak Indians used to escape the torments of their Spanish overlords was to commit suicide by eating raw cassava.

Sweet cassava when boiled has a bland, pleasant flavor, something like a moist white potato. In the islands today it is a frequent accompaniment to meat and is at its best when sprinkled with salt, freshly ground black pepper and a bit of lime juice. It can also be prepared in all the ways Irish potatoes are —mashed, creamed, fried, or made into croquettes. But the most important product of cassava is bread. It is sold on all the islands and can be obtained in the United States in cities where there is a sizable Puerto Rican, Jamaican or Mexican population. Baked in a flat, round shape, it has an earthy flavor and is eaten plain or, in a favorite Jamaican variation, is fried in butter as a breakfast dish. Slightly different from the bread are the wafers made of cassava and served as accompaniments to soups. These chips (Recipe Index) are also round and flat, but they, unlike the bread, have a crisp, airy lightness.

Although the Indians in the Carib reserve on Dominica have very few possessions, every woman owns the necessary equipment for making cassava bread. I watched it being used by Faustulus Frederick's mother during my visit to her village. A stately woman in her mid-40s, Mrs. Frederick lived in a two-room cabin that was spotlessly clean and tidy, and very sparsely furnished: just a table and chairs, a chest of drawers and a wood-slatted bed without a mattress. She did have a radio, as did all her neighbors, and it was to the sound of "The Blue Danube" waltz that we inspected her kitchen.

Like the old Carib kitchens, it was outside the house itself—part of it simply outdoors, among the banana and coconut trees, and part of it in a separate cook shack so that if the open cooking fire spread, it would not destroy the house proper. In the shack were a few pots and pans, a three-foot-tall wooden mortar for grinding coffee beans, and the utensils for making cassava bread. First Mrs. Frederick showed me the grater, a wooden-backed steel device with jagged teeth. I feared for her hand when she demonstrated it but she laughed at me; I should have seen her mother's grater, she said; that one was just rusty nails hammered into a piece of wood.

Then Mrs. Frederick explained the bread-making process. After the cassava is grated it is heaped in a cassava canoe, a wooden receptacle shaped like the dugout canoes for which the Caribs are famous. Later the gratings are thoroughly squeezed through a cloth to press out the poisonous juices, and are left to dry in the sun. Next they are passed through a sifter made of woven roots to get the meal to a consistent fineness. The cassava is then ready for "baking." Actually it is not baked but is cooked on a griddle pancake style. (Like her neighbors, Mrs. Frederick uses a rough-edged circular piece of miscellaneous metal as a griddle.) Finally the bread is thoroughly dried in the sun until it has a hard, crusty texture throughout. Although non-

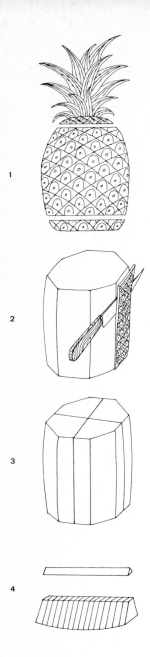

HOW TO PREPARE PINEAPPLE WEDGES
A quick way to peel, core and cut a
fresh pineapple into wedges is shown
in these drawings. First lay the fruit
on its side and, grasping it firmly
with one hand, slice off the leafy
crown and the base with a large, sharp
knife (1). Then stand the pineapple
on end and slice off the prickly rind
in seven or eight downward strokes,
cutting deep enough each time to
remove the eyes (2). Now divide the
fruit into quarters (3), and cut the
triangular section of core away from
each quarter. Lay each quarter on its
side and slice it crosswise into wedges
of the desired thickness (4).

Carib islanders use more modern methods—they may grate the tubers in a
blender and cook them on greased griddles over a gas flame—local cookbooks still recommend drying the bread under the tropical sun.

In the outdoor part of Mrs. Frederick's kitchen is her work surface, a
board nailed between two trees at a convenient height, and her larder, consisting simply of a tomato plant and a hot pepper plant, one growing at
each end of the work table. She needs only to reach out her arm, she showed
me, to obtain the best fresh ingredients for her soups and stews.

Both these plants figure strongly in Caribbean cooking, but the pepper is
perhaps the single most important ingredient in the cuisine. The Indians
were using capsicum peppers in their cooking when the Spaniards arrived.
The plant grows profusely on the islands, and its fruit comes in every imag-
inable shape, size, color and degree of pungency and is turned into
innumerable varieties of pepper sauces by the islanders. The Caribs were accomplished pepper-sauce makers. Not knowing how to extract salt from the
sea, they flavored their food with *coui,* a sauce of hot peppers and cassava
juice. The addiction has persisted: All West Indians like hot peppers in their
food, and when a dish is not spicy enough they reach for the ever-present bottle of hot sauce. This is made in most homes by steeping diced hot peppers
in vinegar. They may also be soaked in rum or sherry, but every island, indeed every Caribbean kitchen, has its own variation on the theme.

There are few records of other seasonings used by the Indians in their cooking, though it is known that sweet basil, purslane and watercress grew on
the islands. The Europeans found another spice, one they had never seen before, growing wild on many of the islands. They decided it tasted like a combination of cinnamon, nutmeg and clove, and so it got its name—allspice.
Also known as Jamaica pepper, allspice still grows in profusion on that island, which supplies a good share of the world's supply.

There is another now-popular spice that the Indians put to curious use.
The seed of the annatto, a graceful, red-flowering tree, makes an excellent
dye; the Indians mixed it with oil and used it to paint their bodies. Its purpose was partly decorative—some historians think it was the American
Indians' use of this dye that earned them the name "redskins"—but also functional: The Indians wore no clothes and were constantly exposed to the sun
and to insect bites. Annatto oil protected them from both.

In time annatto achieved a culinary importance. Like saffron, it lends a delicate flavor and a strong color to food, and on the Spanish-speaking islands,
where it is called *achiote,* the seed came to be used as a base for sauces.
Today it is an essential ingredient in a great many Puerto Rican dishes. The
dried seeds are stirred into a small amount of lard or oil until a vivid red-
orange color is obtained. The seeds are then removed and into the reddened
oil go the chopped leaf of the coriander plant (which in Spanish is called *cilantro*), tiny sweet peppers, onions, garlic, tomatoes and sometimes salt pork.
These are simmered in the oil to make a sauce called *sofrito.* (There is a Spanish sauce of the same name that does not include annatto.) Now Puerto
Rican cooking begins. *Asapao, arroz con pollo,* Puerto Rican *ropa vieja,* and
all kinds of vegetable dishes start with the making of *sofrito.* Annatto is used
on other Caribbean islands as well (it is called *rou-cou* on Trinidad, Martinique and Guadeloupe) but on Puerto Rico it is as essential as salt is to us.

The Indians' culinary legacy to the modern Caribbean cuisine includes two methods of cooking. To cook a fish or bird, the Indians coated it with mud and baked it in an ash fire made in a pit dug into the sand. When the creature was sufficiently done its mud jacket was scraped away; this pulled off the scales or feathers as well, leaving the flesh clean and unaffected by contact with the fire. On Guadeloupe, among people who live in beachfront houses, the method is still popular for cooking fish for twilight picnics. A large fish, generally a red snapper, is preferred. Thyme and hot peppers are placed between its skin and flesh, then mud is tightly packed around the fish; it is placed on hot ashes in a pit, covered with sand and slowly baked while the guests laze in the evening's cool.

The Indians' other cooking legacy is one to which every enthusiastic backyard chef in America owes an appreciative salute. For it is from the Caribbean Indians that the word barbecue comes. An Arawak *barbacoa* was a grating of thin green sticks upon which meat was grilled above an open fire. (The Arawaks also used the word for a stick-frame bed they made in the same fashion.) The Indians sliced their meat into thin strips, laid it upon the *barbacoa* and cooked it slowly, exposing it to the smoke of the wood fire below, which was constantly enhanced with the fat of the animal. Cooked and cured in this way, meat took on a more interesting flavor than that obtained by the South American Indians, who cured their meat by drying it in the sun. Some writers have suggested that our word barbecue comes from the French *barbe à queue,* or beard to tail, reasoning that barbecuing sometimes involves spitting whole animals across a cooking fire. I prefer the view of most authorities, that we took the word from the Arawak.

To cook meat on a *barbacoa* was, in the language of the early settlers, to boucan. By another curious etymological twist, it is from this word that the pirates who plagued Spanish shipping of the 17th Century took their name —buccaneers. Except for the few who struck it rich, these adventurers lived among the Indians in almost as wild a fashion. They sustained themselves by boucaning the islands' birds, small game and fish just as the Indians did.

One of the first men to report on the Indian methods of cooking was Père Labat, an extraordinary French priest who lived in the Caribbean in the late 1600s. Garrulous, argumentative, humorous, inquisitive about everything from priestly intrigue to gardening, Labat wrote a memoir of life in the islands that is one of the most fascinating of all travel books. An inordinate number of Labat's stories deal with food, and I was puzzled by his preoccupation until I saw a portrait of him. Round-faced and fat as any Chaucerian priest, Labat was plainly a man for whom food was Experience.

My favorite Labat story is one he tells about the day he gave a boucan picnic for some fellow priests. It was held in a forest on Martinique, and all the guests had to pretend to be buccaneers. Their fare was a pig, barbecued in Indian and pirate fashion. No metal implements were permitted, no plates, dishes, spoons or forks. "Even tablecloths are forbidden," the priest's rules read, "as they are too much at variance with buccaneer simplicity."

The guests arrived at 9 a.m. and were immediately put to work constructing the *barbacoa* and building a fire under it. After the fire burned down to charcoal the pig was laid on its back upon the *barbacoa,* its belly up and open and sprinkled with lime juice, salt and crushed allspice. When the pig was ready, the priests said a blessing and "sat down at a table so solid that noth-

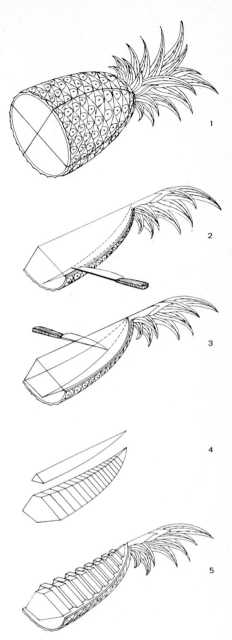

HOW TO PREPARE PINEAPPLE BOATS
A fancy way to serve fresh pineapple is to cut it apart and then reassemble the fruit in four boatlike pieces of rind. First lay the pineapple on its side and cut off the base with a large sharp knife. Then, slicing right through the leafy crown, divide the pineapple lengthwise into quarters (1). Make diagonal cuts into the quarters from each side to separate the fruit from the rind (2 and 3). Lift out each strip of fruit, cut away the core along the top, and slice the fruit crosswise into wedges (4). Return the fruit to the rinds, staggering the wedges decoratively (5).

ing but an earthquake could have shaken it, for our table was the earth itself." There were a few unauthentic touches at the picnic for which Labat apologized: "I had provided napkins and bread though this is really contrary to the rules, for real buccaneers know not the meaning of napkins and use only baked plantains for bread."

But in one respect there was total authenticity. The priests played their roles of buccaneers to the hilt by drinking their wine neat—not, as in their usual fashion, mixing it with water. It must have been a hilarious afternoon, and Labat is at his wittiest describing it. "I do not think it necessary to inform the reader that one of the essential things in a boucan is to drink frequently. The law compels it, the sauce invites one to do so, and few err in this respect. But since man is frail and would often fall if he had no one to remind him of his duty and correct him, the master of the boucan has to watch his party. Should he find anyone idle or negligent he must at once call everybody's attention to the fact. The delinquent must then do penance by drinking from the large calabash, no mean punishment since this calabash is always kept full of wine."

Like Labat, the Indians considered pork the most desirable meat for boucaning—though it has been said that the savage Caribs preferred the barbecued limbs of an enemy. Visitors among the Caribs testified to this, and one writer even discussed with the Indians their favorite victims. He reported that they found the French to be the most delicate in flavor, the Spanish stringy and likely to produce indigestion.

The few Indians remaining today rarely barbecue or boucan anything because it is increasingly difficult to obtain game on the islands and they are too poor to buy meat. However, they have developed over the years one dish that is a highlight of Caribbean cuisine and has been adopted and adapted by all other comers to the island: pepper pot *(Recipe Index)*. If you are traveling in the islands and haven't been invited to someone's home to discover its delights, the best place to sample pepper pot is in the Trinidadian restaurant called The Tropical, which serves some of the finest West Indian food in the islands. The Tropical offers curried chicken, stuffed crab back, crisp akkras, thick vegetable soups. But its best dish is pepper pot, the gift of the Indians.

The traditional pepper pot is a stew, not to be confused with a soup of the same name widely popular on Jamaica and other islands today. The latter has vegetables in it, which Indian pepper pot has not. What it does have is meat, though one never knows what kind it might be—sometimes a wild creature, sometimes beef or pork, sometimes chicken or oxtail and calf's head. Or all of these.

Pepper pot does have one ingredient besides the meat, however, that makes it different from any other stew. This is cassareep, a juice obtained from cassava root. Cassareep gives pepper pot a flavor that is almost impossible to describe; a flavor often called "subtle" or "haunting" or simply "indescribable." I decided to try to be more specific one day, and prepared some cassareep and carefully tasted it. It was bitter, certainly, but more, a mysterious something I could not define. Just then my daughter Jessica came in and asked to taste, too. I warned her she wouldn't like it—and, indeed, she didn't, but she said, "It isn't bitter, Mommy; it's sweet, too sweet." And then she said, with a five-year-old's certainty, "It's both. It's sweet and bitter. How strange." And I realized that that was it, the haunting, subtle flavor of pepper pot—a finely balanced tug of war between bitter and sweet.

I find it ironic that the basis of pepper pot is the juice of cassava roots: The substance that brought death for suicide-bent Arawaks prolongs life for the last lingering Caribs. I was moved by this thought when I went to the small town of Arima on Trinidad, and visited the ancient lady who is the titular "queen" of Trinidad's remaining Caribs. She is Edith Martinez, a wizened woman in her late 70s whose mother was queen before her. The hereditary title passes through the maternal line, so Queen Edith expects her eldest daughter to become queen too. Not too soon, though, she cautions. Her own mother lived to 113 and she herself feels as sprightly as a girl.

The day I met her she had dressed for the occasion. She was wearing three-inch spike-heeled shoes and a pink lace dress, undoubtedly bought years ago when she was not so stooped, that came down almost to her ankles. I was glad, for my daughter was with me, and when she first saw the queen's one-room wooden house she refused to believe we were going to meet a queen; but she suspended all her disbelief when the old woman appeared. The length of the dress convinced Jessica that here indeed was a queen.

I myself needed only to speak with her to be convinced. She spoke about her people with royal concern, and we talked of the help she longed to give

Fresh from a Trinidadian garden, this bouquet displays some of the spices, herbs and roots available to Caribbean cooks. Most of them are used for flavoring; the basilisk, worm grass and jumbie balsam, however, are steeped to make tea.

1 Parsley	8 Annatto
2 Thyme	9 Anise
3 Broad-leaved	flowers
thyme	10 Chives
4 Thyme	11 Spanish
5 Basilisk	thyme
6 Worm grass	12 Geranium
7 Jumbie	13 Anise
balsam	14 Bay leaf

her people—food, education, a place in the town of Arima that would offer them shelter when they came down from the hills. Then we talked about cooking, one of Queen Edith's favorite occupations. She showed me her dirt-floored kitchen. Despite its meager equipment, its open fireplace and crude cassava-grating tools, it was clearly a well-loved province.

"What do you like to cook?" I asked. "Cassava bread," she said proudly. "That's our own bread. The Caribs' bread. Although lots of other people eat it now too." I nodded to show that I knew about it. "What do you have with it?" I asked. "A stew we make with cassava juice," she said. "Some people call it pepper pot. We make it whenever we can afford to buy meat. Or if we catch some." She explained further: "We keep it going on the fire a long time so when there's a pot of it if someone's hungry he can eat any time of day." Then, looking troubled, she added: "And if we don't have pepper pot, we have whatever we can find."

The Indians are finding less and less. They are the poorest outcasts of the islands; quite possibly, despite belated governmental efforts to honor and protect them, the Caribs will be as extinct as the Arawaks within a few generations. Yet both peoples live on—in the sense that their foods live on as part of the present. For barbecuing, for cassava bread and hot pepper sauce, for pepper pot and a host of herbs and fruits, all the islanders today, of whatever background, owe the Indians a debt of gratitude.

The Arawak Indians, who were part of the aboriginal population of the Caribbean islands, produced pottery and sculptures marked by a lively expressiveness. This water jug, showing a distorted human form, was found in an ancient burial mound in southern Trinidad. It had been placed there, along with food and other domestic amenities, to help ease the passage of an Arawak soul to the world of the dead.

Sopa de Frijol Negro (Cuba)

BLACK BEAN SOUP

In a large sieve or colander, wash the beans under cold running water until the draining water runs clear. Transfer the beans to a heavy 3- to 4-quart casserole, add 1 tablespoon of salt, and pour in enough water to cover the beans by at least 2 inches. Bring to a boil over high heat, reduce the heat to low, cover partially and simmer for 2 to 3 hours, or until the beans are tender enough to be mashed against the sides of the pan with a spoon.

Drain the beans through a large sieve or colander set over a bowl and put them aside to cool to room temperature. Add enough chicken stock to the bean-cooking liquid to make 6 cups.

When the beans have cooled, combine 1 cup of beans and 1 cup of the liquid at a time in the jar of an electric blender. Blend at high speed until the beans are pulverized, but do not purée them too finely. As you proceed, scrape the mixture into a large bowl or pan with a rubber spatula. (To purée the beans by hand, rub them through a food mill into a deep bowl or press them through a fine sieve with a spoon. Stir the liquid into the purée.)

In a heavy 4- to 5-quart casserole, heat the annatto oil over moderate heat until a light haze forms above it. Add the onions and garlic and, stirring frequently, cook for 5 minutes, until they are soft and transparent but not brown. Stir in the ham, tomatoes, vinegar, cumin and a few grindings of pepper. Bring to a boil and, stirring frequently, cook briskly until the mixture thickens enough to coat the spoon heavily. Add the bean purée and simmer over low heat for 15 minutes, or until the soup is heated through.

Taste for seasoning. Ladle the soup into a large tureen or individual soup plates and serve it at once.

Sopa de Gandules (Puerto Rico)

GREEN PIGEON PEA SOUP

In a heavy 3- to 4-quart casserole, fry the salt pork over moderate heat, turning the dice about with a spoon until they are crisp and brown and have rendered all their fat. Remove the dice and discard them.

Add the onions and garlic to the fat remaining in the casserole and, stirring frequently, cook over moderate heat for 5 minutes, until they are soft and transparent but not brown. Drop in the tomato, green pepper and ham; cover and simmer for 5 minutes longer. Stir the pumpkin, stock and green pigeon peas into the casserole. Bring to a boil over high heat, reduce the heat to low, cover tightly, and simmer for 20 minutes, until the soup thickens and the pumpkin is soft and begins to fall apart. The soup should still be somewhat lumpy. Taste and season with salt and pepper. Ladle into a heated tureen or individual soup plates, and serve at once.

NOTE: To prepare fresh tomatoes, drop the tomato into a pan of boiling water and remove it after 15 seconds. Run it under cold water, and peel it with a small, sharp knife. Cut out the stem, then slice the tomato in half crosswise. Squeeze the halves gently to remove the seeds and juice, and chop the tomato coarsely.

To serve 6 to 8

2 cups (1 pound) dried black beans
Salt
2 to 4 cups chicken stock, fresh or canned
2 tablespoons annatto oil *(page 47)*
1 cup finely chopped onions
2 teaspoons finely chopped garlic
8 ounces finely chopped lean cooked ham (about 2 cups)
1 large firm ripe tomato, peeled, seeded and finely chopped *(see sopa de gandules, below)*, or ½ cup chopped drained canned tomatoes
2 tablespoons malt vinegar
½ teaspoon ground cumin
Freshly ground black pepper

To serve 6

4 ounces lean salt pork, cut into ¼-inch dice (about 1 cup)
1 cup finely chopped onions
1 teaspoon finely chopped garlic
1 large firm ripe tomato, peeled, seeded and coarsely chopped, or substitute ½ cup chopped drained canned tomatoes
1 medium-sized green pepper, seeded, deribbed and finely chopped
4 ounces lean boneless cooked ham, cut into ¼-inch dice (about 1 cup)
1 pound fresh West Indian pumpkin (calabaza, *see Glossary, page 197*), or substitute Hubbard or other winter squash, peeled, seeded and cut into ½-inch dice (about 3 cups)
1 quart chicken stock, fresh or canned
A 1-pound can of green pigeon peas *(gandules)* with their liquid
Salt
Freshly ground black pepper

These three steamy soups are almost meals in themselves. Jamaican callaloo, with crabmeat, is at top left and center right. *Saucochi di gallinja*, a chicken-vegetable soup of Aruba, is at top right and center left. Cuban black bean soup is in the middle.

To serve 6 to 8

A 5- to 5½-pound stewing fowl,
  trimmed of excess fat and cut
  into 8 to 12 serving pieces
1 fresh pig's foot (about ½ pound)
2 quarts water
2 teaspoons salt
3 pounds boneless fresh pork
  shoulder, or lean boneless beef,
  cut into 2-inch cubes
½ cup cassareep (*opposite*)
1 large onion, peeled and cut
  crosswise into ¼-inch-thick slices
2 tablespoons dark-brown sugar
2 whole fresh hot chilies (*caution:
  see page 46*)
A 2-inch piece of stick cinnamon
4 whole cloves
¼ teaspoon crumbled dried thyme
1 tablespoon malt vinegar

Pepper Pot (*Trinidad*)
CHICKEN AND PORK STEW

Place the fowl and the pig's foot in a heavy 8- to 10-quart casserole and pour the water over them. The water should cover them by about 1 inch; add more if necessary. Add the salt and bring to a boil over high heat, skimming off the foam and scum as they rise to the surface. Reduce the heat to low, cover partially, and simmer for about 1 hour, or until the bird is almost tender and shows only the slightest resistance when pierced with the point of a small, sharp knife.

With a large spoon, skim as much fat as possible from the surface of the soup. Stir in the pork cubes, cassareep, onion, brown sugar, chilies, cinnamon, cloves and thyme. Bring to a boil over high heat, reduce the heat to moderate and, stirring occasionally, cook partially covered for about 30 minutes longer, or until the fowl and pork are tender. Remove the chilies, cinnamon and cloves with a slotted spoon and discard them. Stir in the vinegar and taste for seasoning.

Mound the pieces of pork, pig's foot and fowl attractively on a deep heated platter and pour the sauce remaining in the casserole over them. Serve the pepper pot at once, accompanied, if you like, by boiled potatoes, yams or cassava biscuits (*Recipe Index*).

44

Callaloo (Barbados)
CRAB AND GREENS SOUP

Wash the callaloo greens (or spinach or chard) under cold running water and discard any discolored leaves. Leave the callaloo greens whole but, if you are using spinach or chard, bunch the leaves together and shred them into fine strips.

In a heavy 4- to 5-quart casserole, melt the butter over moderate heat. Add the onions and garlic and, stirring frequently, cook for 5 minutes, until they are soft and transparent but not brown. Add the greens and turn them about with a spoon for 4 or 5 minutes, until they glisten with butter and become somewhat limp.

Stir in the stock, coconut milk, salt and a few grindings of pepper. Bring to a boil over high heat, reduce the heat to low, and simmer uncovered for about 10 minutes, or until the greens are tender. Add the crab meat and A-1 or Pickapeppa, and stir for 2 or 3 minutes to heat the crab through.

Taste for seasoning and serve at once, from a heated tureen or in individual soup plates.

Cassareep

With a small, sharp knife or swivel-bladed vegetable parer, peel the brown fibrous bark off the white flesh of the cassava root. Cut the cassava root in half and with a stand-up hand grater, finely grate one half of it into a deep bowl lined with a double thickness of dampened cheesecloth. Bring the ends of the cheesecloth together to enclose the pulp, and wring the cloth vigorously to squeeze the cassava juice into the bowl. Discard the pulp (or use in cassava biscuits or *brazo gitano, Recipe Index*). Grate and squeeze the remaining half of the cassava in a similar fashion.

Transfer the entire contents of the bowl to a small, heavy skillet. Stirring constantly, cook over moderate heat for about 1 minute, until the cassareep is smooth and thick enough to hold its shape almost solidly in the spoon.

NOTE: The amount of liquid in the cassava may vary, depending on the age and quality of the roots available. If there are any small dark flecks or spots of mold in the flesh of the cassava, the root is old and will yield little if any juice.

Saucochi di Gallinja (Aruba)
CHICKEN AND VEGETABLE SOUP

Combine the chicken and fresh stock (or canned beefstock and water) in a heavy 6- to 8-quart casserole and bring to a boil over high heat. With a large spoon, skim off the foam and scum as they rise to the surface. Reduce the heat to low, cover partially, and simmer for 45 minutes.

Skim as much fat from the soup as possible, then add the tomatoes, corn, yams, boiling potatoes, pumpkin (or squash), peas, chilies, salt and pepper. Bring the *saucochi* to a boil again, reduce the heat and simmer partially covered for about 20 minutes longer, or until the chicken and vegetables are tender but still intact.

Taste the soup for seasoning and stir in the chives. Serve at once from a heated tureen or individual soup plates.

To serve 4 to 6

½ pound callaloo greens (dasheen or Chinese spinach, *see Glossary, page 197*), or substitute fresh spinach or Swiss chard
3 tablespoons butter
½ cup finely chopped onions
½ teaspoon finely chopped garlic
3 cups chicken stock, fresh or canned
½ cup coconut milk *(see Recipe Booklet)*
1 teaspoon salt
Freshly ground black pepper
½ pound fresh, canned or frozen crab meat, picked clean of all bits of shell and cartilage
A dash of A-1 or Pickapeppa sauce

To make about ½ cup

1 medium-sized (about 2 pounds) young cassava root

To serve 6 to 8 as a main course

A 3- to 3½-pound chicken, cut into 6 to 8 serving pieces
3 quarts freshly made beef stock or 6 cups canned beef broth combined with 6 cups water
4 large tomatoes, peeled, seeded and coarsely chopped *(see sopa de gandules, page 43)*, or 2 cups chopped drained canned tomatoes
2 medium-sized ears fresh or frozen corn, cut into 3-inch rounds
2 medium-sized yams (about 1 pound), peeled and cut crosswise into ½-inch-thick slices
2 small boiling potatoes, peeled and cut into ½-inch-thick rounds
¼ pound West Indian pumpkin or Hubbard squash, peeled and cut into ½-inch dice (about 1 cup)
½ cup fresh or frozen green peas
2 small fresh hot chilies, stemmed, seeded and thinly sliced *(caution: see page 46)*
1 tablespoon salt
Freshly ground black pepper
2 tablespoons finely cut fresh chives

How to Handle Chilies

Hot peppers, or chilies, require special handling. Their volatile oils may burn your skin and make your eyes smart. Wear rubber gloves if you can, and be careful not to touch your face or eyes while working with chilies.

To prepare chilies, rinse them clean and pull out the stems under cold running water. Break or cut the pods in half, and brush out the seeds with your fingers. In most cases the ribs inside the pods are thin and may be left intact, but if they seem fleshy, cut them out with a small, sharp knife. The chilies may be used at once or soaked in cold, salted water for an hour or so to make them less hot. After handling hot chilies, it is advisable to wash your hands thoroughly with soap and warm water.

The hot chili pepper that adds so much pungency to Caribbean cooking is part of a large and wonderfully diverse family called *Capsicum*. The plant, not the least of Columbus' discoveries in the New World, now grows all over the world. Its innumerable varieties range from the familiar bell and sweet red peppers to the fiery little *habaneros* shown being picked here, and others so hot that their oil is literally lethal.

All pepper sauces contain chilies, but the other ingredients for recipes like those on these pages may vary every time a cook makes a new supply. In the islands pepper sauce is universally served as a condiment with boiled, broiled or roasted meats, poultry and seafood.

To make about ½ cup

1 tablespoon finely chopped fresh
  hot chilies *(caution: see box above)*
2 tablespoons finely chopped onions
½ teaspoon finely chopped garlic
3 tablespoons malt vinegar
¼ cup water
½ teaspoon salt
1 tablespoon olive oil

Saba Pepper Sauce

Combine the chilies, onions and garlic in a small bowl. Bring the vinegar, water and salt to a boil in a small enameled, stainless-steel or glass saucepan and, stirring constantly, pour them over the chili mixture. Pour the oil over the top.

Tightly covered and refrigerated, the Saba pepper sauce can be kept safely for about 3 to 4 weeks.

Sauce Ti-Malice (Haiti)
CHILI, ONION AND LIME-JUICE SAUCE

To make about 1 cup

1½ cups finely chopped onions
¾ cup strained fresh lime juice
2 tablespoons butter
2 teaspoons finely chopped fresh hot
  chilies *(caution: see box above)*
1 teaspoon finely chopped garlic
2 teaspoons salt

Drop the onions into a small bowl, stir the lime juice into them, and marinate at room temperature for at least 30 minutes. Drain the onions in a fine sieve set over a bowl, tossing them with a fork to remove as much liquid as possible. Reserve the marinade.

In a heavy 8- to 10-inch skillet, melt the butter over moderate heat. When the foam begins to subside, add the onions and, stirring frequently, cook for 5 minutes, until they are soft and transparent but not brown. Watch carefully for any sign of burning and regulate the heat accordingly.

Stir in the chopped chilies and the garlic, reduce the heat to low, cover the skillet tightly, and cook for about 10 minutes, or until the chilies are tender. Off the heat stir in the reserved marinade and the salt. Cool to room temperature before serving.

Covered tightly and refrigerated, *sauce Ti-Malice* can be kept safely for about 5 to 7 days.

Pepper Wine

Wash the chilies under cold running water and pat them completely dry with paper towels. Place the whole chilies in a 1-quart bottle or jar and pour the rum over them. Cover tightly and marinate at room temperature for at least 10 days before using.

A drop or two of pepper wine is a fiery flavoring for such soups as callaloo and *saucochi di gallinja (Recipe Index)*.

To make ½ pint

3 whole fresh hot chilies, each about 3 inches long *(caution: see box opposite)*
½ pint light rum, or substitute pale dry sherry

Mrs. Bessie Byam's Mango Relish *(Trinidad)*

With a small, sharp knife, peel the mangoes and cut the flesh away from the large seed inside each fruit. Discard the seeds and chop the fruit as fine as possible. In a deep bowl, combine the mangoes, chilies, garlic and salt, and turn them about with a spoon until thoroughly mixed.

Ladle the relish into a serving bowl or a clean jar, and trickle the oil over the top so that it floats on the surface. Cover tightly with plastic wrap until ready to serve.

Covered and refrigerated, the mango relish can be kept safely for about 4 to 6 weeks.

To make about 1 pint

2 large (about 1 pound each) unripe mangoes *(see box, page 116)*
2 tablespoons finely chopped fresh hot chilies *(caution: see box opposite)*
2 teaspoons finely chopped garlic
1 teaspoon salt
1 tablespoon olive oil

Annatto Oil

Pour the oil into a small saucepan or skillet and heat it over moderate heat until a light haze forms above it. Stir in the annatto seeds and, when they are evenly coated with oil, reduce the heat to medium and simmer for about 1 minute. Remove the pan from the heat, uncover, and let the oil cool to room temperature.

Strain the annatto oil into a jar, cover tightly with plastic wrap, and refrigerate it until ready to use. Discard the seeds.

Annatto oil will keep for several months, but its flavor and color will diminish with age. The oil is used to give a reddish-orange color and a mild flavor to meat, poultry and seafood sauces in many Caribbean islands as well as in Latin America.

To make about ½ cup

½ cup vegetable oil
¼ cup annatto *(achiote)* seeds

Sauce Créole *(Martinique)*

In a deep bowl, combine the tomato purée, lime juice, onions, celery, chilies, salt and a few grindings of pepper, and stir until they are thoroughly blended. Then stir in the olive slices.

Serve at once, or cover the bowl tightly with plastic wrap and refrigerate it until ready to use. The sauce can be safely kept in the refrigerator for about 5 to 7 days.

Sauce créole is traditionally served as an accompaniment to seafood dishes, such as broiled lobster and *pescado asado (Recipe Index)*.

To make about 2 cups

1 cup canned tomato purée
¼ cup strained fresh lime juice
1 cup finely chopped onions
1 tablespoon finely chopped celery
1 teaspoon finely chopped fresh hot chilies *(caution: see box opposite)*
1 teaspoon salt
Freshly ground black pepper
3 pimiento-stuffed olives, drained and cut crosswise into paper-thin slices

III

The Laborer's Life: Magic from the Soil

The vegetables that are the staples of the Caribbean cuisine, the spices that enliven it and the fruits that dress it up all grow easily in the verdant hills of Grenada. Everything in this basket, posed against the sweep of Grand Anse Beach, was purchased in Market Square in the island's capital, St. George's *(pages 18-19).*

Throughout the Caribbean there are still villages so primitive, so untouched by the modern world that one thinks on seeing them, "This could be Africa," or, "This could be 100 years ago." And both are true. One such village I visited is near St. Anne on the southern coast of Martinique. It was Sunday but the men were at work mending fishing nets laid out upon the ground. The women were chatting in front of their houses, or cooking the Sunday meal—also in front of their houses. One woman sat cross-legged before an outdoor fire, stirring a thick, leafy garden of a soup. Another was preparing tiny round flour dumplings, called *dombé,* to add to the pot of peppery black-eyed peas already simmering on her one-burner kerosene stove. The houses were wooden shacks, windowless and bare. There were no cars in the village; there were not even any streets. On wooden platforms, sardines lay drying for tomorrow's bait. A few chickens and an occasional skinny pig—*cochon planche,* the Martinicans say, to distinguish it from fatter, rounder pigs —rooted about in the sandy yards.

Children played among the fishing boats lined up on the shore, the boys pretending to fish, the girls playing house. In one boat six little girls, with calabash bowls and stirring twigs in hand, were feeding two blond-haired dolls. I stopped to talk to them and they asked me where I came from—France? The United States, I said. One of them had heard of my country and she asked me about the snow: "Does it hurt when it falls on you?" I tried to explain that it was like rain. "Does the rain hurt?" But she didn't believe me. Then I asked them what they were feeding their dolls. One answered, *"Farine,"* which is what the Martinicans call cassava meal, "and then she'll have

West Indian Standbys: Squashes and Roots

The quintet of vegetables below may look unfamiliar to many mainland cooks, but all of them are staples in a Caribbean kitchen. Left to right:

CALABAZA, OR WEST INDIAN PUMPKIN
Though their shapes and colors vary, large squashes like the one on the left are all called calabaza. Usually boiled, they have firm, delicately flavored flesh somewhat like that of a butternut or Hubbard squash.

CHRISTOPHENE
This small, pale pear-shaped vegetable, which varies from white to yellow to green, is also a kind of squash. It is cooked, and tastes, like a tender young zucchini.

TARO ROOT
Under its brown skin, the taro's flesh is white but may turn gray, green or violet when boiled. Whatever the color, it has a faintly nutty taste.

CASSAVA ROOT
This all-purpose vegetable with its barklike skin and starchy white flesh is not only boiled as a vegetable, but also used for the cassareep in Trinidadian pepper pot (*Recipe Index*) and for manioc meal and tapioca.

YAM
This tropical tuber—not the familiar orange sweet potato often confused with it—is the genuine yam. Its skin is tough and thick; its flesh may be white, yellow or, in some roots, red.

rice, this one. And this one fish if the catch is good. Otherwise I'll give her salt fish. And nice, sweet plantains."

The menu of the doll and the menu of the children are the same. It is not too different from what was eaten in this village and villages like it 100 or even 200 years ago. During the two centuries when the majority of people on the islands were enslaved, they ate what the plantation owners found economical. This almost never included meat and rarely included fresh fish. One early traveler to the Caribbean noted that, although the islands lie surrounded by the sea and its wealth of fish, the planters "tend their profits so much they will not spare a Negro's absence so long as to go to the Bridge and fetch it." Dried salt fish—mackerel or cod—was more convenient. It was cheap, it did not spoil in the tropical heat, and it came down from New England in the same ships that carried the islands' rum and molasses back to America. The salt fish sent to the West Indies was generally of second quality —the finest product of the Yankee fisheries went to European markets—but it was consumed in great quantities in the islands and was the main source of protein for generations of slaves. Otherwise the vast majority of the Caribbean's people got along—and rather well you discover when you taste their dishes—on vegetables, usually starchy ones rich in carbohydrates.

This emphasis on vegetable cooking was reinforced in the 19th Century when slavery ended and laborers from India and China were brought over to work the fields as indentured servants. They were almost as poor as the African slaves had been, and many observed religious restrictions in what they ate. So they, too, made their meals chiefly of local vegetables.

Soul food? Yes. Like our American soul food, the food of most Caribbean islanders was composed of cheap, starchy and filling ingredients. Despite these limitations, and perhaps because of them, the islanders learned to make superb dishes that were cleverly flavored with herbs and tingling with spices. Even today, when meat and fish are available, the islanders continue to lavish their attention and imagination on soups and vegetable dishes.

It was a meal on Guadeloupe that first made me realize meat or fresh fish was not essential to a satisfying dinner. My husband and I have a French friend there, a man who loves and understands island food. After he had taken us to several of the small, red-tableclothed restaurants on the island to eat sea eggs and land crab and conch, he announced on our last night, "Now you are ready for the true Creole food." There was something a bit ominous in what he said. Was it to be the mucilaginous Caribbean cactus soup I had read about? No, that was from Curaçao. Or would it be *vers-palmiste*, the palm-tree caterpillar some islanders particularly admire when roasted?

But no, it was vegetables he meant. And salt fish. There was a restaurant of which he was very fond, owned by an ancient Guadeloupian lady who in his opinion served the finest callaloo and the best vegetables in the islands.

The restaurant turned out to be the narrow veranda of an old wooden house. Several bare tables, a few wire-backed chairs and a single fluorescent light were the only furnishings. But Madame Touchin, a strikingly beautiful woman who greeted us at the foot of her porch steps, waved us graciously up the stairs. Eighty years old or more, she was dressed in the splendid costume—a blend of Africa and 18th Century France—that only a generation or two ago distinguished all the women of the French islands. Today only the very old still wear it, and Madame carried it off magnificently. Her dress was a floorlength printed cotton, from under which peeked her petticoats, one of lace, another of silk. Around her shoulders was a vivid red and purple and yellow silk scarf, fastened by a big gold pin whose glitter matched her long, dangling earrings and the bangles on her arms. Crowning all was her "madwas," a bright Madras turban stiffly tied with four extended points. The protruding points of a French Creole's Madras were once a semaphore of love: If a girl displayed only one point, it meant, "I am free"; two points signified, "My heart is already taken"; three points said, "I am happily married"; four points meant, "Although that may be the case, there may yet be a place for you."

At Madame Touchin's there is no menu. One stops by to arrange for dinner a day ahead because Madame must rise early to go to market. Our friend had discussed the meal with her, and she had decided to prepare what she liked to prepare. We would have callaloo to start, of course. The principal ingredients of her callaloo are taro leaves and okra, which came to the islands from Africa. Taro leaves look like green elephant ears and grow on a bush whose edible root is called dasheen; sometimes, however, taro leaves are called callaloo after the soup made from them. Not so well known in the United States as okra, taro is nevertheless available; however, it is sometimes confusingly called dasheen, leaves and all. The Americans I know who like callaloo usually avoid the problem by substituting spinach for the taro.

Callaloo is eaten throughout the Caribbean, but the people of the French islands are especially fond of it. Listen to one Guadeloupian cookbook: "To relish and appreciate the subtlety and refinement of this preparation, one must be on the shaded shore of one of our beautiful rivers . . . sitting on a stone, feet in the water, or plunged up to the shoulders in a blue basin, the plate in one's hand and the soul impregnated with sun and euphoria."

We waited for the soup on the dimly lit porch, the palms around us scarcely stirring in the dense, hot August night. Soon a barefoot girl appeared with a big earthenware tureen from which she began to ladle for each of us an almost overflowing bowl. The color of the soup was exactly the same deep forest green as the leaf-laden soup I had seen cooking outdoors in the little fishing village on Martinique, but Madame had mashed the leaves by twirling and twirling them with her *baton lélé*—the African wooden swizzle stick that Caribbean cooks use as a whisk—until the soup was smooth in texture.

In my first spoonful I tasted peppers, cloves and the pungent sharpness of the taro leaves. But our friend advised me to wait—there was more to come. The girl reappeared with a dish of marinated slivers of salt fish, onions and bright red peppers. She scooped spoonfuls of each into our soup bowls, and then left us to our eating. The soup was softly fragrant as a somnolent tropical forest, yet it tingled with vinegary, peppery onions and salt fish. Marinated salt fish, in soup or by itself, is perhaps the most popular of dozens of fascinating ways in which the islanders use salt cod. (They always soak it first to soften it and reduce its saltiness.) The Spanish-speaking islanders serve marinated salt fish with sweet peppers and call it *serenata;* the French make it with hot peppers and call it *féroce.*

Later we had more of Madame's repertoire of vegetables: breadfruit cooked in two ways, plantains and a variety of roots. All the vegetables were placed on our plates at once, but they were so varied in texture and flavor that they in no way resembled one another. It was easy to taste the differences among the roots, all steamed and buttered: nutlike yams, sugary sweet potatoes and delicate malanga, mealy and mild like a Maine potato. One portion of the breadfruit was creamy; it had been mashed with chives, thyme, parsley, garlic and bacon fat. It bore little resemblance to itself in another guise, fried *beignets* (fritters) that were puffy and airy. The plantains, my favorite, had been sautéed in such a way that they were crusty outside, but as soft as baby food inside.

Madame came and stood in the doorway of the porch. I smiled at her and she at me, and she said something in the Creole patois that I could not understand and I said something in my French that she could not understand. But we were communicating: I our pleasure in her food, she her pleasure in our pleasure. She stood for a while, proudly watching us eat, and when she was satisfied she withdrew into her house.

The dessert she sent out to us, a cake poetically called "the torments of love," was rich and chewy with coconut. It originated on the nearby islands called Les Saintes, and only a few old women remember how to make it. Madame Touchin was justly proud of her version, as she had been of her soup and vegetables, but we had eaten so well that we could not finish it.

Root vegetables such as cassava and yams existed in the islands when Columbus discovered them, but many others that are now important to Caribbean cooking came from the Old World. For a long time it has been believed that this was true of one of the region's most useful vegetables, the plantain, cousin of the banana. (Although it is really a fruit, the plantain must be cooked to be palatable and so is usually considered a vegetable.) The plantain had reached Southern Europe via Africa in the caravans of Arab traders who had discovered it growing in India; when a Spanish friar named Tomás de Berlanga went as a missionary to the New World in 1516 he took plantain shoots with him, thinking they would do well in the tropics. Berlanga's plantains did indeed thrive in the Caribbean, but it is now believed that his botanical experiment was unnecessary. Many experts think plantains already grew on some islands when the Spanish arrived, since research shows they were growing at the time in Peru, Mexico and other parts of Central America.

Whatever their origins, plantains now grow throughout the islands; they are also becoming increasingly available in the United States and can be bought not only at specialty fruit shops but also in some supermarkets. Americans are beginning to show the same sort of enthusiasm for them that

Akee *(left),* one of the Caribbean fruits treated as a vegetable, grows to about the size of a peach. When ripe, its woody shell bursts, revealing shiny black seeds and three segments of edible flesh. In the Jamaican salt fish and akee shown below *(Recipe Index),* the bland scrambled-eggs flavor of the fruit is contrasted with cod, onions and peppers.

turned bananas, in the course of the last 50 years, into one of the country's biggest fruit imports.

Plantains, though less sweet than bananas, are more versatile. They can be cooked and eaten at various stages of ripeness, and each stage has its own taste and treatment. Green or unripe plantains, which are almost as hard as potatoes, are often simply boiled in salted water and served with meat, as we serve boiled potatoes. They taste starchier than potatoes, however, and to be really appetizing should be accompanied by lots of pepper and onion and spices or made into a casserole or a hot salad. They are also good cut into slivers, deep-fried and served as chips *(Recipe Index);* they make an interesting change from the standard potato chips at parties.

The half-ripe plantain is the main ingredient in a superb Puerto Rican appetizer, *mofongo.* Not yet sweet but no longer merely bland and starchy, the plantain is fried, then mashed with pork cracklings and garlic into a delicious avocadolike creaminess and may be served on bread.

But it is when the plantain is fully ripe that it is at its most glorious. It is served most often as Madame Touchin served it, sliced into rounds and sautéed in butter, crisp outside and soft inside. Its mild but definite sweetness blends magnificently with pork or chicken and it makes beef more interesting, too. Chopped beef and ripe plantains are, in fact, the basis of another special Puerto Rican dish, *piononos.* In this ingenious creation, ripe plantains that have been sliced, fried and wrapped around a mixture of meat and cheese are dipped into beaten eggs and refried until the plantains taste flaky and sweet as pastry *(Recipe Index).*

It is easy to be enthusiastic about plantains, but breadfruit, the Caribbean's next most important vegetable mainstay, takes getting used to. It has a bland standoffish personality and must be carefully handled if it is to display its best qualities. The first time I ate it boiled, which is the way it frequently is served, it seemed completely flavorless. But when one gets to know the breadfruit and explores its possibilities, it becomes more interesting. French fried, made into chips, roasted with butter, served cold with mayonnaise, onions and sweet peppers as a salad, it is versatile and friendly and gets on with everything. It is at its most enticing when it is scraped from its skin, boiled, then stuffed back into its own prickly green round vaselike shell with onions, spices and salt fish. It is frequently the centerpiece at Caribbean buffets, the handsomest dish at the party.

The breadfruit's history is entangled with some of the most dramatic incidents of 18th Century exploration—and has played a central role in some. It first came to the attention of Europeans when Captain Cook encountered it on Tahiti, where it was a staple. He himself did not care for its flavor, "as disagreeable as that of a pickled olive generally is the first time it is eaten." But the botanist who accompanied him on the voyage did like it and wrote that the rest of the crew agreed with him; they ate it for several months on the return voyage to England as a substitute for bread and found it consistently tasty and nourishing. Perhaps the cook on that first voyage knew the breadfruit's shy secrets. In any case, the botanist wrote, "No one of the whole ship's Company complained when served with breadfruit in lieu of biscuit; and from the health and strength of whole nations, whose principal food it is, I do not scruple to call it one of the most useful vegetables in the world."

A humanitarian, he urged that no expense be spared in attempting to grow breadfruit in other tropical regions where hunger was a problem.

The West Indian planters, always on the lookout for filling foods that would grow with a minimum of care and demand as little of their valuable sugar land as possible, were intrigued with his description. One Jamaican landholder traveled to England especially to petition King George III to dispatch an expedition to the South Seas to carry breadfruit to the Caribbean. The King was amenable, and in 1787 Captain William Bligh was chosen to lead the expedition. His ship was H.M.S. *Bounty*.

His crew's famous mutiny is a familiar story, but less well known is the fact that one of the chief causes of the men's hatred for their captain was his devotion to the breadfruit. First he delayed too long in the South Seas in his efforts to gather perfect and well-established breadfruit saplings. Then, during the homeward voyage he denied water to his crew in order to keep the precious breadfruit alive. Also little known is the story of what Bligh did after he was cast overboard by the mutineers and made his way hundreds of miles to safety in an open boat. Almost as soon as he got back to England he set out once again to fulfill the mission. This time he succeeded. In 1793 he sailed into Jamaica's Port Royal Harbor with a ship so crowded with beautiful leafy saplings that the Jamaicans rowed out toward the ship to inspect with greatest enthusiasm this "floating forest," "the ship that have the bush."

The breadfruit tree, one of the Caribbean's most attractive, tall and crowned with intensely dark green leaves, took hold and spread miraculously. Now it is found on virtually every Caribbean island; its sustaining qualities are so highly thought of that the men on St. Vincent have a saying, "Give me a good working woman and a breadfruit tree and I need never work again."

The saying is somewhat fanciful because breadfruit is not, all by itself, nourishing enough to keep a man fat and lazy. But the islanders have a whole spectrum of other vegetables to fill out their menu. Among them corn and okra are particularly favored. Corn was native to some of the islands; Columbus saw it growing on Hispaniola and early Spanish writers described how it was boiled, then fried into cakes, one sort for the common Indians, another for their chiefs. Today it is often prepared as a peppery companion to soups or stews. In this form it is called funchi or fungee; both names are African, although the dish closely resembles polenta, Italy's cornmeal pudding.

On Curaçao, funchi and fish chowder inevitably go together. In a country restaurant where my husband and I sat on a patio at a big rough-hewn table shaded only by an awning made of fish nets, we sampled funchi at its best.

HOW TO PEEL A GREEN PLANTAIN
Ripe plantains can be peeled as easily as bananas. But the green ones used for plantain chips or for *banane pesé* *(Recipe Index)* require special handling, since the thick skin clings tightly to the fruit and tends to break off in little pieces. The diagram below illustrates an efficient—and unfrustrating—way of removing the peel. With a sharp knife, slice off the ends and cut the plantain in half. Make four evenly spaced lengthwise slits in the skin of each half, cutting through to the flesh from one end to the other. Then, starting at the corner edge of one slit, lift the skin away a strip at a time—pulling it off crosswise rather than lengthwise.

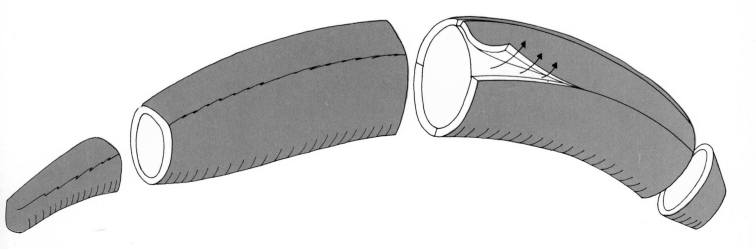

The restaurateur, Janchi, would not even begin to make the dish until we were ready to eat. "It has to be springy and soft," he said, "and it grows hard if it waits for you. You must wait for it." We did, sipping rum and contemplating the fierce cactus, the *cadushi*, that grows in quantity on Curaçao and makes a meal for those too poor for funchi and chowder. The funchi finally arrived, pale yellow and as puffy as a pillow. We cut into its steaming center, dunked great chunks of it in a savory snapper-filled chowder and discovered its earthy moistness. Sometime later I read an 18th Century poem in which a slave whose wife has deserted him mourns her absence. He complains, "My fungee, alas! is unboil'd. . . ," and I felt sympathy for him. No doubt he missed his wife, but I could see that it might be easy to miss fungee more.

Okra, though now as prevalent as corn, was not indigenous to the Caribbean; it came over with the slaves from Africa. It is often combined with funchi to make a dish known as coo-coo. Or it is cooked into a soft pudding of mashed plantains called foo-foo, which, in the words of a song sung by Jamaican folk singer Louise Bennett, is a very good dish "for when you lose your teeth." Funchi, coo-coo and foo-foo all entered the Caribbean cuisine via Africa, and are found on all the islands regardless of their colonial backgrounds; they offer fascinating evidence of the basic homogeneity of the islands' cuisine. Curiously, their names in the original African usage referred to consistency rather than to ingredients. Funchi is from a word that means mush or meal, while foo-foo described the paleness of pounded, doughy food. A similar case is duckunoo, another Caribbean dish of African descent, which can be made from any of several vegetables, as long as they are grated, then wrapped up for steaming in a banana or plantain leaf. Duckunoo may be spicy and eaten with meat or soup or it may be sweetened with coconut, sugar and vanilla and eaten as a dessert.

Also from Africa came the most exotic among those Caribbean fruits that, like the plantain, masquerade as vegetables. This is the akee, which a friend of mine once described as looking "like a one-pot meal." Split, its yellow flesh resembles a plateful of scrambled eggs, its seeds a garnish of shiny black olives and its mottled red skin a glazed pottery casserole; its texture is soft and its flavor mild. It first crossed the Atlantic in slave ships bound for Jamaica, and was undoubtedly carried along by Africans anxious to take with them some familiar flavor of home to the unknown they faced.

Oddly, akee never caught on anywhere in the Caribbean except Jamaica. "Akee, rice, salt fish are nice," goes a verse in the song "Jamaica Farewell," "And the rum is fine any time of year." All the islands have fine rum, but only Jamaica has akee and salt fish *(Recipe Index)*, which, as any Jamaican will tell you, is one of the best dishes anywhere in the Caribbean. The cod is soaked overnight to reduce its saltiness; then it is boiled and shredded. A sauce of sautéed garlic, onions, sweet or hot peppers and bits of bacon punctuates the mildness of the akee. But stubbornly, the fish stays salty and the akee stays mild, and the combination is so felicitous that they seem an ideally married pair, able to accommodate to any course that follows.

It was long believed that akee was poisonous if not picked at a precise stage of ripeness and then boiled for many hours. This view, which may account for its absence on the other islands, is contested by agricultural

Opposite: These Muslim women, who live in Port of Spain, Trinidad, have gathered for a lunch of some of the traditional Indian dishes that are gradually becoming part of the Caribbean's cookery. Among the foods being offered here are chicken *biriani (foreground)*, a kind of saffron-colored chicken *pelau* served with hard-cooked eggs; *polouri*, deep-fried balls of chick-pea meal, and curried shrimp with tomato *(center)*.

researchers at the University of the West Indies in Kingston; they maintain the notion is superstition. Nevertheless, the belief is still widely held and no one will eat raw akee or pick it before the fruit has begun to split and show its shining seeds. Fortunately cooks in the United States do not have to worry about the problem, since only canned akee is available there.

Akee, breadfruit and plantain, however familiar in the islands, all seem a bit exotic to Americans; but there is another classic Caribbean vegetable staple that is, in our eyes, a good deal more humble: beans and rice. Each large island has its preferred version of this combination, and each version, far from being humble, is memorable.

On Jamaica, the dish is known as rice and peas—what Jamaicans call peas, we know as beans; in this dish they are either red kidney beans or small red beans native to the island. (Throughout the islands the words pea and bean are often used interchangeably.) Jamaican rice and peas is always made with coconut milk, but beyond that requirement every cook is on her own; the variations in recipes are countless. Some call for adding sweet peppers and tomatoes, some for bacon, some for soup beef or stewing beef, some for onions or chives or hot peppers, some for any combination of these *(Recipe Index)*.

I became a devotee of Jamaican rice and peas the very first time I tasted it. It was in New York. My daughter had just been born, and I was feeling weak, nervous about this first baby, and determined to have for a while no responsibilities except toward her. So we hired a young Jamaican nurse-housekeeper. I planned that I would feed the baby and Vivian would feed my husband and me. She knew a little American cooking, she said, so my husband obligingly went to the supermarket and bought easy things, steaks and a roast. But after three days he began to complain and after the fourth he was miserable. The steaks were always too well done; the roast beef was garlicky. And Vivian herself looked disdainfully at her own handiwork and wouldn't eat it.

So I pleaded with her: "Vivian, make something you like to make. If you make something you like I'm sure we'll like it too." "Oh, no," Vivian insisted. "Americans don't like West Indian food." "What is it?" I asked weakly. "Well, it's rice and peas." I told her to make it, whatever it was, tottered off to bed, and napped self-indulgently while Vivian went out shopping. She came back laden with chunks of beef, scallions, sweet peppers, red kidney beans and a hairy coconut. From my bedroom I heard her banging at this last with my husband's hammer, and I went into the kitchen to see what was happening. The red beans had been put on to simmer with the beef; the coconut was split open, and Vivian began grating it on a small hand grater. Then she squeezed what she had grated between her fingers, picking up lump after lump of coconut, moistening it with water, and pressing and struggling with it until its juices flowed and a white milk was obtained. It seemed terribly slow and painstaking to me, but I could tell she was absorbed in a way she had not been by the dishes I had asked her to cook. As I saw how involved she was in her work, my own interest in cooking revived and for the first time since my daughter's birth I found myself becoming curious about something outside myself and the baby.

Ultimately, Vivian threw away the coconut mash and used only the liquid she had so patiently squeezed from it, which she called coconut cream. She poured this into the beans and beef mixture when the water had boiled down, and followed it with the onions and peppers that she had prepared separately, and finally with the rice. That night we sampled the dish. The rice came out of the pot fluffy, but dappled with the beans' earthy redness; in each hearty forkful there was the barest hint of coconut, a sweet tropical teasing. "We love it," we told Vivian. And she smiled and said incomprehensibly, "I knew you would."

Another Jamaican favorite—a partiality shared also by the Trinidadians—is rice and pigeon peas, small yellow peas that came originally from Africa and are known in the Caribbean by names, Congo or goongoo peas, that point to this origin. Jamaicans cook the goongoo peas either with rice or into dumplings; they also sing about them, as they so often sing about food in their folk songs. (Indeed, love and food receive almost equal emphasis in the hauntingly sad Jamaican songs of deprivation.) "Catch up the fire, Martha; pass me the goongoo peas. Rub up the flour, Sarah. Lord, feel the evening breeze!" sings a field laborer in "Evening Time," expressing his relief that at last at day's end he may return home to the good things of life, "to go walk on the mountain side" and "to eat, sing, dance and play."

In Cuba black beans are the specialty. These are to my mind the heartiest and meatiest of beans. Ordinarily they are not cooked with rice but are served with it, and one shovels great coal-dark scoops of the beans onto snowy soft rice. One without the other is a disappointment. There is also a Cuban dish in which the beans and rice are cooked together and this black and white combination is known colloquially as *Moros y Cristianos*.

Haiti too has its own distinctive rice and bean dish, rice *djon djon*, a dish made nowhere else in the islands because it calls for an ingredient found only on Haiti—black mushrooms. Haitian black mushrooms are small, and only their earthy-tasting caps are edible. But the stems make a deep-black dye; they are used to color the water in which the rice is cooked, then discarded. The caps are added to the rice and so are lima beans. European dried mushrooms have virtually the same taste as the Haitian ones, but they do not lend as interesting a color to the dish.

The ubiquitous bean appears often in another universal Caribbean specialty: soup. There are dozens of rich, vegetable-and-bean-laden brews that tempt the traveler from one end of the Caribbean to the other. They are almost always hot, both in temperature and taste, for islanders believe that a hot soup, by causing one to perspire, is a healthful and cooling affair. One feels warmer while eating it, but cooler afterward; the bland, chilled concoctions that tourists prefer may whet the appetite but they merely forestall cooling off.

Martinique's opulent *soupe à Congo* starts with a large assortment of mixed local beans or peas and is then laden with eggplant, yams, green beans, cabbage, avocado, carrots and okra, and flavored with garlic, onion, cloves, hot pepper, a single sweet potato and a pig's tail. Jamaica has red-pea soup, deliciously flavored with salt pork. But it is Cuba's black-bean soup that I find most memorable of all. Thick and dark and highly spiced, the beans as satisfying as any meat, it is usually served with side dishes of rice and cut-up raw onion; you thicken the soup to suit yourself by ladling in rice and sharpen it as you like by sprinkling on the onions.

Continued on page 66

Carnival Capers in Port of Spain

For complexity and sheer spectacle, even Rio de Janeiro would be hard put to match the pre-Lenten carnival in Port of Spain, Trinidad. For two days, thousands of masked and costumed revelers surge through the streets, miming, singing, making music, joking and soliciting tips from the onlookers. The marchers are organized into groups, or bands, each representing a specific theme that is either traditional (Bad Behavior Sailors, Red Dragons) or topical (a local murder case, a new film). Carrying on around the clock, the celebrants replenish their energies at food stalls that spring up all around town to serve them.

Expert carnival-goers can distinguish the many different bands that march the streets by their costumes and antics. The fright wig and face paint on the masker at left identify him as one of the African Warriors. The brilliantly costumed marchers at right all belong to a vast (1,200 members) carnival band called Psychedelic Latin America, which came in third in the 1969 band-of-the-year competition. The Tambourine Dancers are at the right in the picture, and the Magnificent Matadors are at left. Maskers' outfits are generally elaborate and expensive, but a way has been found to ease the financial strain: after carnival participants can often sell their costumes to tourists as souvenirs.

60

At carnival time in Port of Spain, Mrs. Sookday Maharaj works in a stall preparing *polouris* and other hot Indian fritters.

To make *sahinas*, her favorite fritters, Mrs. Maharaj spreads taro leaves with batter, then stacks, rolls, slices and fries them.

Indian fritters, shown in the making on the opposite page and at left, have been adopted as a carnival treat by Trinidadians. Three varieties displayed in the wooden tray above are, from left, *polouris*, small balls of split pea meal; *sahinas*, made of a batter of ground split peas and saffron; and *kachouris*.

Overleaf: Dozens of food stalls like Mrs. Maharaj's ring the savanna in Port of Spain during carnival, and do a brisk business among the marchers and dancers who fill the town's central square to overflowing with gaiety, movement and color.

Kachouris (being fried) are chick-pea fritters flavored with scallions and served with pepper sauce.

Pervasive as the African influence is throughout the islands, it is not everywhere supreme. In some areas the culinary effects of the Oriental influx of the 19th Century are also strongly felt. To the beans and starchy vegetables basic to the African people's cooking, the Indians and Chinese added a taste for leafy and green vegetables. The Orientals have long been recognized as the finest gardeners on the islands, and in many places they supply the demand they created for lettuce, cabbage, cucumber and green beans by cultivating and selling them. Trinidad, where nearly all the commercial gardeners are Indian, has the most verdant vegetable markets of the Caribbean. In Kingston, Jamaica, if one wants really fine vegetables one goes to the Chinese vendors on Barry Street. Sitting on folding chairs in the street, their wares displayed beside them, the sellers boast as great a variety as can be found in the city's big covered marketplaces; and the green of their lettuces and extra-long "Chinese" string beans is dazzling.

Aside from their magic with vegetables, the Chinese have affected the culinary habits of the islanders chiefly through the proliferation of Chinese restaurants all over the region. Virtually every island has at least one, simple or grand. In Cuba, where the Chinese have intermarried with the rest of the population, Chinese food became so popular that an entirely new restaurant fashion developed: Cuban-Chinese restaurants specializing equally in standard Cuban dishes and standard Chinese dishes. Now, run by émigrés, they have mushroomed all over New York City and Florida.

Even more than the Chinese, the Indians have had a deep effect upon Caribbean cuisine, primarily through their enthusiasm for curry, which is becoming as much a part of Caribbean cooking as it is of Indian. The method is different: Islanders do not mix a curry paste for themselves the way the Indians do, but always employ prepared curry powder. But in many parts of the area, curry is regularly used to flavor chicken, meats, potatoes, even Africa's akee. Indeed, on Jamaica, the national party dish, eaten whenever there is something special to celebrate or just to be happy about, is curried goat. On Trinidad *pelau* has equal status as a "national" dish, and many people claim it was popularized by Indians. Similar to pigeon peas and rice, Trinidad's *pelau* also contains chicken or meat and can be embellished with saffron and raisins and tomatoes.

The Indian influence on Caribbean cuisine is a quite recent development, and its impact is steadily spreading. Usually the study of how one people's food affects another's is a study of the past, but in the Caribbean the process is going on right now. I saw convincing evidence of this influence at work in Port of Spain, Trinidad, during a recent carnival week.

Carnival is celebrated all through the islands, though nowhere more exuberantly than in Trinidad. It began as a French Catholic custom, an indulgent celebration before the strict fasting required during Lent. The colonialists attended lavish parties and wore masks and finery; the slaves celebrated with mimicking versions of the festivity back in their own quarters. After emancipation the Africans began to participate in carnival openly and their mimicry became public. They donned homemade papier-mâché masks and, too poor for fine robes, whatever costumes they could devise, and they paraded and cavorted, reciting witty satires in which a man's or woman's most embarrassing foibles were pointed out. Certain of the costumed figures became traditional, and they can still be seen in today's carnival—some French, like Pierrot Granad, a pompous grandee in tattered robes, and some straight out of African mythology, like Moko Jumby, a witch doctor on stilts, or the Shango men with nut and seed necklaces about their necks. Now, though, the festivities are organized on a far grander scale, with expensive costumes and elaborate, carefully rehearsed presentations.

The essence of carnival is embodied in the celebrants' ecstatic, rapturous dancing and their spirit of joyous self-expression. Carnival is a time for the assertion of freedom, for giving free flow to primitive urges. At carnival no one complains about drunkenness, exhibitionism, or even fighting, and every November, nine months later, there seems to be a sudden increase of babies born in the islands.

Yet one basic urge, eating, was long underplayed at carnival. It is only now becoming an exciting part of the event, and this is because of the Indians. They participate only sparingly in the actual pageantry of carnival; but they come to the savanna, the central park in Port of Spain where the carnival shows take place, and there they set up rough wooden stands with grand names like Taj Mahal and Ali's Caribbean Restaurant, from which they dispense sustenance to the carnival players. Although traditional Creole food is sold around the savanna, the wares of the Indian food sellers seem especially matched to the enthusiasm for the exotic that *is* carnival.

On Tuesday of the carnival week I spent in Port of Spain, when it seemed to me the entire population of the city had been either making music or dancing to it nonstop for more than 30 hours, I went to the savanna to watch the climax of the festivities, the masqueraders' grand, marathon march. For months before they had been rehearsing for this final parade. Now the singers, bandsmen and masqueraders came pouring into the savanna in a whirl of silks, feathers and sequins. Renaissance princes, cruel pirates, African warriors and fierce mythical animals swarmed in exuberant conviviality. And when they were not dancing, they besieged the Indian food sellers behind their counter fortresses that ringed the savanna. The vendors met the onslaught bravely with trays of triangular meat pies and stacks of *roti,* the flat Indian bread. Beef stewed in tomatoes, chicken caramelized with brown sugar and made fragrant with lime, steaming split-pea purée and chunky potato curry were packed into the *rotis* as fast as agile hands could move. At the sweets stalls the crowds were full of children reaching up for cakes and candies spiky with coconut, sandy with sugar and dripping with honey.

But the crowds were thickest at the stalls dispensing Indian vegetable fritters: golden balls of ivory-smooth chick-pea batter, sparkling with oil and studded with little emerald treasures of split peas and spinach.

I spent an hour that morning watching one Indian woman, Mrs. Sookday Maharaj, deftly squeeze and roll, pet and pat an endless flow of fritters through her fingers. Like many of the food sellers, Mrs. Maharaj lives in the country and comes into Port of Spain only for special events like carnival or the horse races held in June and December. Her husband drives a taxi in their country village, an occupation that does not pay much; but at the races and carnival, the Maharaj family, feeding the throngs with the same dishes they favor at home, makes sufficient money to assure a fairly comfortable life. There are 12 children, and all, except one son who had emigrated to London, were helping out at carnival. The teen-age sons took charge of the soda and beer, and laboriously peeled and diced potatoes for the curry and green mangoes for the mango pickle. The daughters, under their mother's fierce tutelage, mixed the batter for the fritters and did the selling. Mrs. Maharaj herself did all the frying, though, for the trick of her fritters is to keep the oil at exactly the right temperature and to remove the fritters at exactly the right moment. When she was talking to me at one point, her teenage daughter, fearing that her mother was distracted and that the fritters might get too dark, made a movement toward the red clay cooking stove. Mrs. Maharaj saw it all from the corner of her eye and uttered a resounding, "Nah, nah, nah! Only I will take them out."

She and the other Indian women who do the cooking around the savanna in their sandals, earrings and golden armbands are very proud of their work. The most popular fritter is *polouri*, made of preground split-pea meal, flour, baking powder, salt and saffron. These are sold by the bagful, and it is rare that the vendors can keep up with the demand. Equally good are *kachouri*, fritters made of hand-ground chick-pea meal, flour, salt and scallions. *Kachouri* are meant to be spicy, but Mrs. Maharaj does not put hot pepper into her *kachouri* batter at the stand as she does at home—she hand-mixes so much batter in the course of a day that a peppery mixture would burn her skin. Instead the spiciness is supplied separately by pepper sauce. She also makes *bara*, similar to *polouri* but shaped differently, and *baigani*, made of eggplant.

Her own favorite is *sahina*, made from taro leaves. She and her children pick these (the plant seems to grow wild on much of the island), and set them to dry on the roof of the stand. When the leaves have turned a bit brown, they are spread individually with a batter of split peas, flour, baking powder, salt and saffron and stacked on top of one another. When the stack is a few inches thick, it is rolled up like a jelly roll, and then it is spread with batter and sliced crossways. The slices are fried and produce the most exquisite of her fritters. I bought a collection of all Mrs. Maharaj's fritters, but when she was filling my bag with *sahina* she said sharply, "These you must eat yourself. Don't give any away. Even to your daughter."

I hurried away with my treasures, pushing through the throng of dancers to find a place to stop and taste them. Watching her cook and all the celebrants dance had made me extremely hungry. I found a bit of unoccupied grass and expectantly opened my brown paper bag. I was not disappointed: The *polouri* was soft within, the batter airy and sweet; the *kachouri* had a more assertive taste, nutlike and salty; but the *sahina*, as Mrs. Maharaj had promised, was the best. With each bite, it was at once pungent and sweet, chewy and crisp. Its many-layered texture reminded me of when I was a child, all mouth, and used to go to my grandmother's for nut strudel, when it seemed that counting all the thicknesses of that flaky delicacy would have meant counting higher than I could add.

Indians form only a tiny percentage of the Caribbean population, of course, and the legacy from Africa will always predominate. But those ebullient crowds of carnival dancers swarming around the Indians' food stalls made me realize how dynamic the Caribbean cuisine is, and how it continues to expand and grow more exciting as it draws upon the culinary imagination of all who come to the islands.

Opposite: A Christmas favorite in the English-speaking islands of the Caribbean, the refreshing drink called sorrel is made not from the pot herb of the same name but from a member of the hibiscus family. Parts of the blossoms (seen behind the pitcher) are combined with various flavorings and steeped in water for a day or so to produce a spicy, somewhat tart drink. In Trinidad, it is lightly fermented and rum is added to produce a headier concoction.

Piononos (*Puerto Rico*)

DEEP-FRIED PLANTAIN RINGS WITH SPICED GROUND-BEEF FILLING

To serve 4

2 large ripe plantains (about 1 pound each)

3 tablespoons butter

1 tablespoon vegetable oil

3 tablespoons annatto oil *(page 47)*

1 pound lean ground beef, preferably ground top round

½ cup finely chopped onions

¼ cup finely chopped green pepper

1 tablespoon finely chopped fresh hot chilies *(caution: see page 46)*

1 teaspoon finely chopped garlic

2 tablespoons flour

4 ounces boiled ham, cut into ¼-inch dice (about 1 cup)

3 medium-sized firm ripe tomatoes, peeled, seeded and finely chopped *(see sopa de gandules, page 43)*, or substitute 1 cup chopped drained canned tomatoes

¼ cup water

1 teaspoon salt

Freshly ground black pepper

3 large pimiento-stuffed olives, thoroughly drained and finely chopped

1 tablespoon finely chopped capers

2 tablespoons malt vinegar

Vegetable oil for deep frying

4 eggs

Peel the plantains and cut each one lengthwise into 4 thick strips. In a heavy 10- to 12-inch skillet, melt the butter in 1 tablespoon of vegetable oil. When the foam begins to subside, add the plantain. Turning the strips with a slotted spatula, cook them for about 4 minutes on each side, or until golden brown. As they brown, transfer the strips to paper towels to drain and cool.

In the same skillet, heat the annatto oil over moderate heat until a light haze forms above it. Drop in the beef and, mashing it constantly with the back of a spoon to break up any lumps, cook until all traces of pink disappear. Add the onions, green pepper, chilies and garlic and, stirring frequently, cook for 5 minutes until the vegetables are soft but not brown. Add the flour, and stir for 3 or 4 minutes to remove any taste of raw flour. Stir in the ham, tomatoes, water, salt and a few grindings of black pepper. Stirring occasionally, cook briskly until most of the liquid in the pan evaporates and the mixture thickens enough to hold its shape lightly in the spoon. Off the heat, stir in the olives, capers and vinegar, and taste for seasoning.

To make the *piononos,* shape each strip of plantain into ring about 3 inches in diameter, overlapping the ends by about ½ inch and securing them with a wooden toothpick inserted lengthwise. Lay the rings side by side and spoon about ⅓ cup of the beef mixture into the center of each one. Pat the meat firmly into place and gently press the top as flat as possible.

Fill a deep fryer or large saucepan with vegetable oil to a depth of 2 to 3 inches and heat the oil to a temperature of 350° on a deep-frying thermometer.

In a small, shallow bowl, beat the eggs with a fork or whisk until they are thoroughly combined. One at a time, place the filled plantain rings on a slotted spatula and dip them into the eggs, coating them completely. Immediately slide each ring into the hot oil and deep-fry it for about 3 minutes, gently turning it about with a spoon until golden brown on both sides. As they brown, transfer the rings to paper towels to drain. Serve at once with *riz et pois* or *riz au djon djon* (*Recipe Index*).

Sautéed plantains are curved into rings and filled with meat *(below, left),* then coated with egg and deep-fried to produce the crusty Puerto Rican favorite *piononos,* shown opposite arranged around a mound of red beans and rice and accompanied by beer.

Riz au Djon Djon *(Haiti)*
SAUTÉED RICE WITH DRIED BLACK MUSHROOMS

To serve 6

1 cup dried Haitian *djon djon*
    mushrooms *(see Glossary, page 197),*
    with stems removed, or dried
    black European mushrooms
2 cups boiling water
1 tablespoon vegetable oil
1 ounce salt pork, cut into ¼-inch
    dice (¼ cup)
¼ cup finely chopped green pepper
¼ cup finely chopped fresh parsley
1 tablespoon finely chopped
    scallions, including 1 inch of the
    green tops
1 teaspoon finely chopped garlic
1 cup uncooked long-grain white
    rice
¼ teaspoon crumbled dried thyme
A pinch of ground cloves
1 teaspoon salt

Place the mushrooms in a small enameled, stainless-steel or glass saucepan and pour in 2 cups of boiling water. Let the mushrooms soak for 30 minutes, then bring them to a boil over high heat. Reduce the heat to low and simmer uncovered for 15 minutes. Drain the mushrooms in a sieve set over a bowl, and measure and reserve the cooking liquid. If you are using European mushrooms chop them coarsely; leave the Haitian mushrooms whole.

In a heavy 3- to 4-quart saucepan, heat the oil over moderate heat until a light haze forms above it. Fry the pork in the oil, turning the pieces about with a spoon until they are crisp and brown and have rendered all of their fat. With a slotted spoon, transfer the pork to paper towels to drain. Add the green pepper, parsley, scallions and garlic to the fat remaining in the pan and stir for about 2 minutes, until the vegetables are soft but not brown.

Add the rice and stir constantly for 2 or 3 minutes, until the grains turn somewhat milky and opaque. Do not let them brown. Combine the reserved mushroom cooking liquid with enough boiling water to make 2 cups and pour the mixture over the rice. Stir in the mushrooms, pork, thyme, cloves and salt, and bring to a boil over high heat. Reduce the heat to low, cover tightly, and simmer for about 20 minutes, or until the rice has absorbed all the liquid in the pan and become a rich walnut-brown color. Taste for seasoning, fluff the rice with a fork, and serve at once.

Banane Pèsé *(Haiti)*
TWICE-FRIED PLANTAIN SLICES

To serve 4

½ cup vegetable oil
2 medium-sized green plantains,
    peeled *(page 55)* and cut crosswise
    into ½-inch-thick slices

In a heavy 12-inch skillet, heat the oil over moderate heat until a light haze forms above it. Add as many plantain slices as you can without crowding the pan, and brown them for about 2 minutes on each side. As they brown, transfer them to paper towels to drain. On a board, using a broad solid (not slotted) spatula, press each slice into a flat round about ¼ inch thick and 2 inches in diameter. Heat the oil and fry the rounds again for about 1 minute on each side. Drain on paper towels and serve at once. Traditionally, *banane pèsé* is served as an accompaniment to *griots (Recipe Index).*

Frituras de Ñame *(Dominican Republic)*
FRIED YAM CAKES

To make about 20 two-inch round
    cakes

1 pound fresh yams, not sweet
    potatoes *(see Glossary, page 197),*
    peeled and finely grated
1 tablespoon butter, melted and
    cooled
1 tablespoon finely grated onion
1 tablespoon finely chopped fresh
    parsley
1½ teaspoons salt
Freshly ground black pepper
2 egg yolks
¼ cup vegetable oil

In a deep bowl, combine the yams, butter, onion, parsley, salt and a liberal grinding of pepper, and mix well. Drop in the egg yolks and beat vigorously with a large spoon until the mixture is fairly smooth and thick enough to come away from the sides of the bowl in an almost solid mass.

Line a large shallow baking dish with paper towels and place it in the oven. Preheat the oven to the lowest setting. In a heavy 10- to 12-inch skillet, heat the oil over moderate heat until a light haze forms above it. For each cake, drop about a tablespoon of yam mixture into the hot oil. Cook 4 or 5 at a time, leaving space between them so that they can spread into 2- to 2½-inch rounds. Fry the cakes for about 4 minutes on each side, or until golden and crisp around the edges. As they brown, transfer the *frituras de ñame* to the lined dish to drain and keep warm. Serve at once.

Riz et Pois (Haiti)
RED BEANS AND RICE

In a large sieve or colander wash the beans under running water until the draining water runs clear. Transfer them to a heavy 3- to 4-quart saucepan, add ½ teaspoon of the salt and a few grindings of pepper, and pour in 6 cups of water. Bring to a boil over high heat; reduce the heat to low, and simmer partially covered for about 1½ hours, or until the beans are tender but still intact. Drain in a sieve set over a deep bowl and put the beans aside. Measure the cooking liquid and add enough water to make 4 cups.

In a heavy 2½- to 3-quart saucepan, melt 1 tablespoon of the lard over moderate heat. When it is very hot but not smoking, add the rice and stir for 1 or 2 minutes, until the grains turn somewhat milky and opaque.

Stir in the 4 cups of reserved liquid and water, the remaining teaspoon of salt and a liberal grinding of pepper, cover tightly, and reduce the heat to the lowest possible point. Simmer undisturbed for about 20 minutes, or until the rice is tender and has absorbed all the liquid. Taste for seasoning and set aside off the heat, partially covered to keep the rice warm.

Working quickly, melt the remaining 2 tablespoons of lard in a heavy 8- to 10-inch skillet. Drop in the beans and stir until they are heated through. Watch carefully for any sign of burning and regulate the heat accordingly.

Fluff the rice with a fork, mound it on a heated platter, and surround it or top it with the beans. Serve at once.

To serve 6

1 cup dried red kidney beans
1½ teaspoons salt
Freshly ground black pepper
6 to 8 cups water
3 tablespoons lard
2 cups uncooked long-grain white rice

Moros y Cristianos (Cuba)
BLACK BEANS AND RICE

In a large sieve or colander, wash the beans under cold running water until the draining water runs clear. Transfer the beans to a heavy 3- to 4-quart saucepan, pour in 7 cups of water, and bring to a boil over high heat. Reduce the heat to low and simmer partially covered for 2½ to 3 hours, or until the beans are tender but still intact. When the beans are done, almost all of the cooking liquid should have cooked away; if the liquid seems to be evaporating too quickly, add more boiling water when necessary.

Drain the beans in a sieve or colander. Mash 2 tablespoons of them to a smooth paste with a mortar and pestle or in a small bowl with the back of a fork. Set the beans and bean paste aside.

In a heavy 10- to 12-inch skillet, heat the oil over moderate heat until a light haze forms above it. Fry the pork in the oil, turning the dice about with a spoon until they are crisp and brown and have rendered all their fat. Remove them from the pan with a slotted spoon and drain on paper towels.

Add the garlic, onions and green pepper to the fat in the skillet. Stirring frequently, cook for about 5 minutes, until the vegetables are soft but not brown. Watch carefully for any sign of burning and regulate the heat accordingly. Stir in the bean paste, then add the beans and pork bits, reduce the heat to low, and simmer uncovered for 10 minutes.

Return the entire contents of the skillet to the saucepan and add the rice, salt and 2 cups of water. Stirring constantly, bring to a boil over high heat. Reduce the heat to low, cover tightly, and simmer for about 20 minutes, until the rice is tender and all the liquid has been absorbed. Taste and season with salt and a few grindings of pepper. Serve at once.

To serve 6 to 8

1 cup dried black beans
9 to 10 cups water
4 tablespoons vegetable oil
1 ounce lean salt pork, cut into ¼-inch dice (¼ cup)
½ cup finely chopped onions
¼ cup finely chopped green pepper
1 teaspoon finely chopped garlic
1½ cups uncooked long-grain white rice
1½ teaspoons salt
Freshly ground black pepper

To serve 4

1 pound salt cod
4 ounces salt pork, cut into ¼-
    inch dice
1 cup finely chopped onions
1 teaspoon finely chopped fresh
    hot chilies (caution: see page 46)
A 1-pound 2-ounce can of akee
    (about 1 cup), thoroughly drained
    (see Glossary, page 197)
A pinch of crumbled dried thyme
Freshly ground black pepper
1 firm ripe tomato, cut lengthwise
    into 8 wedges

Salt Fish and Akee (Jamaica)

Starting a day ahead, place the cod in a glass, enameled or stainless-steel pan or bowl, cover it with cold water, and soak for at least 12 hours, changing the water 3 or 4 times.

Drain the cod, rinse under cold running water, place it in a saucepan, and add enough fresh water to cover the fish by 1 inch. Bring to a boil over high heat. (Taste the water. If it seems excessively salty, drain, cover with fresh water, and bring to a boil again.)

Reduce the heat to low and simmer uncovered for about 20 minutes, or until the fish flakes easily when prodded gently with a fork. Drain thoroughly. With a small knife, remove and discard any skin and bones and separate the fish into coarse flakes. Set aside.

In a heavy 8- to 10-inch skillet, fry the salt pork over moderate heat, turning the dice about with a spoon until they are crisp and brown and have rendered all of their fat. Discard the pork.

Add the onions and chilies to the rendered fat in the skillet and, stirring frequently, cook for about 5 minutes, until they are soft but not brown. Watch carefully for any sign of burning and regulate the heat accordingly. Add the flaked cod, akee, thyme and a few grindings of pepper, and cook for a minute or two to heat them through.

To serve, transfer the entire contents of the skillet to a heated platter and garnish with the wedges of tomato.

To serve 4

A 1-pound 2-ounce can of akee
    (about 1 cup), thoroughly drained
    (see Glossary, page 197)
3 tablespoons butter, plus 1
    tablespoon butter, softened
3 tablespoons flour
1 cup milk
1 teaspoon Worcestershire sauce
½ teaspoon salt
¼ teaspoon white pepper
4 egg yolks
5 egg whites

Akee Soufflé (Jamaica)

Drop the akee into a small skillet or saucepan and slide the pan gently back and forth over moderate heat for about 5 minutes, or until all of the liquid has evaporated. With the back of a large spoon, force the akee through a fine sieve set over a deep mixing bowl or purée it through a food mill. Set the akee aside.

In a heavy 1½- to 2-quart saucepan, melt 3 tablespoons of the butter over moderate heat. When the foam begins to subside, stir in the flour and mix thoroughly. Pour in the milk and, stirring constantly with a whisk, cook over high heat until the mixture thickens heavily and comes to a boil. Reduce the heat to low and simmer for about 3 minutes to remove any taste of raw flour. Stir in the Worcestershire sauce, salt and white pepper.

Remove the pan from the heat and beat in the egg yolks, one at a time. Stir in the akee and cool the mixture to room temperature.

Preheat the oven to 375°. With a pastry brush, spread the tablespoon of softened butter evenly over the bottom and sides of a 1½-quart soufflé dish.

In a deep bowl, beat the egg whites with a whisk or a rotary or electric beater until they are stiff enough to stand in unwavering peaks on the beater when it is lifted from the bowl. Stir about one quarter of the whites into the akee mixture, then pour it over the remaining egg whites. Gently but thoroughly fold them together with a rubber spatula, using an over-under cutting motion rather than a stirring motion.

Pour the soufflé mixture into the prepared dish and lightly smooth the top with the spatula. Bake in the middle of the oven for about 35 minutes, or until the soufflé puffs above the rim of the dish and the top is lightly brown. Serve at once.

74

Bakes *(Trinidad)*
FRIED BISCUITS

Sift the flour, baking powder and salt together into a deep bowl and drop in the lard. Working quickly, use your fingertips to rub the flour and fat together until they look like grains of coarse meal. Pour in the sugar-and-water mixture all at once, toss together, and gather the dough into a ball. If the dough crumbles, add a little more cold water, a teaspoon or so at a time, until the particles adhere. For each biscuit, pinch off about 2 tablespoons of dough and pat it into a ball. On a lightly floured surface, roll each ball into a round about 3 inches in diameter and ¼ inch thick.

Pour oil into a heavy 10- to 12-inch skillet to a depth of about ¼ inch and heat until it is hot but not smoking. Fry the biscuits, four or five at a time, for about 3 minutes on each side, turning them with a slotted spoon and regulating the heat so they color richly and evenly without burning. As they brown, transfer them to paper towels to drain.

Serve the bakes warm, or at room temperature, with butter or cheese.

To make about 9 three-inch round biscuits

2 cups flour
2 teaspoons double-acting baking powder
1 teaspoon salt
2 tablespoons lard, chilled and cut into ¼-inch bits
2 teaspoons sugar dissolved in ¼ cup cold water
Vegetable oil for frying

Cassava Biscuits *(Barbados)*

Preheat the oven to 400°. With a sharp knife, peel the brown barklike skin from the cassava, then grate it finely on a hand grater. Wrap the grated root in a double thickness of cheesecloth and squeeze vigorously to extract its liquid. The liquid may be reserved for use as cassareep in pepper pot *(Recipe Index)*.

In a deep bowl, cream the butter, lard and sugar together, beating and mashing them against the sides of the bowl with a large spoon until the mixture is light and fluffy. Beat in the egg and the cassava and coconut.

Combine the flour and baking powder, and sift them onto a sheet of wax paper. Add about ½ cup at a time to the creamed mixture, beating well after each addition. The dough should be firm enough to be gathered into a compact ball; if necessary, add a little more flour a tablespoon at a time. When the dough becomes too stiff to stir, knead in the remaining flour with your hands.

On a lightly floured surface, knead the dough for 2 or 3 minutes, pushing it down with the heels of your hands, pressing it forward, and folding it back on itself. Then roll it into a circle about ¼ inch thick. With a biscuit cutter or the rim of a glass, cut the dough into 2-inch rounds. Gather the scraps into a ball, roll it out into another circle, and cut out rounds as before.

Place the rounds about 1 inch apart on one or two large ungreased baking sheets and bake in the middle of the oven for 20 minutes, or until the biscuits are firm to the touch and golden brown. Serve at once.

To make about 2 dozen 2-inch round biscuits

1 pound sweet cassava, or yuca *(see Glossary, page 197)*
4 tablespoons butter, softened
4 tablespoons lard
½ cup sugar
1 cup sugar
1 egg
1½ cups finely grated fresh coconut *(see Recipe Booklet)*
2 cups flour
1 teaspoon double-acting baking powder

Sorrel Drink *(Trinidad)*

Place the sorrel sepals, cinnamon stick, orange peel, whole cloves and sugar in a large jar or crock and pour the boiling water over them. Cool, cover with foil or plastic wrap, and set aside at room temperature for 2 or 3 days. Strain the liquid through a fine sieve, return it to the jar, and stir in the rum, ground cinnamon and ground cloves. (Discard the seasonings left in the sieve.)

Let the liquid stand at room temperature for another 2 or 3 days. Then strain it through a fine sieve lined with cheesecloth and refrigerate until thoroughly chilled. Pour into chilled glasses with or without ice; serve at once.

To make about 2 quarts

1 ounce dried Jamaica sorrel, or roselle, sepals *(see Glossary, page 197)*
A 3-inch piece of cinnamon stick
A 3-by-1-inch strip of fresh orange peel
3 whole cloves
1½ cups sugar
2 quarts boiling water
¼ cup medium-dark rum, such as Appleton Estates or Mount Gay
½ teaspoon ground cinnamon
¼ teaspoon ground cloves

IV

The Planter's Life: Rich, Plentiful Fare

Once only the rich families in the greathouses of the islands could afford meat, and the cooks devised many imaginative dishes to treat tropical foods in a Continental style. One favorite is baked papaya with spicy beef filling, shown next to a salad of watercress and onion rings.

The Caribbean's colonial era was a time of contrast. While those who worked the fields lived on vegetables, the planters who owned the fields enjoyed a life style as elegant as any back home in Europe. Their plantations had huge kitchens and large household staffs, and they combined Old World culinary traditions with the New World's plenty to produce legend-inspiring meals. They served all the vegetables that their lands produced, but the keystones of their generous cuisine were the meats and poultry raised on the plantations. And today, long after that opulence has gone, there remains a tradition of hearty eating and a treasury of fanciful meat recipes.

I first sensed the richness of this heritage at a farm on Jamaica. A friend had invited me to visit a family in a remote area of the island, two hours from Montego Bay along treacherous winding roads. Now I was seeing the variety of terrain that makes Jamaica different from many of the smaller islands. They are counties at best; Jamaica is a *country,* a collection of disparate elements. It has dozens of beaches, coral-reefed and silver-sanded, as well as palm trees that grow as much as 20 feet in five years. But Jamaica also has a dramatic interior—mountains and hills, fertile upland valleys with precariously perched villages. Here is the heart of the country and it dominates whatever occurs along the shores, from politics to weather.

We set out for the farm in daylight, but drove along roads so closely hemmed in by huge ferns and trees that we seemed to ride through dimly lit tunnels. Then the cane-scented tropical darkness descended quite as abruptly as the travel books say it does. The road got rougher and the houses farther apart, and soon the only lights to be seen were those of occasional roadside stalls. We stopped to treat ourselves to a "polismun," as the Jamaican Red Stripe beer is called, after the red stripe on the island's police uniforms. Soon there were no longer any stalls nor many people along the roads. For we had come to duppy country—ghost country—where many people still believe that the human personality is divided threefold into body, soul and shadow, and the shadow arises after death and wanders forth to terrify the living. Duppies do their wandering at night, so people stay at home, and all the houses we passed were tightly shuttered against ghosts.

When we finally reached the farm it was too dark to see the land and, surprisingly to me, too chilly up there in the hills to want to stay outside. The farmhouse was inviting, its kerosene lamps flickering defiance at the night and the duppies. Our hosts gave us some homemade sweet-potato wine, thick and warming, with a faint flavor of the raisins that had steeped in it. The potion soon took away our chill, and we toured the house, which turned out to be stuffed with the furniture of another era, when human beings liked to be dwarfed by their possessions. There were chairs in which I got lost and armoires that threatened me with their height, and an island-made table of mahogany, a grandiose four-footed creature, that took up the entire dining room. I wondered what my hostess could put upon it to fill all that space; for this was a table worthy of the massive silverware that was found everywhere on Jamaica in the days of piracy. (One Frenchman of the time suggested his countrymen would do better to plunder the tables of the English than the galleons of the Spanish silver fleet.)

But when dinner came I understood why such gigantic tables are still used in so many island homes; whenever afterward I sat down at one, whether on a plantation, a small farm like this one or even, once, in the city home of a Trinidad family that had once been farmers, I knew its entire surface would soon be covered with an astonishing array of dishes.

The display was one that spoke of the generosity of both the farmer and his fields. We began that night with Jamaican pepper-pot soup, thick and green with the farm's cultivated spinach and okra and the leaves of the prickly susumber bush that grows wild where other things will not. When the soup was cleared away, my hostess and the woman who helped her cook (and who had worked in this house for 40 years) carried in from the outside kitchen platter after platter of farm produce. There were vegetables in profusion, of course: roasted white yams; tender boiled chocho, a member of the squash family that combines the flavors of zucchini and cucumber; vivid orange carrots to complement the chochos' paleness; tomatoes; fried white breadfruit slices; baked plantains golden with butter.

But it was the meat dishes that were most exciting. In the center of the table, confusing me by an embarrassment of riches, were a plump roasted chicken, a baked loin of pork and a high-heaped casserole of goat. The chicken had been imaginatively stuffed with mashed bananas *(Recipe Index),* the pork was glazed with brown sugar *(Recipe Index),* and the goat, cut into cubes, had been curried.

I couldn't decide where to begin my meal or what combinations to put on my plate: The pork and plantains went together naturally, I knew, but what else? The chicken with chochos and carrots? The goat with the rice and breadfruit? My hostess solved the problem for me—there was no beginning; everything must be sampled, and all at once. This is customary in many island homes, and at first I found it as disconcerting as the traditional Oriental way of ending a meal with soup. There is no arbitrary separation of courses in the Caribbean. I have had fish and meat on my plate at once, bananas between them and vegetables all around. One keeps the tastes separate by following one's own order; a heaping plate is the ideal.

My plate certainly achieved the ideal that night. From among the wealth of tastes offered by the feast, the one that intrigued me most was the goat. I had never eaten it before and, like a lot of Americans, expected it to be stringy and gamy. I was wrong. First of all, the meat was incredibly tender—partly because, I discovered later, the cook had softened it in the old country fashion, rubbing it with green papaya, which has tenderizing juices. As for flavor, I have since affirmed what I then suspected through the dominant curry, that goat tastes mild and rather like lamb. In fact, because goat is hard to get in the United States, lamb makes a good substitute for it in curried goat *(Recipe Index)*. For this dish, with its coconut-flavored curry, is too good to miss for want of a goat. (The real thing is best, of course; but you are not likely to get it in Jamaica unless you leave the beaten tourist path. By all means do so—but be warned that the meat there is sometimes less carefully prepared than here and you are likely to encounter some bones.)

The venerable ancestry of many farm dishes is documented in a remarkable treasure that belongs to one of the oldest English families on Jamaica, the Pringles. It is an unpublished collection of recipes going back almost two centuries, compiled by a Pringle lady in the 1840s from the many instructions and scraps of paper she had inherited from aunts and grandmothers. The recipes—still being used by Pringle descendants—reveal how much attention and imagination the colonial planters' wives brought to bear on their unfamiliar surroundings. Ways to enhance the local foods share a place with ways to translate favorite European dishes. There is one recipe for squab pie so charming that I have long admired its unknown inventor. It is, she notes, a Devonshire dish, a poultry pie cooked with apples. But she is forced to "rearrange" it, substituting pork for the squab and chochos for the apples. Undaunted, she still calls it squab pie.

This antique collection also contains warnings that are clearly as valuable a contribution as the recipes themselves, for what not to eat had to be learned too. A note with the recipe for mutton with guinea-hen weed reads: "Avoid this altogether. The people soak the meat in vinegar which they fondly hope destroys the detestable taste of the weed; but it cannot do so completely and once smelt and tasted it cannot be mistaken. Sometimes beef tastes and smells of it too. Avoid that also."

Mutton with guinea-hen weed was presumably not on the menu at the plantation dinners enjoyed by Lady Janet Schaw, a Scottish lady who visited Jamaica and other islands in 1774. She was so impressed by her first plantation meal that she wrote, "In England it might figure in a newspaper, as if it were given by a Lord Mayor or the first Duke in the kingdom," but on her host's plantation it was merely "a family dinner." She was at first critical of such extravagance, but she concluded, "Why should we blame these people for their luxury? Since nature holds out her lap, filled with everything that is in her power to bestow, it were sinful in them not to be luxurious."

Continued on page 82

A Substantial Jamaican Favorite

India's culinary influence on the Caribbean has produced one dish that is an
island-wide party specialty in Jamaica: curried kid. In the United States, where
goat meat is a rarity, the curry may be made with lamb, as shown above *(Recipe
Index)*. With curry, islanders often serve *(counterclockwise from bottom right)* grated
fresh coconut, fried plantains *(Recipe Index)*, saffron rice and fresh pineapple.

In Lady Janet's day the expression "rich as a Creole" was as common as "rich as Rockefeller" is in our own. Mansions, called greathouses, that rivaled in spaciousness and furnishings the finest homes in Europe were built in the Caribbean, and even kings were awed by the wealth of their West Indian subjects. King George III once had his afternoon drive in London spoiled because he saw a coach more magnificent than his own. Learning it was the property of a Caribbean planter, he grumbled, "Sugar, eh?" and then, with jealousy, "All *that* sugar?"

Unfortunately for the Caribbean planters, in the mid-18th Century a German scientist succeeded in making a loaf of sugar from beets. (The Chinese had made a crude sugar from beet juice for centuries, but Europe and America had relied on sugar cane.) By the end of the century several European countries had begun to manufacture their own sugar right at home. This, combined with the antislavery movement and growing import duties on Caribbean sugar, began to shake the wealth of the planters.

So in the early decades of the 19th Century a period of decline set in and most of the Caribbean became, until after World War II, a sleepy and forgotten region. Small farmers once again obtained a foothold on many islands, as they had done before the great days of sugar. While they were not so rich as the estate owners, they nevertheless retained many of the traditions of the landholders of the past. My host's farm in the Jamaican hills had been in his family a hundred years. Once productive commercial acreage, it now provides only vegetables for local sale and sufficient meat for the family. It is neither a plantation nor even a very profitable farm, yet I found there pleasurable proof that dinner in such island households is still a momentous affair.

Unlike vegetables, which generally are prepared, cooked and eaten in quite similar ways on all the islands, meats have come to be handled quite differently on different island groups. Indeed, it is in meat dishes that the Caribbean cuisine best reflects the different geographic and cultural forces that have shaped the various islands. Because some islands are damp and some are arid, some hilly and some flat, and because some were owned by Spain and some by France, some by England and some by Holland during colonial times, important individual characteristics developed.

The Spanish, the earliest colonizers in the Caribbean, viewed their new possessions—once it was apparent that gold was not to be had from them—as supply houses from which to feed the busy conquistadors on the mainland. And so from the beginning of their settlement on Hispaniola they imported cattle, pigs, sheep and horses from Spain. So great was their success with livestock that as early as 1503 Hispaniola became self-sufficient, and by 1521 Jamaica, then a Spanish possession, was supplying not only its own meat needs but also those of the new colony of Panama. The Spanish continued to maintain diversified farming on their islands, including Cuba and Puerto Rico, producing proportionally less sugar and using fewer slaves than did the French and English. These powers entered the Caribbean later, at the time of Northern Europe's commercial interest in sugar cane. They went after the profit that sugar yielded and put almost all their land into cane, neglecting livestock even in areas where herds could flourish.

Thus to this day there are more beef dishes on the Spanish-speaking islands than on the others. Many are Caribbean translations of recipes from

Spain, but like all translations they take on a character of their own, changing the original in subtle but important ways. Cuba's popular *picadillo (Recipe Index)*, made of chopped or shredded beef, is clearly descended from an old Moorish dish cooked with olives and raisins, but it also contains the New World prizes of tomatoes and peppers—which in turn the modern Spanish have since adopted. *Ropa vieja (Recipe Index)*, which means old clothes, differs from its Spanish ancestor in having tomatoes and peppers and a handsome orange color derived from the annatto seeds used in its preparation.

Also found on all the Spanish-speaking islands is *sancocho*, a stew that can be made with anything from goat and chicken to pork and beef. I once helped a friend from the Dominican Republic shop in New York for the ingredients she needed for *sancocho*. We were all day about it. We went to the Puerto Rican market in Spanish Harlem on a cold snowy Saturday, wearing boots and furs and scarves, and I had to pause several times to buy hot coffee while waiting for Ilka to find what she had told me were "just a few essentials." These turned out to be plantains and chili peppers, cassava roots, sweet potatoes, yams and *lerenes*, a small tuber that looks like a new potato but has the crunchiness of a water chestnut. Her *sancocho*, which we ate next day (after it simmered for almost 3 hours), was superb. Its beef chunks and thick broth, almost imperceptibly sweetened with coconut, were the foreground of a tropical still life, a garden of roots and tubers. I forgot completely that we had nearly frozen the day before while she rummaged through the market's vegetable bins seeking the perfect companions to the meat.

The Spanish-speaking islands have also contributed excellent poultry and pork recipes to the Caribbean cuisine. *Lechon asado*, whole spit-roasted young pig, and *chicharrones*, crisp flavorful pork cracklings, are good examples. Less well known is *chicharrones de pollo*, small bits of crisp fried chicken, a specialty of Cuba and the Dominican Republic. The chicken is cut into perhaps 20 small pieces, marinated in lime juice and soy sauce, then dipped into flour and quickly deep fried. It is succulent within, crusty without, and is less messy to eat with the fingers than American fried chicken.

When a whole bird—a turkey, for instance—is roasted in the Spanish islands it is usually stuffed with an intriguing combination of chopped pork, ham or beef, olives, raisins and peppers, a kind of *picadillo*, a recipe within a recipe *(Recipe Index)*; in Puerto Rico, where the American custom of serving turkey at Thanksgiving has caught on, the ceremonial bird is always filled with a Spanish stuffing—a culinary demonstration of the two cultural ties that pull at the island.

A spectrum of meats—chopped pork, ham and beef—mixed with raisins, olives, capers, almonds and various other flavorings form the stuffing of another holiday favorite on Puerto Rico, *pasteles*. The meat mixture is placed on a plantain leaf spread with cornmeal or mashed plantains; then the leaf is folded to make an envelope and the whole thing is steamed. The slightly sweet fragrance of the plantain leaf gives *pasteles* a more enticing flavor than do the cornhusks that often wrap the similar Mexican tamales. Although *pasteles* can be eaten all year round, they are essential at Christmas time. In the country, carolers go from house to house, starting their rounds in the dead of night and singing hopefully at each stop, "Esta casa tiene puertas de acero, pero el que vive en ella es un caballero"—"This house has doors of

Continued on page 88

Elegance Paid For by Sugar Cane and Slavery

For the most part only the legends remain. The balls, the splendid dinners, the clothes and furniture and paintings brought at huge cost from Europe are no more. The legions of servants are gone. The greathouses that were a mark of the wealth of 18th Century planters have nearly all succumbed to hurricanes, termites and the inexorable pressures of modern economics. One of the few left is Whim Greathouse *(above)*, now restored as a museum, standing much as it did when it was erected around 1790 on the outskirts of Frederiksted on St. Croix in what was then the Danish Virgin Islands. (The U.S. bought the islands in 1917.) Relatively small and jewellike, the house was built in neoclassical style with a surrounding "moat" that allowed light to reach the cellar. Reputedly the original owner was a Dane with the un-Danish name of McEvoy—a somewhat mysterious figure, but obviously, since the place was built to order, a man of refined and expensive tastes. Not every greathouse can have been as exquisite as Whim, because not every owner shared its builder's sophistication. But it survives with some of its outbuildings *(left)* as a testament to the kind of life sugar cane and slavery once provided for a favored few.

While the greathouse served as a showplace, the real business of the estate went on elsewhere—in the fields, chimneyed boiling houses and cane-crushing windmills *(opposite)*. Even the cooking for the master's meals was customarily done in a separate kitchen building *(above)* equipped with a large stove and brick ovens. Here, using utensils like those on the table in the foreground, slaves prepared the food that was enjoyed in the stately dining room shown below.

Planting the cane in sections diked to hold rain water.

Cutting the tall cane and loading it on carts.

In 1823 an Englishman named William Clark published a handsome volume entitled *Ten Views in the Island of Antigua, in Which Are Represented the Process of Sugar Making, and the Employment of the Negroes, in the Field, Boiling House and Distillery.* Clark's pictures, five of which are reproduced here, illustrate the basic steps of sugar production in the Caribbean 150 years ago. They also indicate the essential role played by slaves in the West Indian economy of the time. Large numbers of workers were needed for every stage of the operation, from the hand planting of cane to the production of raw sugar. One contemporary observer reckoned that to run the smallest possible plantation profitably required a minimum of 250 slaves.

Boiling down the juice. In one step of the process a skimmer (left) ladles liquid sugar out of a vat.

Squeezing juice from the cane in a wind-powered mill. Two crushing rollers are visible in the mill.

Rolling hogsheads of dry sugar into boats—a tricky maneuver—for loading onto bigger vessels and eventual shipment abroad.

Whipping up the master's omelet was made easier for the 18th Century cook who was equipped with this wooden egg beater. Pushing and pulling the notched, horizontal rod causes the beater, bristling with pegs, to revolve rapidly.

Another piece of 18th Century kitchen equipment on exhibit—like the egg beater in the top picture—in the Whim Greathouse kitchen is this herb mill. Fresh or dried herbs were placed in the vessel, then pulverized by the toothed wooden disk.

steel but he who lives within is a gentleman." If he is, he opens his doors to the carolers and rewards them with a *concoco,* rum with coconut water, or a *con-limon,* rum with lime juice, and a heaping platter of *pasteles.* These must be hot even though it is the middle of the night, for another Puerto Rican folk song warns the host, "If you give me *pasteles* give me hot ones, for cold *pasteles* cause indigestion." When served piping hot, the little packages of highly seasoned meat are indeed like Christmas gifts themselves.

Farther down the Caribbean chain from the main Spanish-speaking islands lie the French jewels, Guadeloupe and Martinique, where the early planters, rich in sugar and rum and proud of their ties to the cultural center of Europe, lived in a cosmopolitan comfort that in many cases has lasted to this day. Here the lovely land seems to have a particular affinity for the sea; the low curving hills, called *mornes,* succeed one another like the gentle waves of the water beyond. And dotting the *mornes* like whitecaps on the sea are the sheep that contribute prominently to the cuisine of the French islands.

A current Martinican cookbook still gives an 18th Century recipe for barbecued sheep that calls for stuffing the animal with onions, spices, orange juice, wild ducks, sandpipers and other small birds, then pit-roasting it. More practical and familiar today is *mechoui,* spit-roasted sheep, which the islanders borrowed from their colonial cousins in Algeria. Their own unique contribution is, however, a lamb or mutton dish called *pâté en pot.*

It was the highlight of a meal I had during a visit to a Martinican plantation house. My host, Charles Clément, the owner of a cane and banana plantation and a distillery that produces one of the finest Caribbean rums, belongs to a distinguished Creole family long prominent on Martinique. With the enthusiasm for their island's history that marks the French Creoles, he took me early one morning to see the ruins of St. Pierre, the New World Pompeii. Once the most elegant city in the Caribbean, it was destroyed on May 2, 1902, when the volcano Mont Pelée erupted and destroyed the town and its inhabitants. The jumbled remains—broad, curving staircases that go nowhere, carved stone arches decorated with fleur-de-lis, bits of exquisite French floor tiles, a marble nude—are fascinating to explore; but I left depressed. So little in the Caribbean seems to last, I thought. Tiny destroyers like termites and vast ones like volcanoes, yearly hurricanes and the occasional uprisings of people too long oppressed demolish the old before the new can take hold. But back in my host's house, called Acajou, there was a sense of a past still vibrant. The building is 200 years old. Its floors are made of delicately tinted pale blue, gray and yellow tiles brought as ballast in French sailing ships. Its crystal chandeliers, gilt-edged mirrors and velvet chairs were carefully selected in Paris by people who meant to make their mark on Martinique, to stay and last out the violence of the tropics.

We sat on the red-bricked porch, surrounded by ferns and flowers, drinking a prelunch punch made with M. Clément's fine fragrant rum. It was 1 o'clock, not the best time for a hot meal, I thought; surely stuffed avocados or an iced breadfruit vichyssoise would have been better. But my host had made a special point of inviting me to taste *pâté en pot,* so I dutifully accompanied him to the mahogany-paneled dining room.

From the kitchen building came the cook carrying her offering in a huge china tureen. Soup? Well, yes, but also more than soup. *Pâté en pot* is made from many parts of a sheep or lamb—tripe, heart, belly, lungs and the meat from the feet and head, all finely chopped. It is one of the thickest soups I know. But it is not quite a stew; nor is it a pâté as we have come to use the word. Probably the name of the dish comes from another form of the word, *pâtée,* which denotes a pulpy consistency, a mash; to confuse things further, one French island gourmet suggests the name is a corruption of the word *patte,* which means paw. The confusion extends, in a delightful way, to the taste of the concoction. Mingling in fascinating complexity with the meat are cloves, garlic, hot pepper, thyme, bay leaf and celery, a kaleidoscope of textures and flavors that changes with every spoonful. In my enjoyment of the *pâté en pot* I stopped worrying about the origin of its name and forgot that it was a hot day in the tropics.

I didn't have time to think about that anyway, for the soup bowls were quickly followed by thick slices of a roast lamb that was as rare and juicy as any *gigot* I had eaten in Paris. The rest of the meal continued to mingle France and the Caribbean: The lamb was accompanied by a kind of plantain pudding; we then had coconut ice cream escorted by *petites madeleines* imported from France and followed by a tray of French blue and Camembert cheeses that we ate with sweet slabs of guava jelly. The conversation, too, was cosmopolitan. M. Clément had met Franklin Roosevelt and had also known many of the Caribbean independence leaders, Cheddi Jagan of Guyana and Bustamante of Jamaica among them. But like most of the French Creoles, he was in favor of continuing the French West Indies' close ties with their mother country; he cited a favorite French proverb: "God, I don't ask you to make me a rich man, but merely always to keep me close to one."

After lunch we sat in the parlor with its many remembrances of Madame Clément, my host's wife, who had died a few years before, but whose presence still seemed to dominate the house. In tribute to her, because she loved flowers, the room is filled each day with hibiscus blossoms carefully perched upon slender reed stalks. French in his romanticism, my host showed me his wife's photograph, a beautiful dark-eyed woman in a white ruffled gown. "Like Josephine," he said, for all the Martinicans talk often of Napoleon's adored empress, Josephine, who was born on this island.

We drank what my host called a "shrub," sometimes known as "shrob," a homemade liqueur, bittersweet with the flavor of sour oranges; then when the sun had lost its midday fierceness, we set off to view the ruins of Josephine's home. Only the foundation stones remain of La Pagerie, as the home was called. It was destroyed by a hurricane in 1766, when the future empress was a small girl. Later her father, a prosperous sugar planter, built a second, smaller house. Part of this house still stands, but it is the gardens, beautifully recreated, that best suggest Josephine's girlhood. Resplendent with red and white bougainvillea, climbing oleander bushes and pink amaryllis, the gardens evoke an image of the future empress running barefoot and free across the grass. She admired the Martinican countryside and once wrote with a burst of poetic enthusiasm, "Nature, rich and sumptuous, has covered our fields with a carpeting. . . . I love to hide myself in the green woods that skirt our dwelling place."

I asked the director of the restoration whether Josephine had served any favorite Martinican dishes when she was empress. He did not know, he said,

Continued on page 92

Now Cattle, Not Sugar, Brings Wealth to the Land

About 40 per cent of Jamaica's cultivable land is still occupied by vast estates, a legacy of the colonial past. But sugar is no longer the keystone of the plantation economy. Estate Braco, owned by V. C. Parnell, comprises 1,800 acres of rolling pastures, orchards and scrub woods in the northeast corner of the island. Cattle is now the big money enterprise; 600 head are sold from the ranch annually. And although this restored plantation house is not quite as grand as the greathouses of the past—it was originally built for the estate overseer—its graciousness proves that some of the old traditions of wealth from the land still live on.

Parnell and his wife entertain guests from England in the dining room at Braco, with a meal built around estate-grown beef. Most of the furniture is Jamaican mahogany, but the silver is antique English. Judging by the date of an overseer's journal found during renovation, the Parnells believe the house was built about 1790.

Most of "Val" Parnell's 900 head of cattle are Jamaican Brahmans, a hardy breed first taken to Jamaica from India in the early 19th Century to haul sugarcane wagons. At left, Parnell *(standing)* checks over part of his Brahman herd with head cattleman Percy Johnson. Nestled against the hill beyond them is the Braco Great House and, at the far left, an old sugar works now being used to distill allspice oil. Parnell also raises Aberdeen Angus *(below)* that have been "tropicalized" by crossbreeding with the Brahman strain.

but he did know that when Napoleon was exiled on St. Helena the one dish that roused his appetite was a fritter made of bananas marinated in rum. Perhaps, said the director, it was because it reminded Napoleon of his lost empress. She had retained throughout her days in Europe a lifelong passion for Martinican fruits and when she was living in Paris wrote home to ask her mother for supplies of guavas, mangoes, oranges and bananas.

Josephine was not the only princess the island produced. Madame de Maintenon, who became the last wife of Louis XIV in 1684 and died in the palace at Versailles, was born and raised on one of the tiniest, sleepiest islands in the Caribbean, Marie Galante. Throughout Europe, in fact, the women of the rich island families were thought to possess unequaled languid grace. ("Beautiful as a Creole" was a companion expression to "rich as a Creole.") It was undoubtedly the slow pace of their lives that gave them so much time to focus upon feminine grace. Many were surrounded by slaves and had little real work to do, and sometimes 18th Century artists poked fun at their lazy lives. One famous print shows a planter's wife demanding of her slave, "Mimbo, tell Quashebah to tell Dido to tell Sue to come and pick up my needle." The slave replies, "But Quashebah is gone to market and won't be back for three hours—and Sue is scratching the master's legs for two." "Oh, dear me," is the reply, "one must have the patience of Job to live in this world with any comfort. Here I must wait two hours for my needle."

Certainly there were women like that in the islands, but the satirists overlooked many others who were industrious and self-reliant. They not only took an ardent interest in running their homes and kitchens, but were adventurous souls ready for disasters of weather, war or sea. Père Labat, the French priest who lived on and wrote about Martinique, tells a delightful story about two planters' wives he encountered under trying circumstances. He was on his way from Martinique to St. Thomas, sailing, of all things, aboard a pirate vessel, when bad weather blew the ship off course, forcing it to put in for repairs at a tiny desert island in the eastern Caribbean. He was amazed to discover that another ship, beset while en route to Antigua, had abandoned two Barbadian ladies and their servants on the same island.

The priest and the ladies spent several days in each others' company and they indulged in the favorite sport permitted to Labat: eating. Exchanging recipes, the ladies taught Labat how to cook brisket of Irish beef, pâtés, turtle steaks and ragouts, and he taught them various methods of boucaning, or barbecuing, meats and in particular how to boucan a turtle. "Our two ladies took charge of everything in connection with the culinary department and performed wonders," Labat wrote admiringly, after the ship was repaired and the pirates had dropped the ladies off at Antigua. "I could write a volume on the subject," he declared, "telling how to serve 125 dishes at no cost on a desert island in magnificent style."

Among the recipes the two ladies may have taught the priest is one for conkies, a very old Barbadian specialty. Conkies are little banana-leaf envelopes filled with chopped meat, raisins and coconut, similar to the *pasteles* of the Spanish-speaking islands. Traditionally they were served on Barbados to celebrate that most English of holidays, Guy Fawkes Day. The island's post-colonial government, anxious to be independent of England in all ways, stopped the celebration of Guy Fawkes Day; but conkies have not gone out of favor, and they are served today for any special occasion on Barbados.

Barbados was in many ways the most aristocratic of the islands, for it was here that sugar cane was first planted and that the greatest sugar fortunes were made. The island was often called "Little England," because of the stuffy determination of its colonists to maintain the customs of home and because the landscape of Barbados bears an odd resemblance to England. Neat and tranquil, the Barbadian cane fields are set out remarkably like English wheat fields; manor houses dot the countryside, completing the illusion. It is only when you notice that the trees dividing the fields are tall palms that you remember that this island is a tropical one.

Here, in placid surroundings, the planters lived the most luxurious life in all the islands. In 1700 a visitor wrote, "The opulence and good taste of the inhabitants may be remarked in their furniture, which is magnificent, and in their silver, which they have in considerable quantities. . . . They eat much meat and little bread, and their tables are well served. They have excellent cooks and very fine linen and much order and cleanliness. . . . Their houses are well-stocked with every kind of wine and liqueur and they are delighted if their guests are hard put to it to find their way home."

Today's traveler finds many reminders of this way of life on Barbados. Every mile or so the sugar cane is interrupted by an arcade of trees leading to a graceful manor house with impressive double staircase and pillared porticos. Within, carefully carved doorways open into spacious, cool rooms with furniture in the style of Sheraton and Hepplewhite, beautifully copied by Barbadian craftsmen in local lignum vitae, mahogany and cordia.

I stopped one afternoon to visit a family in one of these homes, not to eat but just to talk. The house looked much as it must have looked when it was built in 1840, shortly after a hurricane had destroyed all the really old homes on the island and virtually all its trees. Delightful touches of the past were everywhere. The kitchen tables still have little cups of water at their feet to drown any ants ambitious enough to attempt to climb the table legs. The water container once found in all island homes but rarely seen now was still in use, a large, porous limestone vat through which rain water slowly seeped into a handsome pottery jug. And the native mahogany table inlaid with whalebone was set with delicate china and massive silver for dinner that evening. I asked what would be served and was told that the meal was to be a traditional plantation one, like the one I had eaten on Jamaica. There would be pepper pot, lots of farm vegetables, glazed roast pork and—a Barbadian specialty at the turn of the century—duck with tomatoes, chives, thyme and garlic, all simmered in local rum.

While planters in the English and French colonies of the 18th Century were cultivating their sugar crops and grooming their plantations, quite a different, though still affluent, life style was developing on the various Dutch-owned islands. Small and few in number, they had an economic and culinary effect on the Caribbean area out of proportion to their size. Here there was never a strong plantation tradition. When the Dutch entered the scramble for Caribbean territory they were not seeking agricultural lands but salt for their North Sea fisheries and, being already a mercantile people, bases from which they could trade. They established commercial ports on Statia in the northeast corner of the Caribbean, and Curaçao in the south, and both is-

Radial steps lead gracefully to the entrance of Acajou, paternal home of the Clément family on Martinique. *Acajou* means mahogany, a tree that grows in abundance locally. The Clément plantation produces bananas and several of Martinique's splendid rums; it exports the bananas and much of the rum to Europe.

lands soon became very rich, handling large numbers of slaves and European goods. Statia was destroyed by the British in 1781 and never recovered its prosperity, but Curaçao remained the key trading island in the Caribbean for three centuries. The capital, Willemstad, with its Dutch-style gabled buildings painted in picturesque pastel shades, became the most European-looking city in the Caribbean.

The prominent Curaçaoans even today are merchants. The ancestors of many of them were Sephardic Jews who went to the island in the early 1600s, fleeing the Inquisition that had driven them from Spain and Portugal. Deeply rooted in the island's history, they are secure and generous and their life has a placid pace. Because for centuries there was considerable wealth on the tiny island and little opportunity to spend it, people had to rely on one another for diversion. Two food-oriented social customs resulted. One is the birthday reception, an open house held from dawn to dusk and attended by everyone who knows the person whose birthday it is, however slight the acquaintance. The other social event, teatime, has become less important now than it was 50 years ago, when society was smaller and everyone knew everyone. In those days teatime was known as the "gossip hour" by the maids of the well-to-do, and tea itself in the Papiamento dialect was called *awa di redu*, "gossip water."

Papiamento, a second language spoken everywhere on the Dutch islands, is a combination of Spanish, Dutch and English, with a smattering of Portuguese, French and African words. But if one knows Dutch and English and has no Spanish, Papiamento is hard to understand, while if one knows Spanish and not the other two there is little difficulty. Similarly, Curaçaoan cooking, while a mixture, is more Spanish than anything else, largely because Spain held the islands for more than a century before the Dutch took over in 1634. I was invited one afternoon to the "gossip hour" at the home of a Curaçaoan merchant. My hostess' friends had helped prepare the typical teatime treats. These were flaky, buttery little pastries and leaf-wrapped parcels containing meat, fish or cheese. The cheese-filled *pastechi,* the chopped beef, banana-leaf-wrapped *ayacas* and the cornmeal and beef *cachapas* that we ate at teatime differed little from the *pasteles* of Puerto Rico and the *hallacas* and *arequipas* of the mainland.

My hostess' house, built in the fashion favored on Curaçao, was three-sided, with a large inner garden providing access to all rooms. Curaçao has so little rainfall that its people use their gardens as integral parts of their living quarters. The gardens are difficult to keep green, however, and the only time a Curaçaoan lady loses her temper is when one of the hundreds of goats that roam the island gets into her garden to gorge on the carefully nurtured grass. There is, my hostess told me, constant battling in the newspaper between the garden-minded who want the goats restricted and the tourist-minded who claim that snapping pictures of the goats is a major enjoyment for visitors. All of which is beside the point, she said, for without the goats Curaçaoans would be deprived of one of their favorite dishes, *stobá.*

This complex stew has been immortalized in a folk song as common among the island's children as "Mary Had a Little Lamb" is among ours. It sings the praises of a certain Alberta, the cook of Shon (Madame) Rica Tutuchi:

> *Alberta of Shon Rica Tutuchi*
> *Only has one eye*
> *One eye alone has she.*
> *But with that eye she sees the onions*
> *Sees the tomatoes*
> *Sees all the seasonings*
> *to throw into stobá.*

And, as one of the guests asserted, seeing all the seasonings for *stobá* is no easy matter, even with two eyes, for the stew requires capers, cumin, celery, garlic, ginger, olives, limes, sweet peppers, hot peppers, cucumbers and shallots, as well as goat or lamb.

I sat all afternoon in the garden, listening fascinated to the lore of Curaçao, and when the day had grown cool we went into town. It was late afternoon and the Dutch houses were daintily pink and blue and yellow in the waning sunlight. My hostess explained the reason the houses are pastel-painted: An early Dutch governor of the island suffered from severe headaches and, deciding they were caused by the strong sunlight glaring on white houses, issued a decree forbidding the use of white paint. The results of this autocratic fiat are lovely, and they form a delicate background for the dazzling goods displayed in Willemstad shops, which are as sumptuously stocked as the finest stores in New York and Paris. Precious stones, china, silver, cameras, watches, tape recorders, luxury item after luxury item line the display windows. Whether I was overstuffed with *pastechi* and *cachapas,* or merely held by the fascination all shoppers feel in Curaçao, I was reluctant when

With the wealth amassed over several centuries as the Caribbean's foremost traders, the burghers of Willemstad, Curaçao, built these shops and houses, whose Dutch-style façades might well grace a canal in Amsterdam. They stand in the city's Punda Quarter, looking out on St. Anna Bay. At right is the Queen Emma pontoon bridge, which opens at least 30 times a day to let vessels pass on their way to or from the sea.

my hostess told me it would soon be time for dinner. I felt a bit like a visitor to the islands of many years ago, a Lady Nugent, who, overfed on exotic foods, complained, "I am doomed to go to dinner."

Yet I made a remarkable recovery that night when I was introduced to what is perhaps the Caribbean's most unusual and exciting dish, *keshy yena (Recipe Index)*. The name is Papiamento and very close to the Spanish words *queso* (cheese) and *llena* (filled). I thought it was a pale-yellow casserole my hostess was carrying to the table, but it turned out to be a huge Edam cheese that had just spent almost an hour baking in the oven and yet had retained its firm roundness. The top of the cheese had been sliced off to be used as a cover and the inside had been hollowed out as one scoops a pumpkin, then mixed with chopped beef, olives, tomatoes and onions and put back inside the cheese.

My hostess set the cheese before me and asked me to lift the cover. An entrancing aroma leaped out, and the taste of melted cheese and meat within was even better. I decided then and there to try to make *keshy yena* when I returned to New York, and eventually I did so, but I altered the Curaçaoan method by baking a small cheese for each guest, so that all could have that enchanted moment of surprise, lifting the lid to let the genie of delicious smells escape. I labored long over the small Edams, peeling the wax off and hollowing them out to a half-inch thickness. But it was fun, reminding me of the childhood pleasure of modeling bowls of clay to be fired in the oven. When you make *keshy yena*, I thought, you really make something. The cheese and meat filling is very savory (and may be interestingly varied to in-

96

clude shrimp, fish or chicken instead of meat), but the thrill of this dish lies in its look as well as its flavor. Unfortunately this advantage is lost when *keshy yena* is served in another way that is sometimes dictated by practicality: the meat filling is surrounded by slices of Edam, rather like a giant cheeseburger. This version is quicker, perhaps, and more convenient, but it seems to me rather like giving someone a Christmas present that hasn't any wrapping paper or ribbon.

My own *keshy yena* was a success, but there were two things I could not give my guests at home that were given me on Curaçao. One was the refreshing local beer, whose distinctive taste may come from the distilled sea water that is the only potable water the island has. The other was my host's entertaining, nostalgic tales of life on Curaçao when he was a boy, when the tram went into town only once a day and people stopped the driver to ask him to deliver their messages and packages all over town, and when the island's one telephone operator listened in on everyone's calls so that she could serve as a central source of news of people's health or whereabouts.

In fact, wherever I have been in the islands, nostalgic stories and the foods and flavors of the past are on everybody's tongue. In this part of the world, which is changing every day, perhaps the past serves as a source of personal and even social stability. New governments, new industries are dramatically altering the Caribbean, and much that is connected with the past is disappearing. But when it comes to food, dishes that were once enjoyed only by the very rich are not disappearing, but are being revived, gradually forming a heritage for all who live on the islands.

Being semiarid, Curaçao must depend on its neighbors for fresh fruits and vegetables. Fortunately its neighbors—Venezuela and the islands of Aruba and Bonaire—are well able to fill the need. At the "schooner market" along the Ruyterkade in Willemstad trading vessels put up canvas flies for shade, and sell their cargoes—which also include dry goods—directly to housewives and shopkeepers.

To serve 6 to 8

A 5- to 6-pound lean pork loin,
    preferably center cut
2 cups chicken stock, fresh or canned
1 cup light-brown sugar
2 tablespoons dark rum
2 teaspoons finely chopped garlic
2 teaspoons ground ginger
½ teaspoon ground cloves
1 medium-sized bay leaf, crumbled
1 teaspoon salt
¼ teaspoon freshly ground black
    pepper
¼ cup light rum
2 teaspoons arrowroot combined
    with 1 tablespoon cold water
3 tablespoons strained fresh lime
    juice

Roast Pork Calypso *(Jamaica)*

Preheat the oven to 350°. With a sharp knife, lightly score the pork loin by making diagonal cuts ¼ inch deep at 1-inch intervals on the fat side. Place the pork scored side up in a shallow roasting pan just large enough to hold it comfortably. (If you prefer to use a meat thermometer, insert it into the loin after you have scored the fat side. Be sure the tip of the thermometer does not touch any fat or bone.) Roast the loin in the middle of the oven for 1 hour, or until the pork is golden brown. Remove the pan from the heat and transfer the loin to a cutting board or platter. Skim the fat from the juices in the pan, pour in the stock, and set the pan and its liquid aside.

With a large mortar and pestle or in a small bowl with the back of a spoon, mash the brown sugar, 2 tablespoons of dark rum, the garlic, ginger, cloves, bay leaf, salt and pepper to a smooth paste. With a metal spatula or your fingertips, spread the paste evenly over the scored side of the pork. Return the loin to the pan scored side up, and roast in the middle of the oven for another 30 minutes, or until the surface is crusty and brown. (The thermometer should reach a temperature of 160° to 165°.)

Transfer the loin to a heated platter and let it rest for 10 minutes for easier carving. Meanwhile, warm the ¼ cup of light rum in a small skillet over low heat. Off the heat, ignite the rum with a match, then slide the skillet gently back and forth until the flames die out.

Bring the liquid remaining in the baking pan to a boil over high heat. Give the arrowroot-and-water mixture a quick stir to recombine it and add it to the pan. Stirring constantly, cook briskly until the sauce thickens enough to coat the spoon heavily. Remove the pan from the heat and stir in the flamed rum and the lime juice. Taste for seasoning and pour the sauce into a heated bowl or sauceboat. Serve accompanied by cornmeal coo-coo *(below)* or *christophene au gratin (Recipe Index).*

To serve 4 to 6

½ pound fresh okra or a 10-ounce
    package frozen okra, thoroughly
    defrosted
2 cups water
1 teaspoon salt
1 cup yellow cornmeal
2 tablespoons butter, softened

Cornmeal Coo-Coo *(Barbados)*
FLAT CORNMEAL AND OKRA CAKE

Wash the fresh okra under cold running water and, with a small, sharp knife, scrape the skin lightly to remove any surface fuzz. (Frozen okra needs only to be defrosted.) Cut ⅛ inch off the stem at the narrow end of each pod, and slice the okra crosswise into ¼-inch-thick rounds. Combine the okra, water and salt in a heavy 1½- to 2-quart saucepan, and bring to a boil over high heat. Reduce the heat to low, cover tightly, and simmer for 10 minutes, until the okra is tender but still intact.

Stirring constantly, pour in the cornmeal in a slow thin stream. Cook over moderate heat, still stirring, for about 5 minutes, or until the mixture is thick enough to leave the bottom and sides of the pan in a solid mass.

Spoon the mixture onto a heated serving plate and, with a metal spatula, shape it into a round cake about 1 inch thick and 8 inches in diameter. Spread the top with the softened butter and serve at once. Cornmeal coo-coo is a traditional accompaniment to meat dishes such as roast pork calypso, *chicharrones de pollo,* or *pollo a lo agridulce (Recipe Index).*

Jamaica's roast pork calypso, shown at top, is a
succulent loin coated with a crunchy glaze of brown
sugar, rum, garlic and ginger, garnished with slices
of fresh lime and served *(right)* with a spoonful of
lime and rum sauce. Balancing the spiciness of the
pork is a mild coo-coo from Barbados, a cornmeal
cake studded with okra and brushed with butter.

To serve 6

3 pounds lean boneless shoulder of
   lamb, trimmed of excess fat and
   cut into 1½-inch cubes
4 tablespoons butter
2 tablespoons vegetable oil
3 cups finely chopped onions
3 tablespoons curry powder
1 tablespoon finely chopped fresh
   hot chilies (caution: see page 46)
½ teaspoon ground allspice
2 teaspoons salt
Freshly ground black pepper
1 cup coconut milk made from
   1 cup coarsely chopped fresh
   coconut and 1 cup milk (see Recipe
   Booklet)
1 cup chicken stock, fresh or canned
1 medium-sized bay leaf
2 tablespoons strained fresh lime
   juice

To serve 4

A 1½- to 2-pound flank steak,
   trimmed of excess fat
1 large onion, peeled and coarsely
   chopped
1 medium-sized bay leaf
3 teaspoons salt
Freshly ground black pepper
2 quarts water
3 tablespoons annatto oil (page 47)
1½ cups finely chopped onions
1 teaspoon finely chopped garlic
1 cup finely chopped green pepper
½ teaspoon finely chopped fresh hot
   chilies (caution: see page 46)
1 large carrot, scraped and finely
   chopped
6 medium-sized firm ripe tomatoes,
   peeled, seeded and finely chopped
   (see sopa de gandules, page 43), or
   substitute 2 cups chopped drained
   canned tomatoes
⅛ teaspoon ground cinnamon
⅛ teaspoon ground cloves
1 tablespoon capers, washed and
   drained
1 whole canned pimiento, drained
   and finely chopped

Curried Lamb (Jamaica)

Pat the lamb cubes completely dry with paper towels. In a heavy 10- to 12-inch skillet, melt 2 tablespoons of the butter in the oil over moderate heat. When the foam begins to subside, drop 6 or 7 cubes of lamb into the hot oil. Turn them about with a spoon until the cubes are brown on all sides, regulating the heat so they color richly and evenly without burning. As they color, transfer the cubes to a plate and brown the remaining lamb similarly.

Melt the remaining 2 tablespoons of butter in the skillet, add the onions and, stirring frequently, cook for about 5 minutes, or until they are soft and transparent but not brown. Add the curry, chilies, allspice, salt and a few grindings of pepper and, stirring constantly, simmer for 2 or 3 minutes.

Return the lamb and the juices that have accumulated around it to the skillet, stir in the coconut milk, stock and bay leaf, and bring to a boil over high heat. Reduce the heat to low, cover tightly, and simmer for 1¼ hours, or until the lamb shows no resistance when pierced with the point of a sharp knife. Remove the bay leaf and stir in the lime juice. Taste for seasoning.

To serve, mound the lamb on a deep, heated platter or in a heated bowl and pour the sauce over it. Curried lamb is traditionally accompanied by plain boiled or saffron rice and mango chutney (Recipe Index).

NOTE: In Jamaica, this curry is prepared with goat meat rather than lamb —and you may substitute kid or goat if it is available.

Ropa Vieja (Cuba)
SPICED BOILED FLANK STEAK

Place the flank steak in a heavy 4- to 5-quart casserole, add the coarsely chopped onion, 1 bay leaf, 2 teaspoons of the salt and a few grindings of pepper, and pour in the water. The water should cover the steak by at least 2 inches; if necessary, add more water. Bring to a boil over high heat, reduce the heat to low, partially cover the casserole, and simmer for 1½ hours, or until the meat shows no resistance when pierced with the point of a sharp knife.

Transfer the steak to a plate to cool. Strain the cooking liquid through a fine sieve set over a bowl, and discard the onion and bay leaf. When the steak is cool enough to handle, cut it along the grain into ¼-inch-wide strips and slice the strips crosswise into 2-inch-long pieces. Set the meat and cooking liquid aside.

Pour the annatto oil into the casserole and heat it over moderate heat until a light haze forms above it. Drop in the 1½ cups of finely chopped onions and the garlic, green pepper, chilies and carrot. Stirring frequently, cook for about 5 minutes, until the vegetables are soft but not brown. Watch carefully for any sign of burning and regulate the heat accordingly.

Stir in the tomatoes, cinnamon, cloves, the remaining 1 teaspoon of salt and a few grindings of pepper, and cook briskly until most of the liquid in the pan evaporates and the mixture is thick enough to hold its shape lightly on the spoon. Return the meat to the casserole, add 1½ cups of the reserved stock, and the capers. Stirring constantly, cook for 2 or 3 minutes to heat the meat through. Taste for seasoning.

To serve, transfer the entire contents of the casserole to a heated platter or serving bowl and sprinkle the pimiento on top. Serve with fried plantains or riz et pois (Recipe Index).

Sancocho *(Trinidad)*
BEEF AND VEGETABLE STEW

Place the corned beef in a heavy 2- to 3-quart saucepan and add enough cold water to cover it by about 2 inches. Bring to a boil over high heat, reduce the heat to low, and simmer partially covered for 1 hour. Drain thoroughly and cut the corned beef into 1-inch cubes.

Meanwhile, lay the plantains in a heavy 12-inch skillet, pour in enough water to cover them completely, and bring to a boil over high heat. Cook briskly for 30 minutes, then drain, peel and cut the plantains crosswise into 1-inch-thick slices. Set them aside.

In a heavy 6- to 8-quart casserole, fry the pork over moderate heat, turning the dice about with a spoon until they are crisp and brown and have rendered all their fat. Discard the pork and drop the beef and corned beef into the hot fat. Brown the meats, turning the cubes frequently and regulating the heat so that they color richly and evenly without burning. With a slotted spoon, transfer the cubes to a plate.

Add the onions to the fat remaining in the casserole and, stirring frequently, cook for 5 minutes, until they are soft and transparent but not brown. Watch carefully for any sign of burning and regulate the heat accordingly. Return the meat cubes to the casserole, add the split peas, stock, salt and a liberal grinding of pepper. Bring to a boil over high heat, then reduce the heat to low, cover tightly, and simmer for 1 hour.

Add the white potatoes, sweet potatoes, dasheen, cassava, yams, chili and coconut cream. Cover and simmer for 15 minutes, or until the meat and vegetables are tender but not falling apart. Add the cornmeal dumplings and simmer partially covered for 15 minutes, until they puff up and rise to the surface. Then gently stir the reserved plantain slices into the stew, and simmer for 5 minutes longer to heat them through.

Serve at once, directly from the casserole or from a large heated tureen.

Cocido de Riñones *(Puerto Rico)*
KIDNEY STEW

In a heavy 8- to 10-inch skillet, heat 3 tablespoons of the olive oil over moderate heat until a light haze forms above it. Add the onions and garlic and, stirring frequently, cook for about 5 minutes, until they are soft and transparent but not brown. Watch carefully for any sign of burning and regulate the heat accordingly.

Add the tomatoes and vinegar and, still stirring, cook briskly until most of the liquid in the pan has evaporated and the mixture is thick enough to hold its shape lightly in the spoon. This mixture is called a *sofrito*. Remove the pan from the heat.

Heat the remaining 4 tablespoons of olive oil in a heavy 10- to 12-inch skillet. Pat the pieces of kidney completely dry with paper towels and sprinkle them with salt and a few grindings of pepper. Drop the kidneys into the hot oil and, turning them frequently, cook for 4 to 6 minutes, or until they are firm and lightly browned on all sides. Pour the *sofrito* over the kidneys and, stirring constantly, cook for a minute or two to heat the *sofrito* through.

Taste for seasoning and serve at once from a heated platter or bowl with plain boiled rice.

To serve 6 to 8

½ pound lean corned beef
2 large green plantains, washed but not peeled
4 ounces salt pork, finely diced
2 pounds lean, boneless beef, preferably beef chuck, trimmed of excess fat and cut into 1-inch cubes
2 cups finely chopped onions
1 cup dried yellow split peas
3 quarts freshly made beef stock, or 6 cups concentrated canned beef stock combined with 6 cups water
2 teaspoons salt
Freshly ground black pepper
1 pound boiling potatoes, peeled and cut into 1-inch slices
1 pound sweet potatoes, peeled and cut into 1-inch slices
½ pound dasheen (taro root), peeled and cut into 1-inch slices
½ pound cassava root, peeled and cut into 1-inch slices
½ pound yams, peeled and cut into 1-inch slices
1 fresh red or green hot chili, about 3 inches long, washed but left intact with stem attached *(caution: see page 46)*
1 cup coconut cream made from 1 cup coarsely chopped fresh coconut and 1 cup heavy cream *(see Recipe Booklet)*
Cornmeal dumplings *(Recipe Booklet)*

To serve 4

7 tablespoons olive oil
½ cup finely chopped onions
1 teaspoon finely chopped garlic
3 medium-sized firm ripe tomatoes, peeled, seeded and finely chopped *(see sopa de gandules, page 43)*, or substitute 1 cup chopped drained canned tomatoes
1 tablespoon malt vinegar
1½ pounds lamb kidneys, trimmed of excess fat, and cut into quarters
½ teaspoon salt
Freshly ground black pepper

Cuba's *brazo gitano*—a baked cassava roll with corned beef filling—is named after a Spanish dessert that is rolled the same way.

To serve 6 to 8

A 5- to 6-pound green papaya *(see box, page 116)*, cut lengthwise into halves and seeded
3 tablespoons vegetable oil
½ cup finely chopped onions
½ teaspoon finely chopped garlic
1 pound lean ground beef
4 medium-sized firm ripe tomatoes, peeled, seeded and finely chopped *(see sopa de gandules, page 43)*, or substitute 1½ cups chopped drained canned tomatoes
1 teaspoon finely chopped fresh hot chilies *(caution: see page 46)*
1 teaspoon salt
Freshly ground black pepper
4 tablespoons freshly grated imported Parmesan cheese

Baked Papaya with Meat Filling *(Jamaica)*

Preheat the oven to 350°. In a heavy 10- to 12-inch skillet, heat the oil over moderate heat until a light haze forms above it. Drop in the onions and garlic and, stirring frequently, cook for about 5 minutes, until they are soft and transparent but not brown. Stir in the beef and, mashing it with a spoon to break up any lumps, cook until all traces of pink disappear. Add the tomatoes, chilies, salt and a few grindings of pepper. Stirring occasionally, cook briskly until most of the liquid in the pan has evaporated and the mixture is thick enough to hold its shape almost solidly in the spoon. Taste for seasoning.

Spoon the meat mixture into the papaya shells, spreading and smoothing the filling with a spatula. Place the shells side by side in a shallow roasting pan. Set the pan in the middle of the oven, and pour in enough boiling water to come about 1 inch up the sides of the papayas. Bake for 1 hour. Then sprinkle each shell with 1 tablespoon of the cheese, and bake for 30 minutes, or until the papaya shows no resistance when pierced with the point of a small knife and the top is delicately browned.

To serve, transfer the papaya shells to a large heated platter and sprinkle them with the remaining 2 tablespoons of cheese.

102

Brazo Gitano *(Cuba)*
BAKED CASSAVA ROLL WITH CORNED-BEEF FILLING

Place the corned beef in a large saucepan or casserole and add enough cold water to cover the meat by about 2 inches. Bring to a boil over high heat, reduce the heat to low, and simmer partially covered for 2½ to 3 hours, or until the corned beef is tender and shows no resistance when pierced with the point of a sharp knife.

Drain the corned beef thoroughly and, when it is cool enough to handle, trim off and discard all its fat. With a small, sharp knife, cut the meat into strips about ⅛ inch wide and 1 to 1½ inches long and set it aside.

Meanwhile, drop the cassava slices into enough lightly salted boiling water to cover them completely. Reduce the heat to moderate and cook partially covered for about 1 hour, or until the cassava is tender but still intact. Drain the cassava in a sieve or colander, return the slices to the pan and slide it back and forth over moderate heat for 10 to 15 seconds, until the cassava is completely dry.

Force the cassava through a ricer set over a deep bowl, or mash it thoroughly with a fork. Then beat in 4 tablespoons of the softened butter, 2 of the eggs (1 at a time), 1½ cups of flour (about ½ cup at a time) and 1 teaspoon of the salt.

Continue to beat until the cassava mixture is smooth and dense enough to hold its shape almost solidly in a spoon. (If the mixture seems too fluid, beat in the remaining flour, a tablespoon at a time.) Cover the bowl tightly with plastic wrap and set aside.

Preheat the oven to 350°. With a pastry brush, coat a large baking sheet with the remaining tablespoon of softened butter.

In a heavy 10- to 12-inch skillet, melt 2 tablespoons of butter over moderate heat. When the foam begins to subside, add the onions and garlic and, stirring frequently, cook for about 5 minutes, until they are soft and transparent but not brown. Watch carefully for any sign of burning and regulate the heat accordingly.

Stir in the tomatoes, chilies, the remaining teaspoon of salt and a few gridings of pepper. Still stirring, cook briskly until most of the liquid in the skillet evaporates and the mixture is thick enough to hold its shape. Off the heat stir in the corned beef and taste for seasoning.

Gather the cassava dough into a ball, place it on a lightly floured sheet of wax paper, and pat it into a thick rectangle. With a floured pin, roll the dough into a rectangle about 12 inches wide, 18 inches long and ½ inch thick. Dust the top from time to time with a little flour to prevent it from sticking to the pin.

Spread the meat mixture evenly over the surface of the dough, to within about 1½ inches of the outside edges. Starting with the long side of the dough, lift the wax paper and, using it for support, roll the dough lengthwise into a thick, compact cylinder.

With 2 large spatulas, transfer the *brazo gitano* to the baking sheet. Beat the third egg with a whisk or fork until it is light and lemon colored, then brush it over the top and sides of the roll. Bake in the middle of the oven for about 1 hour, or until the crust is golden brown.

Transfer the roll to a heated platter, cut it crosswise into 3-inch-thick slices, and serve the *brazo gitano* at once.

To serve 6

1 pound lean corned beef
2 pounds fresh cassava root, peeled and cut crosswise into ½-inch-thick slices *(page 50)*
5 tablespoons butter, softened, plus 2 tablespoons butter
3 eggs
1½ to 2 cups flour
2 teaspoons salt
1 cup finely chopped onions
1 teaspoon finely chopped garlic
6 medium-sized firm ripe tomatoes, peeled, seeded and finely chopped *(see sopa de gandules, page 43),* or substitute 2 cups chopped drained canned tomatoes
2 teaspoons finely chopped fresh hot chilies *(caution: see page 46)*
Freshly ground black pepper

Haiti's *poulet rôti à la créole* is a double-stuffed roast chicken surprise, with banana stuffing in the breast cavity and a bread-crumb mixture in the neck. The stuffing ingredients include *(from left)* garlic, brown sugar, bananas, toasted crumbs, rum, lime and nutmeg.

To serve 4

¼ cup dark rum
¼ cup soy sauce, preferably the
    Japanese type
¼ cup strained fresh lime juice
A 3½- to 4-pound chicken, chopped
    into 16 small pieces by dividing
    the wings, thighs, drumsticks and
    breasts into halves
2 cups vegetable oil
½ teaspoon salt
Freshly ground black pepper
1 cup flour

Chicharrones de Pollo (*Dominican Republic*)
MARINATED FRIED CHICKEN

Warm the rum in a small pan over low heat. Off the heat, ignite the rum with a match and gently shake the pan back and forth until the flame dies. Add the soy sauce and lime juice to the rum. Place the chicken in a deep bowl and pour in the rum mixture, turning the pieces about with a spoon to coat them evenly. Marinate at room temperature for about 2 hours, or in the refrigerator for at least 4 hours, turning the chicken pieces occasionally.

Preheat the oven to the lowest setting and line a large shallow baking dish with a double thickness of paper towels. In a heavy 10- to 12-inch skillet, heat the oil over high heat until it is very hot but not smoking. Pat the pieces of chicken completely dry with paper towels and season them with salt and a few grindings of pepper. Dip them in the flour and shake vigorously to remove the excess.

Fry 5 or 6 pieces of chicken at a time for about 6 minutes on each side, turning them with tongs or a slotted spoon and regulating the heat so they color richly and evenly without burning. As they brown, transfer the pieces to the lined baking dish and keep them warm in the oven.

Serve the chicken as soon as all the pieces are cooked, accompanied if you like with hot boiled rice.

Poulet Rôti à la Créole (Haiti)
ROAST CHICKEN WITH TWO STUFFINGS

To serve 6

Preheat the oven to 350°. In a heavy 6- to 8-inch skillet, melt 3 tablespoons of butter over moderate heat. When the foam begins to subside, drop in the garlic and stir for 10 to 15 seconds. Remove and discard the garlic; add the bread crumbs and stir until they are crisp and brown. Off the heat stir in 3 tablespoons of the lime juice, the lime rind, 1 tablespoon of the rum, the brown sugar, nutmeg, red pepper, 1 teaspoon of the salt and a few grindings of pepper, and taste for seasoning. Set the stuffing aside.

Peel and chop the bananas fine, and drop them into a small bowl. Add the remaining tablespoon of lime juice, 1 teaspoon of the rum, the remaining ½ teaspoon of salt, and a few grindings of pepper, and toss the ingredients about with a spoon to combine them thoroughly.

Pat the chicken completely dry inside and out with paper towels. Fill the breast cavity with the banana stuffing and close the opening by lacing it with skewers or sewing it with a large needle and heavy white thread. Fill the smaller neck cavity with the bread-crumb stuffing and skewer or sew the opening shut. Truss the chicken securely and, with a pastry brush, coat it thoroughly with the 4 tablespoons of softened butter.

Place the bird on a rack in a shallow roasting pan just large enough to hold it comfortably and roast in the middle of the oven for about 1½ hours, basting occasionally with the juices as they accumulate in the pan. To test for doneness, pierce the thigh of the bird with the point of a small, sharp knife. The juice that trickles out should be pale yellow; if it is tinged with pink, roast the chicken for another 5 to 10 minutes.

Transfer the bird to a large, heated platter, cut off and discard the trussing strings, and let the chicken rest for about 5 minutes for easier carving. Meanwhile, skim the fat from the juices in the pan and pour in the cup of stock. Bring to a boil over high heat, stirring and scraping in any brown particles clinging to the bottom of the pan. Cook the sauce briskly for 2 or 3 minutes, taste for seasoning, and pour it into a small bowl or sauceboat. Just before serving, warm the remaining 3 tablespoons of rum in a small pan over low heat. Ignite the rum with a match and pour it flaming over the chicken.

3 tablespoons butter, plus 4 tablespoons butter, softened
1 small whole garlic clove, peeled
1 cup soft fresh crumbs made from homemade-type white bread trimmed of crusts and pulverized in a blender or finely shredded with a fork
4 tablespoons strained fresh lime juice
1 tablespoon finely grated fresh lime rind
4 tablespoons plus 1 teaspoon dark rum
1 teaspoon dark-brown sugar
¼ teaspoon ground nutmeg
¼ teaspoon ground hot red pepper
1½ teaspoons salt
Freshly ground black pepper
3 medium-sized ripe bananas
A 3½- to 4-pound whole roasting chicken
1 cup chicken stock, fresh or canned

Fried Ripe Plantains

To serve 3 or 4

With a small, sharp knife, peel the plantains following the diagram on page 55. After peeling cut each plantain segment in half lengthwise or, if you prefer, slice them crosswise on the diagonal to make ¼-inch-thick ovals.

In a heavy 8- to 10-inch skillet, heat the oil over moderate heat until a light haze forms above it. Fry the plantains in the hot oil for about 4 minutes on each side, turning them with a slotted spatula and regulating the heat so they color richly and evenly without burning. Transfer the plantains to paper towels to drain and serve at once from a heated platter.

2 large very ripe plantains
¼ cup peanut or vegetable oil

V

The Abundant Fruits of Eden

This fanciful fruit tree, which might be found on the Caribbean equivalent of the Big Rock Candy Mountain, was devised by Jasmin Joseph, a young Haitian artist. It shows some of the island's best-known fruits, as well as a few special to Haiti.

1 Mango
2 Star apple
3 Shaddock
4 Orange
5 Apple
6 Mamey apple
7 Apple
8 Melon du France
9 Star apple
10 Mango
11 Fig
12 Star apple
13 Melon
14 Papaya
15 Pepper
16 Melon du France
17 Pomegranate
18 Corn
19 Cashew
20 Mamey apple
21 Star apple
22 Plantain
23 Soursop
24 Star apple

Christopher Columbus was the first to compare the Caribbean islands to the Garden of Eden—and he was convinced they were literally one and the same. Sailing past Trinidad on his third voyage to the New World, he was deeply moved by the sight of shores "so fair and so verdant and full of trees and palms," where "every tree. . .is pleasant to the sight and good for food." Since the authorities of his day placed the Garden of Eden in Eastern Asia, where Columbus thought he was when he got to Trinidad, his mistaking the island for Paradise is understandable.

Though the authorities of my own day know better, I confess that there are times when I agree with Columbus. The stately palms and graceful ferns, the bamboo thickets and trails of creepers, the cascading purple and scarlet and yellow flowers, and especially the fantastically fruitful trees of the Caribbean islands, all fit perfectly my own image of Eden.

Some of the trees in this garden are bizarre, like the jack fruit, which bears gross, malodorous fruits weighing 30 or 40 pounds and sometimes as much as 70 pounds. Some of the trees are deadly, like the manchineel, whose deceptively sweet-smelling apples contain a milky juice that can be fatal and was used, in fact, by the Carib Indians to poison their enemies. But most of the trees of the Caribbean are beautiful, the bearers of beneficent fruits and nuts, and prolific in their uses for men. The stately tamarind not only offers a fruit that makes a sugary, spicy candy and an aromatic drink, but it also provides protection from hurricanes to islanders who plant it beside their houses as a windbreak. The cashew tree furnishes its crisp nut as well as a fruit that, though tart, can be eaten raw or made into sweet wines and syrupy liqueurs.

The pineapple that Columbus saw for the first time in the West Indies has by now spread all over the world. (Special water-storing tissues allow it to grow in dry climates as well as wet.) But it still flourishes in the Caribbean, and is Puerto Rico's largest export fruit crop. The plant above is seen in bud *(top)* and then in flower. The blossoms live only a day; when they wither they leave behind the spots that will become the "eyes" of the mature pineapple.

Over all presides the coconut, the tree that most strongly evokes the lost Eden—a noble palm that gracefully bends and withstands hurricane winds, gives shelter on sun-beaten beaches, and provides a constant supply of food and drink everywhere. The almost clear liquid inside the immature, or green, coconut, called coconut water, is sometimes easier to come by than fresh water in the Caribbean; always pure in its sturdy container, always sweet and cool, the drink could easily qualify, as one Caribbean explorer put it, as "the nectar of the gods." When the coconut is still young its meat is like jelly, with a fresh, fruity flavor, and is eaten with a spoon, as we might eat a melon. When the coconut matures, the meat dries out and, when shredded, has endless uses in such enticing confections as Barbados' chewy coconut custard pie, Puerto Rico's *tembleque,* a trembling coconut flan, or Jamaica's *gisada,* a little coconut tart heady with rum.

It is in the astonishing variety of fruits growing on the islands that nature most conspicuously manifests her bounty, and a visit to a well-supplied Caribbean fruit market confirms the impression that here indeed is Paradise. The fruit displays are overwhelming in their extravagant colors and exotic textures. To the traveler from the north some of the fruits are familiar: mounds of prickly-skinned pineapples, a few cut open to show off their juicy yellow inner secrets; boy-tall stalks of tiny sweet bananas; great pyramids of oranges and limes so scented that peeling one of them perfumes the hands for the rest of the day; piles of papayas and many varieties of mangoes, mottled red and green and yellow like the brilliant birds of the tropics.

There are dozens of other fruits encountered only in the islands themselves. A visitor finds their shapes odd and their names even stranger. Vendors, called higglers in the English-speaking islands, walk about the streets carrying baskets on their heads and chanting the names of their wares like a musical pagan litany: "Cherimoya, carambola, mamey, sapote, monstera, mangosteen, loquat." There are smooth fruits, nubbly ones, delicate and coarse, sweet-smelling and foul. Some have short seasons, some are picked all year round, but there is always a profusion to choose from.

Tropical fruits spoil easily and often do not travel well, and Caribbean fruit-growers are poorly organized, so a relatively small selection of the island fruit delicacies is available elsewhere. But these few are sufficient to give northerners a taste of the islands, and a chance to produce at home some of the exotic desserts found there.

Of the Caribbean fruits available in the United States I think the mango is the most exquisite, although I find its elusive flavor, which seems to combine so many tantalizing, dreamlike hints of other fruits, almost impossible to describe. People always seem able to agree on the flavor of exotic meat; whether it be monkey, iguana or agouti, explorers invariably exclaim, "Hmm . . .tastes amazingly like veal." But when it comes to tropical fruits, and especially to mango, all attempts at definition fail. It is not for lack of trying, though I have listened to dozens of firm and assertive opinions about what the mango tastes like—all different.

A Haitian friend insisted that I describe it as "a combination between a pear and an apricot." A friend on St. Kitts said just as positively, "It's like a melon mixed with a pineapple." A Puerto Rican woman told me, "It has the flavor of an apricot and a texture between that of an avocado and a cassava melon," while her husband contended, "It's a cross between a peach, a melon and a banana." The person who best conveyed its essence was a Jamaican, who said with the particularly poetic turn of speech typical of his people, "You can't describe a mango. Unless you say that it's a delicious, nourishing, breast-shaped delicacy that grown men may nip on in public. It's God's way of making every man outgrow his mother."

One reason it is so difficult to pin down the mango's taste is that there are so many kinds of mangoes. Hundreds of varieties grow in the islands, and they range in size from that of a small plum to that of a big honeydew melon, in form from round to kidney-shaped and in color, when ripe, from pale yellow to scarlet. My supermarket in New York carries only Haitian mangoes; they weigh about a half pound and are kidney-shaped and green. The clerk at the fruit counter often fails to tell buyers what they should know —that a green mango is unripe. A mango can be purchased green but it must be put on the window sill to ripen. It should not be eaten until it blushes pink or yellow and, as with bananas, until it is flecked with brown or black. Green mangoes are used to make mango chutney, a popular accompaniment to curries, but they are picked weeks before they are ripe.

How to cut a mango is a problem as much debated as its taste. It is an extremely juicy fruit, and when one bites into it or cuts it and applies pressure in the wrong places the juice tends to spray. It has often been called a fruit to be eaten in the bathtub. Furthermore, most varieties of mango have a flat pit that, unlike that of a freestone peach, does not come away cleanly from the flesh, but clings with stringy tenaciousness. So getting all the flesh off and staying dry is a feat.

I learned about the many opinions on how best to do this at a meal in Trinidad where I, as guest of honor, was given the last ripe mango my hostess had been able to find in the market. She, her husband and each of their two daughters had a favorite way to eat the fruit. One said peel some of the skin away and suck the fruit; another recommended peeling and eating it with a spoon; the others had intricate systems of cutting and slicing. I ended up cutting off two slabs from the flattish sides of the mango and eating them with a spoon, as you do a melon, and then tackling the rest with knife and fork and, finally, my fingers. Eventually I was covered with juice anyway—and did not mind a bit, because I found the taste so compelling that I ceased to care about anything but eating it. And, of course, I know exactly what it tastes like: mostly peachlike, with hints of banana, melon, apricot and pineapple, and with a little bit of plum.

Another important Caribbean fruit that only recently has begun to claim the attention of Americans is the papaya. Like the pineapple it is a truly New World fruit, one of the first to catch Columbus' interest. In his journal he wrote that the natives of the islands were "very strong and live largely on a tree melon called 'the fruit of the angels.'" It seems an apt name for this sweet, musky fruit. Papaya grows on what looks like a tall tree—15 to 20 feet high—that is really not a tree at all but the woody stalk of a giant plant. This stalk is branchless and at its top is a burst of leaves, a crown carrying the heavy dark-green fruits like jewels.

The papaya has many names in the islands. The Spanish explorers evolved the word papaya from the Carib Indian language, and it came directly into

Seven months after budding, the pineapple is ripe and ready for harvesting. This is done either by breaking it free with a twist of gloved hands, or by slicing it off with a machete, the technique being used here. The golden blush of these pineapples—of the Red Spanish variety—indicates they are too ripe to be shipped whole for any distance: they either will be sold in local markets or will be processed for canning in a Puerto Rican plant.

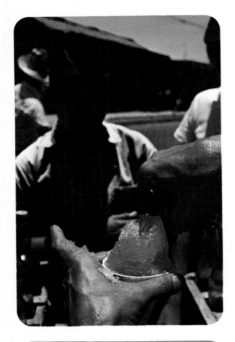

On hot days in the Dominican Republic—that is, most of the time—a favorite inexpensive cooler is a *frio-frio* (*frio* is Spanish for cold). Made by pouring a dollop of fruit syrup over a paper cupful of crushed ice, *frio-frio* goes down especially well with children. These pictures were taken as school was getting out in Santo Domingo, but the same refreshments are found on other islands too—Jamaicans, for instance, call them snow cones or snowballs.

English. But most often on Spanish-speaking islands today the fruit is called either *lechosa* or *fruta bomba* (because in its small varieties it looks like a hand grenade); on the English-speaking islands it is called pawpaw. And the papaya has even more uses than names. Its leaves and fruit contain a valuable enzyme, papain, which breaks down protein tissue in the same way the stomach's digestive juices do. This makes it a natural meat tenderizer. For centuries the islanders have wrapped meat in papaya leaves or rubbed it with a raw young fruit to make it tender, and in recent years the enzyme has been isolated and put into commercial preparations that are widely used around the world. The leaves of the papaya make a boiled green vegetable, with a delicate, slightly bitter flavor reminiscent of dandelion greens. When the fruit itself is not yet ripe, it too is treated as a vegetable that is very popular throughout the islands. It is usually split in half and baked with butter or stuffed *(Recipe Index),* and it has the appearance and flavor of a mild, sweet squash. But papaya is at its best when it is ripe, a juicy, fragrant breakfast or dessert fruit. It is served sliced like a melon, its shiny black seeds clinging decoratively to its firm orange or pink flesh.

Both the mango and the papaya are so good eaten raw that at first I wondered why anyone did anything else with them. But I have learned to love the many other ways the islanders use them for desserts. They make mango pie, mango brown Betty, mango mousse *(Recipe Index)*; they are fond of papaya ices and a confection of baked crushed papaya cooked with vanilla and sprinkled with cinnamon. The Cubans use either mango or papaya in an ambrosial concoction that I find irresistible. The raw fruit is put into a blender with milk and ice and is pulverized to produce a tropical milk shake called a *refresco de papaya,* or, simply, a *batido (Recipe Index).* I often order one at Victor's Café, my favorite New York Cuban restaurant, even after a generous meal of lobster and black beans and fried plantains, and even though I have reached a stage where I try vigorously to avoid desserts. I order guiltily, feeling as if I were 14 again and back in the innocent days when the only thing adolescents were hooked on was milk shakes; and I drink it, my husband says, with a faraway look on my face.

Mangoes and papayas are still rare enough outside the tropics to be considered exotic delicacies, but it may not be long before they become familiar staples, if we can judge from the history of two other once-rare tropical fruits. The banana and pineapple were virtually unheard of in the United States a century ago.

During Civil War days, sailing vessels from the West Indies occasionally reached an American port with a few bunches of blackened bananas left over from the crew's food stores; and sometimes these would be sold in port. Now and then some bananas reached New Orleans from Central America; shipped north to New England, a single piece of fruit wrapped fancily in tinfoil commanded a price equivalent to one dollar today. Then, in 1870, a Cape Cod sea captain named Lorenzo Baker, who sailed regularly to the islands, received two big bunches of bananas as a parting gift from a Jamaican plantation owner. When Baker's schooner reached Boston the bananas were still in good condition, and he discovered a ready market for the exotic fruit. He began bringing bananas back with him regularly from the West Indies, and 15 years later formed the Boston Fruit Company to import the fruit on a large scale. Just before the turn of the century his company merged with that of a railroad entrepreneur in Costa Rica to form the United Fruit Company. By the mid-1920s, with the development of refrigerated ships and railroad cars, bananas were to be found in stores all across the country.

The pineapple, too, was a curiosity to most Americans until the 20th Century, despite its popularity with the Caribbean Indians and their European conquerors. While it was grown under glass as a botanical hobby by gentlemen farmers—a pastime introduced in England in 1690 by the Earl of Portland—few people except those in the upper crust of society or those who traveled to the islands were ever able to taste the fruit. George Washington sampled pineapple on a trip to Barbados in 1751 with his brother Lawrence, who was ill and needed to recuperate in a warm climate. In his diary, Washington listed all the fruits he was served, which included such rarities as sapodilla, forbidden fruit and guavas, but only when it came to the pineapple did he become expansive: "None pleases my taste as do's the pine."

Lady Janet Schaw, traveling in the West Indies at about the same time, described an occasion on which she was served 32 tropical fruits for dessert, and she too wrote that she was most pleased by the pineapple. She had tasted pineapple before, the hothouse variety raised by friends. But apparently a hothouse pineapple was so precious that one ate every bit of it, including the hard center. Lady Janet wrote of Antigua: "When I first came here I could not bear to see so much of a pine apple thrown away. They cut off a deep paring, then cut out the firm part of the heart, which takes away not much less than half the pine apple." But she soon grew accustomed to this wasteful luxury. In fact, like the princess who slept on the pea, Lady Janet became finicky. "Only observe how easy it is to become extravagant," she wrote. "I can now feel if the least bit of rind remains; and as to the heart, heavens! who would eat the nasty heart of a pine apple."

In the islands today both the banana and the pineapple are basic to the cuisine. Pineapple accompanies poultry and pork dishes and is made into cakes, pies and pancakes. Once I had it baked in its shell, sprinkled with rum and cinnamon, and flamed, the most flamboyant tropical dessert I know. Bananas are used in the same ways as pineapple, but there are even more banana recipes: fried bananas, baked and flambéed bananas *(Recipe Index)*, banana pancakes, sweet banana omelets. Many of these have begun to take hold in the United States. Once at a picnic on Jamaica I had a banana dessert that was so superbly innocent that I was astonished the idea had never occurred to me. My friends roasted unpeeled bananas in the ashes of a fire for about half an hour until the skins turned very black. Then we opened the bananas, sprinkled them with sugar and a touch of lime juice, and ate the puddinglike sweet with spoons.

There is another group of fruits, the citrus family, whose absence would change the entire look of the Caribbean and the taste of its cuisine. Citrus groves bloom and bear fruit the year round from Cuba to Trinidad. Yet they are not native to the region. It was Columbus himself who brought the first citrus plants to the New World, oranges from Grand Canary Island, which he planted on Hispaniola in 1493. Indeed, according to John McPhee, author of a delightful and exhaustive book on the orange, the movement of the fruit from its origins near the South China Sea down into the Malay Ar-

Continued on page 116

The bright red fruity part of the cashew *(left)* is called a cashew apple, but is technically the pedicle, or base, of the cashew flower; it produces the nut. The unshelled nuts shown below have been separated from their ripened pedicles. The shelled cashew nut at right is freshly picked; when it has been roasted, it will be the familiar tan color, crisp and ready for eating.

From Curious Cashew to Ugly Ugli, The Yield Is Fruitful

Reina Reynoso adds to her family's income by selling cashew apples and nuts to motorists in the countryside near Santo Domingo in the Dominican Republic. The tart cashew apple can be eaten stewed, but it is usually made into jelly, wine or liqueur.

In a way the cashew tree sums up both the magnanimity and the general unpredictability of nature in the Caribbean. While it is enough for most trees to produce either a fruit or a nut, the cashew bears both. But it also tempers its generosity; because it is botanically related to—of all things—poison ivy, one part of its nutshell will cause a rash. As a whole, the output of the groves and orchards and jungles of the Caribbean islands is more richly varied and more delectable than that of almost any other region on earth. Some fruits are well known—bananas, pineapples, certain citrus species. Others never go abroad, or so deteriorate in traveling that most northerners can have little notion of their true quality. Part of the abundance antedates the coming of the Spanish galleons. Long before them the coconut palm, for example, was everywhere in the Caribbean. But settlers impressed by the climate and soil introduced wholly new plants, such as the breadfruit, mango, orange and lime. Even today, as if in the vast hothouse of some super-botanist, spontaneous crossbreeding of plants keeps bringing fresh hybrids into existence—the tangelo, the tangor, and the splendidly named cross of grapefruit, orange and tangerine, the ugli.

Banana "hands" grow upward. The dangling bud is eaten as a vegetable.

Green coconuts are filled with clear, sweet "water" and savory jellylike flesh.

The papaya may be cooked when green, or eaten raw when ripe.

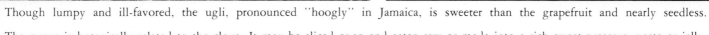

Though lumpy and ill-favored, the ugli, pronounced "hoogly" in Jamaica, is sweeter than the grapefruit and nearly seedless.

The guava is botanically related to the clove. It may be sliced open and eaten raw or made into a rich sweet preserve, paste or jelly.

Despite its name, the starchy-fleshed breadfruit is prepared as a vegetable.

The prickly soursop has a cottony consistency, and makes a tart drink.

The cocoa tree yields chocolate from its nut and cocaine from its leaves.

Many Caribbean fruits are unknown outside the islands, but the star apple is particularly obscure. It is very sensitive to the cold, must be tree-ripened, and has such a short season that even the most determined tourist may never see or taste one. The fruit is about the size of an apple, and its name comes from the fact that the seeds are distributed in a handsome starlike pattern clearly visible when it is sliced open, as at left. The flesh is slightly gelatinous, mild and sweet. It grows throughout the West Indies but is especially abundant on Jamaica and Haiti.

115

A Flaw in the Fruits of Paradise

Like the famous fruit of an earlier Eden, the Caribbean's mangoes and papayas, for all their succulence, present a potential danger. Both can cause allergic reactions in susceptible people, the mango by a fluid secreted beneath its skin, the papaya by an enzyme in its skin and unripened flesh. The chief danger lies not in eating the fruits but in getting their irritating juices on the face or in the eye; they may cause skin eruptions or swelling. Allergy sufferers are well advised to wear rubber gloves when peeling mangoes or papayas and to wash their hands afterward.

Opposite: A hospitable custom of the old-time Jamaican planter was the breakfast fruit bowl, an iced array of local fruits. A number of Jamaican hotels and resorts have restored the tradition, and a fortunate tourist may now wake to an inviting sight like this. It offers bananas, mango slices, black-seeded papayas, oranges, limes, grapefruit, pineapple and, in the center, two naseberry halves.

chipelago, across the ocean to Africa and across the African deserts into the Mediterranean and thence to the Americas "closely and sometimes exactly kept pace with the major journeys of civilization." Arab traders took it to Africa, Islamic warriors to Spain, and Spanish conquistadors to the New World. For centuries the orange was an expensive luxury in Europe; the demand for a new source of supply was great. By the beginning of the 16th Century, orange trees were growing all across the Caribbean.

Most Caribbean oranges look very different from the smooth-skinned, bright-colored product of Florida and California. Some island oranges have bumpy skins, and most are lime green; color is not an indication of the fruit's ripeness or sweetness, and a green orange in a hot climate may be perfectly ripe inside. However they look, Caribbean oranges are sweet and juicy, though some have a tartness that seems a natural antidote to the tropical sun. In Trinidad, oranges are sold on the street cut in half and sprinkled with salt. On many islands they are sold by street vendors who use ingenious hand-turned peeling machines to cut off the skin in a long, thin spiral, leaving the fruit ready to eat then and there.

Lime trees were also planted by the early Europeans, and this fruit has become an ingredient that rivals the pepper in its importance to Caribbean cooking. The West Indian limes bear little relation to the smaller, less juicy specimens that often find their way to northern supermarkets. Caribbean limes seem to be bigger and greener than any I have seen elsewhere. Fragrant and gloriously juicy, they are as much part of the Caribbean experience as sun and sea, and it is almost impossible to imagine island cooking without the lime. Its juice is used in almost every Creole sauce, in countless fish, vegetable and poultry dishes; myriad desserts use lime, and, of course, it is the perfect companion to rum.

Grapefruit is less important to the Caribbean cuisine, but it deserves special notice because it is a West Indian creation. Grapefruit did not even exist before the 18th Century. In the 17th Century a British ship captain named Shaddock sailed into Jamaica, having brought from Polynesia a large citrus fruit with a thick rind and yellowish-red flesh that was aromatic but bitter. Planted in the West Indies, the fruit flourished, and came to be called shaddock (also known as pomelo). Some time later, a fruit began to appear in the islands that was either a natural mutation of the shaddock or the result of some botanist's attempt to cross it with a sweet orange. It resembled the shaddock but its skin was thinner, its flesh yellower, and its flavor sweeter. Thus was born the grapefruit.

Other citrus fruits have been developed, too. Among the hybrids recently evolved are the tangelo, a cross between the tangerine and the grapefruit, the tangor, a cross between the tangerine and the orange, and, most intriguing of all, the ugli, a cross between a grapefruit and an orange. The ugli got its name from its resemblance to a lumpy, misshapen orange. But the appellation is meant affectionately. Jamaicans, who developed the fruit and gave it its unflattering name, have nothing but praise for its inner beauty, its delicate, slightly tart flavor. Also grown on many islands is the citron, which has tough skin and a pulp too acid to eat, but which makes excellent candied peel, and a bitter orange that is also too sour to eat but is the source for Curaçao's world-famous orange liqueur. The ancestors of these bitter or-

Mango chutney is a tart, gingery condiment for roast meats and fowl as well as for curries. Ingredients for the Jamaican version shown above include *(from left)* fresh ginger root, malt vinegar, unripened mango, ground allspice, garlic, sugar, raisins, hot peppers, salt and dried tamarind.

anges were probably Valencia oranges that were planted in the 17th Century by a governor of Curaçao.

From this array of citrus fruits the islanders make spectacular desserts. Cored oranges are stuffed with sugar and butter, and baked and served with cream. Or oranges are pulped, then mixed with dates and nuts and brown sugar, and the mixture is stuffed back into the orange rind, baked, then doused in rum and carried, flaming, to the table. Orange fritters, orange cakes, grapefruit mousse, grilled grapefruit topped with grapefruit marmalade, lime pie, spongy lime puddings—all are popular. Perhaps the most elegant Caribbean citrus dessert is lime soufflé, a fragrant creation whose airiness is punctuated with shredded coconut *(Recipe Index)*.

The crowning Caribbean achievement with citrus fruits is the wedding cake made on all the English-speaking islands. When one says "wedding cake" on Jamaica or Barbados or Antigua, one means a dark fruitcake made with candied lime and orange and citron, and heavily steeped in rum. It is also known as Christmas cake, bride's cake and, most commonly, black cake. The cake's shape may vary. Sometimes there are two—a small, round one for the bride and a tall one for the groom; sometimes there is a single three-tiered cake; sometimes the confection is in the shape of a garden or a house, and is a work of elaborate artistry that demands month-long attention and creativity by the bride's female relatives and friends. One woman I met described the wedding cake she and her friends had made for her niece the winter before. It was built in the shape of a church and, like an architect's model, was perfect in detail: Its roof was made with almond-flavored icing tinted to the reddish-brown color of Spanish tiles, and its steeple actually contained a clock, the watch of one of the women working on the cake.

Whatever the design of the cake, it is made with citrus fruits and rum, and in its rich moistness is very similar to a wedding cake that has been traditional in England since the 18th Century. Comparing a contemporary Jamaican wedding-cake recipe with one I read in an English cookbook written in 1813, I found the recipes almost identical. "Beat in your sugar a quarter of an hour" and the egg yolks "half an hour at least," read the book's stern instructions. The other ingredients, almost all gifts of England's West Indian colonies, were candied orange, lemon and citron peel, mace, nutmeg and brandy. The hand beating and the ingredients are unchanged in the islands today, although local rum is used instead of brandy. It is an interesting example of how the islands' centuries of isolation helped preserve a tradition intact.

The islands are, of course, no longer isolated, and no doubt there will be increasing culinary interchanges. Certainly more and more of the Caribbean's exotic fruits are finding their way to North American tables, and I hope the trend continues. But I have to admit that however quickly modern air traffic can whisk them from tropical tree to urban grocery, many of the Caribbean fruits seem to taste best when eaten right in the Eden where they grow. One of my prime delights in visiting the islands, in fact, is to look for unfamiliar fruits, and I try to find a new one every time I go. It is not difficult. On one trip, in a Jamaican market, I discovered the sapodilla, dusty and brown on the outside but containing a sweet purplish jelly within. At a bar on a sandy beach on Dominica I first tasted passion fruit, a small yellow plum-shaped fruit with too many seeds to make comfortable chewing but delicious in a rum punch. Elsewhere I came to know genip, a pale-green grapelike fruit that grows in clusters and has pink cantaloupelike flesh; and sorrel, a flower that is used to make a deep-red aromatic drink (Recipe Index) that is traditional at Christmas on the English-speaking islands; and soursop, a big bumpy-skinned fruit with juicy white flesh that is unrivaled for making drinks and sherbets; and the star apple, which, when cut horizontally, reveals a magical star of purple seeds in its white interior.

Perhaps my favorite of all is a fruit I found at a roadside stand in the mountains of Trinidad. The Trinidadians call it pomerac and some other islands know it as Otaheite apple. It looks like a fruit from a fairy tale—waxy and bright red, shaped like a pear, with snow-white flesh that smells incredibly of roses. But the roster of fruits in the Caribbean is apparently endless; I have yet to try a sugar apple, a granadilla, a forbidden fruit, a cherimoya, a hog plum. I am sure I'll find a new favorite the next time I go there.

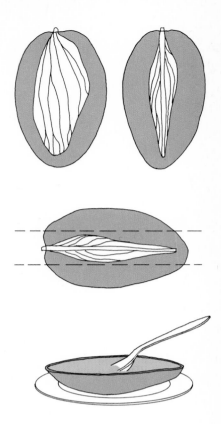

HOW TO TACKLE A RIPE MANGO
The stone, or pit, inside a mango is almost flat and is generally positioned within the fruit as shown in the two cross sections at top; the flesh clings to the stone and must be cut away. The simplest way to do this is to lay the mango on its flattest side and cut a thick slice off the top (center drawing). Turn the fruit over and repeat the process. The two slices may be served like avocado halves and eaten with a spoon. The juicy flesh still attached to the stone can be cut off in chunks, or eaten directly—and messily—from the stone.

119

As the nut ripens, its thick pericarp splits open.

The mature nutmeg is covered with scarlet mace.

Grenada's Marvelous Two-in-One Spice Kit

In 1843, an English sea captain homeward bound from the Spice Islands in the East Indies called at the Caribbean island of Grenada. He carried with him some small nutmeg trees and left them with his hosts when he sailed for England. Fifteen years later, Grenada marketed its first crop of nutmeg and mace. Today the island produces nearly 40 per cent of the world's supply.

Nutmeg and mace are different parts of the nut that grows on the 70- to 90-foot nutmeg tree. As the nut ripens, the spongy outer pericarp splits open and eventually gapes wide enough to allow the mace-covered nutmeg within to fall obligingly to the ground. Plantation workers pick up the nutmegs and strip away the still pliable mace. The mace is dried and graded *(opposite)* and the nutmegs are shelled and then sorted according to their size and oil content—the best being those that are round, heavy and oily. Most nutmegs are ground into powder or pressed for their oil; the most perfect are shipped whole to epicure markets.

The mace webbing stripped from the nutmeg is valued and treated as a spice in its own right. It tastes something like nutmeg, but is stronger, more astringent and less sweet. About one pound of mace is produced for every six pounds of nutmeg. The woman at left is sorting mace at the Gouyave processing station, one of three major nutmeg cooperatives in Grenada. The mace is put through a curing process during which it turns yellow and golden. The best quality is called ''whole pale'' and has a golden color and high oil content. In the picture below, this grade is at the bottom and at top right is broken mace; the rest is fresh, uncured mace. The various grades of mace will be bagged and sold to spice jobbers.

CHAPTER **V** RECIPES

Pineapple Fool *(Jamaica)*

Place the pineapple in a sieve or colander set over a bowl and let it drain for at least 10 minutes.

In a large chilled bowl, whip the cream with a whisk or a rotary or electric beater until it is stiff enough to hold its shape softly. Taste the pineapple and, depending on its sweetness and your own taste, sprinkle the cream with 1 to 4 tablespoons of confectioners' sugar. Add the vanilla and continue beating until the cream is stiff enough to form firm, unwavering peaks on the beater when it is lifted from the bowl.

Chill the whipped cream and the pineapple separately until you are ready to serve them. (Tightly covered with plastic wrap, whipped cream can be kept for an hour or so.) At the last possible minute, fold the pineapple into the cream with a rubber spatula, blending them together gently but thoroughly. Spoon the fool into chilled individual dessert bowls or parfait glasses and serve immediately.

NOTE: Mango may be substituted for the pineapple.

To serve 4

2 cups finely chopped fresh pineapple *(page 38)*
1 cup heavy cream
1 to 4 tablespoons confectioners' sugar
1 teaspoon vanilla extract

Refresco de Coco y Piña *(Dominican Republic)*
CHILLED COCONUT MILK AND PINEAPPLE DRINK

Combine the coconut milk, pineapple and sugar in the jar of an electric blender and blend at high speed for 30 seconds, or until the pineapple is completely pulverized and the mixture is reduced to a smooth purée. Pour the entire contents of the blender jar into a fine sieve set over a deep bowl and lined with a double thickness of cheesecloth. Press down hard on the pineapple with the back of a spoon to extract all its juices before discarding the pulp.

(To make the drink by hand, rub the chopped pineapple through a fine sieve set over a deep bowl or force it through a food mill. Stir in the coconut milk and sugar.)

Taste the *refresco de coco y piña* and add more sugar and a drop or two of almond extract if desired. Cover tightly and refrigerate for at least 2 hours, or until thoroughly chilled. To serve, pour the drink into tall tumblers with or without ice cubes.

To make about 3 cups

2 cups coconut milk, made from 2 cups coarsely chopped fresh coconut and 2 cups hot water *(see Recipe Booklet)*
2½ cups coarsely chopped fresh pineapple *(page 38)*
2 tablespoons sugar
Almond extract (optional)

Refresco de Papaya *(Dominican Republic)*
ICED MILK AND PAPAYA FRAPPE

With a small, sharp knife or swivel-bladed vegetable parer, peel the papaya. Cut it in half lengthwise and scoop out the black seeds inside, then chop the papaya coarsely.

Place the papaya in the jar of an electric blender and add the milk, lime juice, lime rind, sugar, vanilla and crushed ice. Blend at high speed for 20 or 30 seconds, until the papaya is completely pulverized and the mixture is smooth and thick.

Pour the *refresco de papaya* into chilled tall tumblers and serve at once, garnished if you like with thin slices of lime.

To make about 3 cups

1 medium-sized (about 12 ounces) firm ripe papaya *(see box, page 116)*
½ cup milk
3 tablespoons strained fresh lime juice
½ teaspoon finely grated fresh lime rind
¼ cup sugar
½ teaspoon vanilla extract
½ cup crushed ice or 4 ice cubes, wrapped in a kitchen towel and finely crushed with a mallet or heavy pan
Thin lime slices for garnish (optional)

Three fruit-laden Caribbean delights are *refresco de coco y piña (far left)* and *refresco de papaya*, both drinks; and pineapple fool, a dessert.

123

To serve 4

4 large ripe bananas
¼ cup light rum
4 tablespoons butter
½ cup dark-brown sugar
½ teaspoon ground allspice
¼ cup strained fresh lime juice

Flambéed Baked Bananas (*Antigua*)

Preheat the oven to 400°. With the tines of a long-handled fork, pierce the un-peeled bananas deeply in two or three places. Lay them on a baking sheet and bake them in the middle of the oven for 10 to 15 minutes, or until the skins darken somewhat and the bananas feel tender when pressed gently between your thumb and forefinger.

Remove the bananas from the oven and, with a small, sharp knife, slit their skins lengthwise along their inside and outside curves. Gently lift and peel off the top half of the skin, leaving the underside intact.

About 10 minutes before serving, warm the rum in a small pan over low heat. Meanwhile, melt the butter in a heavy 10- to 12-inch skillet over moderate heat. When the foam begins to subside, add the sugar and allspice to the butter and stir until well mixed. One at a time, gently lay the bananas flesh side down in the skillet and carefully lift and peel off the remaining skin. Sprinkle the bananas with lime juice. Then ignite the rum with a match, and pour it flaming over the bananas a little at a time, shaking the skillet gently until the flame dies. Spoon the sauce over the bananas and serve at once.

To make about 1 quart

The meat of 1 medium-sized (about
    1½ pounds) fresh coconut (*see
    Recipe Booklet*)
2 cups warm milk
1 cup sugar
¼ cup water
A pinch of cream of tartar
1 to 3 drops almond extract

Coconut-Milk Sherbet (*Barbados*)

Preheat the oven to 325°. With a swivel-bladed peeler or a small, sharp knife, pare off the brown outer skin from a piece of coconut meat about 4 inches square. (Set the rest of the coconut aside unpeeled.)

Grate the peeled piece coarsely with a hand grater and measure it. You should have about 1 cup. Spread the grated coconut in a thin layer in a large, shallow baking pan and, stirring occasionally, toast it in the middle of the oven for 15 to 20 minutes, or until light brown. Remove the coconut from the oven and set it aside.

Meanwhile, following the directions in the Recipe Booklet, make coconut milk with the remaining coconut meat and 2 cups of warm milk.

124

Antigua's bananas flambéed with rum makes a spectacular dessert. To produce it without burning or bruising the fruit, bake unpeeled bananas until their skins blacken. Slit the skin of each banana from end to end and gently peel off one half as shown in the photograph at far left. The next step is to melt butter and brown sugar in a large skillet. One at a time, lay the bananas in the pan, flesh side down, and carefully lift off the remaining peel *(center)*. To flambé the bananas, pour flaming rum over them slowly, shaking the skillet gently.

In a small, heavy saucepan, bring the sugar, water and cream of tartar to a boil over medium heat, stirring until the sugar dissolves and the syrup becomes completely clear, about 5 minutes. Pour the syrup into a heatproof mixing bowl and let it cool to room temperature.

Stir the toasted coconut and the coconut milk into the cooled syrup and flavor the sherbet with a drop of the almond extract. Taste and add more of the extract if desired. Pour the mixture into 2 ice-cube trays from which the dividers have been removed.

Freeze the sherbet for 3 to 4 hours, stirring it every 30 minutes to break up the solid particles that will form on the bottom and sides of the tray. The finished sherbet should have a fine, snowy texture.

To serve, spoon it into parfait glasses or dessert dishes.

Mango Chutney *(Jamaica)*

Place the tamarind in a small bowl and pour the boiling water over it. Stirring and mashing occasionally with a spoon, let the tamarind soak for 1 hour, or until the pulp softens and breaks up in the water. Rub the tamarind and pour its soaking liquid through a fine sieve set over a bowl, pressing down hard with the back of a spoon before discarding the seeds and fibers.

With a small, sharp knife, peel each mango and cut the flesh away from the large, flat stone. Discard the seeds and cut the mangoes into 1-inch dice.

Combine the mangoes and vinegar in a heavy 4- to 5-quart enameled or stainless-steel pot. Bring to a boil over high heat, stirring occasionally, and cook briskly for 10 minutes. Stir in the sugar, raisins, ginger, garlic, chilies, allspice and salt, reduce the heat to low, and simmer uncovered for 45 minutes, or until the mango flesh is tender.

Remove the pot from the heat. With a large spoon, ladle the chutney immediately into hot sterilized canning jars, filling them to within 1/8 inch of the top. Seal each jar quickly and tightly with sterilized rings and lids.

To make about 3 pints

2 ounces dried tamarind (a piece approximately 2 by 2 by 3/4 inches)
1/2 cup boiling water
4 pounds medium-sized unripe mangoes *(see box, page 116)*
2 cups malt vinegar
1 cup sugar
1/2 cup seedless raisins
1/2 cup peeled, very finely chopped fresh ginger root
1 teaspoon finely chopped garlic
1 teaspoon finely chopped fresh hot chilies *(caution: see page 46)*
1/2 teaspoon ground allspice
2 tablespoons salt

125

Coconut bread *(left)* and banana bread are teatime favorites in the islands; the iced tea usually comes with lime.

Violet Hurdle's Coconut Bread *(Barbados)*

To make 3 small loaves

Preheat the oven to 350°. With a pastry brush, spread 1 tablespoon of softened butter evenly over the bottom and sides of three 3½-by-7-inch loaf pans. Sprinkle 1 tablespoon of the flour into each pan and tip the pans from side to side to spread it evenly. Then invert the pans and rap the bottom sharply to remove any excess flour. Set aside.

Sift the remaining 5 cups of flour, the sugar, baking powder, cinnamon, cloves and salt into a deep bowl. Add the grated coconut and, with your hands or a large spoon, mix all the ingredients together well. Pour in the milk, ½ cup at a time, and blend thoroughly after each addition. Then stir in the 4 tablespoons of melted butter.

Ladle the coconut batter into the prepared pans, filling each of them no more than two thirds full. Bake the bread in the middle of the oven for 1 hour, or until it begins to pull away from the sides of the pans and the top is golden brown and crusty.

Remove the bread from the oven and let it cool in the pans for about 5 minutes, then turn the loaves out onto wire cake racks. Serve the coconut bread either warm or cool.

NOTE: Four cups of packaged or frozen flaked or grated coconut may be substituted for the freshly grated coconut. If the prepared coconut is presweetened (most brands are), reduce the amount of sugar in the recipe from 2 cups to 1½ cups. If you want to reduce the size of the packaged flakes to make the bread less crunchy, pulverize the coconut in the jar of an electric blender by blending it at high speed for a few seconds.

1 tablespoon butter, softened, plus 4 tablespoons butter, melted
3 tablespoons plus 5 cups flour
2 cups sugar
1 tablespoon double-acting baking powder
½ teaspoon ground cinnamon
¼ teaspoon ground cloves
1 teaspoon salt
1 large fresh coconut, opened, peeled and finely grated *(see Recipe Booklet)*
2 cups milk

Banana Bread *(Jamaica)*

To make one 9-by-5-by-3-inch loaf

Preheat the oven to 350°. With a pastry brush, spread 1 tablespoon of softened butter evenly over the bottom and sides of a 9-by-5-by-3-inch loaf pan and set it aside.

Reserve ¼ cup of the most perfectly shaped pecan halves for the garnish. Chop the rest of the nuts coarsely and toss them with the raisins and 1 tablespoon of the flour. Sift the remaining flour with the baking powder, nutmeg and salt.

Peel the bananas, chop them coarsely, and put them into a small bowl. With the back of a table fork, mash the bananas to a smooth purée. Stir in the vanilla and set aside.

In a deep bowl, cream the remaining butter and the sugar together, beating and mashing them with a large spoon against the sides of the bowl until the mixture is light and fluffy.

Add the egg, and when it is well blended beat in the flour and the bananas alternately, adding about one third of each mixture at a time, and continue to beat until the batter is smooth. Gently but thoroughly stir in the chopped pecans and raisins.

Ladle the batter into the loaf pan and arrange the reserved pecan halves attractively on the top. Bake the bread in the middle of the oven for 50 to 60 minutes, or until a cake tester or toothpick inserted into the center of the loaf comes out clean. Remove the bread from the oven and let it cool in the pan for 5 minutes, then turn it out on a wire cake rack.

Serve the banana bread either warm or cool.

9 tablespoons butter, softened
¾ cup unsalted shelled pecans
¼ cup seedless raisins
2 cups all-purpose flour
1 tablespoon double-acting baking powder
¼ teaspoon ground nutmeg, preferably freshly grated
½ teaspoon salt
2 large ripe bananas (about 1 pound)
1 teaspoon vanilla extract
½ cup sugar
1 egg

Fiery hibiscus blooms frame three cold fruit desserts *(from left):* mango mousse, coconut sherbet and lime soufflé.

Lime Soufflé *(Barbados)*

Fold a 24-inch-long piece of wax paper lengthwise in half and again lengthwise into quarters. With a pastry brush spread the vegetable oil evenly on one side of the folded strip. Then wrap the paper strip, oiled side in, around the outside of a 1-quart soufflé dish to make a collar extending about 2 inches above the top edge of the dish. Tie the paper in place with string. Coat the inside of the dish lightly with the remaining oil and set the dish aside.

Pour the lime juice into a heatproof bowl, sprinkle in the gelatin and let it soften for 2 or 3 minutes. Then set the bowl in a skillet of simmering water and stir over low heat until the gelatin dissolves. Remove the skillet from the heat, but leave the bowl in the water to keep the gelatin warm.

In a 1½- to 2-quart enameled, stainless-steel or glass saucepan, heat the evaporated milk over moderate heat until bubbles form around the edge of the pan. Remove from the heat.

With a wire whisk or rotary or electric beater, beat the egg yolks until well blended. Slowly add the sugar and continue beating until the yolks are thick enough to fall in a ribbon when the beater is lifted from the bowl.

Beating constantly, slowly pour the hot milk in a thin stream into the yolks, then pour the mixture back into the saucepan. Stir over low heat until it thickens into a custard heavy enough to coat the spoon. Do not let the custard come to a boil or it may curdle. Remove the pan from the heat and stir in the dissolved gelatin and 3 tablespoons of the lime rind. Transfer the custard to a deep bowl, and set it aside to cool to room temperature.

In a separate bowl, beat the egg whites with a whisk or a rotary or electric beater until they form firm peaks on the beater when it is lifted out of the bowl. Stir about one quarter of the whites into the custard, then pour it over the remaining egg whites and gently fold them together. Pour the soufflé into the prepared dish and refrigerate for at least 3 hours, or until firm.

Meanwhile preheat the oven to 325°. Spread the coconut in a baking pan and, stirring occasionally, toast it in the oven for 15 to 20 minutes, or until light brown. Remove the coconut from the oven and set it aside to cool.

Just before serving, gently remove the wax collar from the dish and garnish the soufflé with the coconut and the remaining tablespoon of lime rind.

To serve 6

1 tablespoon vegetable oil
1 cup strained fresh lime juice
1 envelope unflavored gelatin
1 cup evaporated milk
6 egg yolks
1¼ cups sugar
4 tablespoons finely grated lime rind
4 egg whites
½ cup coarsely grated fresh coconut *(see Recipe Booklet)*

Mango Mousse *(Barbados)*

With a small, sharp knife, peel the mangoes and cut the flesh away from the large, flat stone inside each fruit. Cut the flesh of 2 of the mangoes into ¼-inch dice and set aside. Chop the 3 remaining mangoes fine and purée them through a food mill set over a bowl. Then stir in the lime juice.

In a large bowl, using a whisk or a rotary or electric beater, beat the egg whites with the salt until they are frothy. Sprinkle in the sugar and continue beating until the egg whites are stiff enough to stand in unwavering peaks when the whisk is lifted from the bowl. In a separate, chilled bowl, but with the same beater, whip the cream until it is stiff enough to form firm peaks.

With a rubber spatula, fold the egg whites into the cream. Stir about 1 cup of the mixture into the mango purée, then pour the purée over the remaining cream and fold them together gently but thoroughly. Carefully fold in the diced mango. Spoon the mousse into individual dessert dishes or a large serving bowl. Refrigerate it for at least 3 hours before serving.

To serve 8

5 medium-sized (about 1 pound each) ripe mangoes *(see box, page 116)*
⅓ cup strained fresh lime juice
2 egg whites
A pinch of salt
⅓ cup sugar
½ cup heavy cream

VI

Shining Treasures from a Tropic Sea

Besieged by customers, the owner of the *Sonia*, just in with the morning's catch, turns from fisherman to fishmonger. It is Sunday, the biggest selling day of the week, and buyers have come all the way across Martinique from Fort-de-France to this beach at Vauclin on the island's southeastern shore.

Whenever I am in the islands I love to wander in the early mornings along the quayside markets of the towns where the big fishing vessels dock, or along the shores of the little net-draped villages where fishermen sell directly from their long dugout canoes. For me, nothing in the duty-free shops of the Caribbean, with their pearls from Majorca, silver from India and gleaming gold watches from Switzerland and Japan, can match these local treasures. Lying on the decks or in the bottoms of the boats are exquisite purple-backed flying fish with silver stomachs and fins like dragonflies' wings, enormous sparkling pink and white snappers, glistening gray mullets, and flashing psychedelic fish all cobalt blue or piercing yellow, palest lilac or grape green, diamond marked or zigzag striped or polka-dotted.

Tropical waters have more varieties of fish than northern waters and almost all of them are brilliantly colored. But of course they are more than beautiful; they are also delicious. Travelers seem always to remember with most affection the seafood they eat in the islands. And no wonder, for fish and shellfish are at their best when eaten close to their own environment—on a beach, a boat, or within sight of salty blue-green water—and in the Caribbean one is almost never more than a few minutes from the sea.

My own favorite meals in the islands have come from the sea. I particularly remember the first time I had a deceptively simple concoction of poached fish called blaff. It is a dish that still summons up, when I cook it at home, the fragrant smells, the languid heat, the brilliant clarity of the Caribbean. I have only to taste a spoon of its pale broth to be transported, as Proust was with tea and *petites madeleines,* to another place and time—the day I first sampled blaff on a gleaming beach on Martinique. It was in January, and the sun glaringly affirmed that I was indeed in the Caribbean again, wearing a red bikini and nursing a suntan, while my husband and daughter were sloshing, booted and burdened with coats, through New York's gray snow. Perhaps my own good fortune colored my enthusiasm, but I felt the day was charged with that special aura of exhilarating serenity that makes the islands seem another world.

Creole friends of ours, Max and Denise Elizé, owned a cruiser and had invited me to join them for a day on the water. The Elizés, their children and I set out early, breakfasting aboard the boat on crusty local bread, spicy blood sausage and juicy pineapple. Madame Elizé explained that for lunch we would buy freshly caught fish at one of the villages along Martinique's southern coast and cook blaff on the beach. The dish is named onomatopoeically, she said, after the sound the fish makes when it is thrown into the simmering pot in which it swims its last.

Eventually, when the sun was high and too hot for me (the Elizé family, some dark-skinned and dark-haired, some blond and blue-eyed and fairer-skinned than I, were used to the sun), we stopped at a village, just like many others we had passed, on a flat, narrow shelf of glistening sand tucked beneath curving verdant hills. The fishermen had just come in. Their boats were lying on the sand, still partly in the water as if the crowd of villagers had begun reaching for fish before the men could get the boats any farther ashore. The buyers' excitement was keen. The morning's catch had been good, and men, women and children edged each other aside to examine and probe the brilliant live treasure heaped in the bottoms of the boats. Madame Elizé made her selection, an assortment of small mackerellike fish. Blaff can be made of almost any kind of fish and of any size fish, she said, but she prefers small ones. The fisherman weighed the fish on his simple scale set on the seat across the center of the boat, and then cleaned them for us.

We escaped from the crowd and headed down the beach to where it curved into the sea, and settled on the white sand with rocks behind us and coconut palms and tamarind trees sheltering us from the sun. The grownups drank rum and lime juice while the children hunted coconuts to slake their thirst and wood to build a fire. When they returned their mother emptied the large metal pot that served as her picnic basket of its few contents: allspice, cloves, a scallion, parsley, garlic, peppers and limes. Filling the pot from a container of fresh water she had brought, she mashed down the garlic, scallion and parsley with the back of a spoon, put them and the cloves and allspice back into the pot and placed the pot on a stick fire. She remarked that it was too bad not to have fresh allspice, too, so the children were sent to find some; they soon returned with a twig bearing little dark-green leaves. Madame crushed one and added it and its fragrance to the pot. (I learned later that the berries and leaves of the bay-rum tree are also traditionally used in blaff and other dishes instead of allspice, which bay-rum berries, also called malagueta pepper, resemble in appearance and taste.)

While the pot simmered we rested and the children played in the sand. Soon it was time for the fish to be thrown in—and they did make a sound like *blaff* as they splashed into the steamy water. They came out almost as quickly. There are only two requirements for a perfect blaff: one that the fish be absolutely fresh and the other that they be cooked very briefly. Madame Elizé placed a few fish in each person's bowl and then tasted the broth still in the pot. Her brow furrowed, and she added salt and some generous squeezes of lime to the liquid. Then she stirred it and spooned the broth over our fish and gave each of us a piece of lime and half a fiery pepper, not to eat but to season the sauce with. The fish was permeated with the aromatic scent of cloves and allspice; sometimes a hint of hot pepper, sometimes the fragrant lime would dominate a bite. I felt I could eat blaff forever and never be bored with its simplicity, a taste of the sea gracefully modified by the fruits of the tropical soil. With the blaff we drank coconut water from the big green nuts the children had gathered, a cooling sweetness that complemented the spicy fish.

Blaff, still my favorite Caribbean fish recipe, is a specialty of the French islands, but each island has its own way with fish. On Puerto Rico and in the Dominican Republic the most popular way of preparing it is *en escabeche*, a traditional Spanish technique encountered throughout Latin America. An *escabeche* is made by pouring a tangy marinade of olive oil and vinegar, onions, bay or allspice leaves and spices over fillets of grilled or fried fish; the result is eaten either hot or cold. Virtually the same dish is also popular on Jamaica, where it is called escovitch *(Recipe Index)*. I have heard that many Jamaicans are not aware of its Spanish origins; they joke that escovitch must have been invented by and named after a gourmet Polish sea captain. I like to stop for escovitch when I am driving in the countryside where tourist restaurants are virtually nonexistent. At roadside stalls in the Jamaican hills the dish is made to order and wrapped to take out; to my mind it is better snack food than the hot dog sold in the United States because it is crisp and spicy and all protein.

I asked a cook at one of the stalls how he made his escovitch and, although I have since read many recipes for it, none has been more expressive than the one he recited. "You make sure the fish is dry by patting it with a towel," he said. "Then you make cuts in it and put in black pepper and salt. Use coconut oil in the pan. But it must be hot; it's got to go *shussh* when you throw in the fish. You got to stand back then, it's going *shussh!* Then you turn it and when it's done, you cut an onion and some pepper, green or red pepper this time, but hot, and fry it in the leftover oil. Then add some vinegar to this. Then put it on top of the fish and cover the dish and let it all sweat inside together. And then you have something wonderful! Then you have escovitch."

On Aruba and Curaçao the most distinctive seafood dish is a chowder called *sopito*. Its special flavor is so hard to achieve consistently that one of the big hotels on Curaçao employs a local chef to make just *sopito*. On Mondays, his day off, there is no chowder, for though the hotel has many chefs the others are not from Curaçao and have never mastered the intricacies of *sopito*.

Sopito differs from other fish chowders in being made with coconut milk. Salt pork or corned beef, onions, tomatoes, garlic, peppers, fresh cream and a variety of spices are also included. Any of dozens of kinds of fish found in the local waters can be used—as they can in blaff or escovitch. Curaçaoans buy their fish at the floating market, a fleet of schooners that sails over from nearby Venezuela to supply the island with not only fish but also the food-

Continued on page 136

An Abundance of Fishes for Cooking and Looking

From a commercial standpoint, the waters of the Caribbean are sadly underdeveloped. They are full of fish, but the primitive methods used in most areas fail to harvest enough to satisfy local demands. Even the spiny lobster, held by some to be superior in flavor to its cold-water cousin, is caught in limited quantities. From a sportsman's standpoint, however, the supply of fish is ample. Snorkeling with a spear gun on the coral reefs, trolling in the deep blue of the sea, fly-casting in the shallows of a mangrove inlet—such techniques can yield a delicious sampling of Caribbean seafood. For those interested more in scenery than in sport, there are other possibilities. At St. Croix in the Virgin Islands an underwater "park" rich in tropical marine life has been set aside for fish watchers.

On the beach at Hawksbill Inn on Antigua, an employee dangles two spiny lobsters *(above)* destined for the pot. At right another member of the Hawksbill staff displays two kinds of edible sea urchins, or sea eggs. The dolphin *(below),* which changes colors spectacularly when caught, is a fine-tasting game fish.

stuffs its own arid soil cannot grow. The merchants shout the value of their wares from shipboard while the buyers at dockside jump up and down to get a good look at the grouper, snapper, snook and shark piled on the decks, choosing the ingredients for their *sopito* in a balletic commotion.

At my friend Dolly Delvalle's house on Curaçao, *sopito* is never served as a soup—as it is in hotels and restaurants that scrimp on the fish—but as a main dish. Creamy and white, it seems as laden with fish as the schooners of the floating market, and the coconut milk gives it a special smoothness. With it my friend serves Curaçaoan bread, *pan serra*, a dense loaf perfect for scooping up the fishy scraps in the bowl when all the broth has been drunk. I could smell the sea from Dolly's house and that enhanced my introduction to *sopito*, but I have eaten it since in my New York apartment and found it just as good.

Of the myriad kinds of edible fish in the Caribbean, snapper is the one most often served on restaurant and hotel tables. In the Dominican Republic I ate it with a thick topping of capers, olives, garlic and onions; on Jamaica it came with a stuffing of locally grown cashew nuts. On Trinidad, in fact, a snapper recipe was invented and named for me. Trinidadians are famous for greeting arrivals at the airport with calypsos composed on the spot and featuring ingenious rhymes based on the tourist's appearance—how tired or excited he looks, his clothing, what he is carrying, the color of his hair. The islands' chefs can be just as attentive to the newcomer, and as imaginative, as the calypsonians are. Invited to a special dinner given by the National Culinary Arts Association, I was told by my hosts that they regretted it had rained throughout my visit, that I must certainly return (I did, of course), and that meanwhile they intended to provide me with some vicarious sunshine in the dinner's main dish, "Red Snapper Sunshine Wolfe." It was a seven-pound snapper stuffed with pigeon peas and salt pork, bathed in lime and orange juice, and rubbed on the outside not only with herbs and spices but with mustard and ketchup as well, to give it a gay sunshiny color.

Snapper is just as popular on the French islands and, not surprisingly in those outposts of superb eating, the fish is accorded the utmost respect. One evening on Guadeloupe my husband and I were treated to an unforgettable dinner whose every course came from the sea. Our host was a Parisian who had married into a leading local family and had thrown himself into the spirit and life of the islands and become an accomplished Creole-style cook. Because of the constant failures of telephone service in the Caribbean we had been unable to alert him to our impending arrival; nevertheless, on the day we met he insisted we come to dinner, though it was already late afternoon. He said he was disappointed that he had not known beforehand because he would have liked to make his specialty, a snapper cooked in the style of the Carib Indians—pit-baked, with thyme and hot peppers placed between skin and flesh and a layer of mud packed outside. There was no time for this, he apologized, but he would do what he could.

No apology was needed. Crisply fried little *soleil*, or sunfish, were followed by fish fritters and then by red snapper *court bouillon*, tingling with spices *(Recipe Index)*. (Among the Creoles of Martinique and Guadeloupe, *court bouillon* is the name of a dish, not the herb- and vegetable-flavored liquid in which fish or meat is poached in French cooking.) The dish is begun by marinating fish in lime juice and rubbing it with hot peppers. Later it is browned in scallion-flavored oil, and then steamed with small tomatoes, onions and more hot peppers. Just before the fish is served it is given a final fillip of flavor by the addition of slices of raw garlic and lime. The spiciness of this dish enlivened our conversation and the evening. At midnight we all swam off our host's moonlit beach while he gaily pointed out that Creole *court bouillon* was never really good unless the guests felt moved to take off their shirts after eating it.

The sea, of course, yields other bounty besides fish. The Caribbean lobster is a superb creature. Its chief difference from the lobster of northern waters is that it has no pincerlike claws. It is also called *langouste, langosta* or spiny lobster, and it compensates for its lack of claw meat by the quality of the meat in its tail, acclaimed by its champions as the most delicate meat available from any crustaceans.

Very few of the lobsters caught in the islands are eaten by fishermen and their families because their catch goes to meet the demand of establishments catering to tourists. This demand, in fact, often goes unfilled, even on Jamaica, where half the island's 3,000 fishermen are involved in lobstering; thus the traveler eager for a taste of the famous spiny lobster is sometimes frustrated. This holds true on all the islands except Cuba, which has built up the largest lobster fishery in all the Caribbean and Latin America; lacking a tourist horde to consume the supply, Cubans export lobster in large quantities.

Cuba has also exported a dish—known variously as *langosta enchilada, langosta criolla* or lobster Creole—that is my own favorite way of elaborating on lobster, the only way that is good enough to compete with the natural elegance of broiled lobster with butter sauce. In lobster Creole *(Recipe Index)* the lobster tail is fried in hot oil until the shell barely reddens. Then it is removed, and into the skillet go white wine, tomatoes, onions, sweet green pepper and just enough hot pepper to tangle with the taste of the lobster but not overpower it; finally the lobster is cooked a few minutes longer in this sauce. The result couldn't be more unlike broiled lobster, but it is just as good because the disguise is not too complex—beneath it one is always aware of the real thing, the sweet mild chewiness of the meat.

Shrimp too are consumed as fast as they can be caught in the islands. Unfortunately, shrimp grow in limited quantities in Caribbean waters; in most places shrimping is a local, small-scale operation, and tourism has so increased the demand that there never seem to be enough to go around. Indeed, on those islands with the most tourists, such as Jamaica and Puerto Rico, the visitor is likely to find himself eating frozen shrimp imported from the United States.

This does not mean that shrimp are not highly regarded by the islanders and not brilliantly treated in their kitchens. Shrimp have been considered a delicacy since the earliest days of the region's history. Perhaps the oldest shrimp recipe of the islands is a Jamaican soup that has been handed down in the Pringle family's centuries-old cookbook. The concoction, based on the shrimp meat itself, is strengthened by the addition of the pounded heads, tails and skins of the shrimp and then is given body with a "penny ha'penny worth of salt pork or beef." There is also a host of modern shrimp dishes that are memorable, among them shrimp stuffed with anchovy paste, shrimp

Flying fish are not only exotic but also extremely good to eat. Their wings are actually extended pectoral fins that sustain the fish in a long glide after it leaps from the water when fleeing danger. Common to most tropical waters, flying fish are especially plentiful off Barbados, where this one was caught. The island has even built a cannery and a freezing plant, with the aim of exporting its most elusive delicacy.

curry and shrimp Creole *(Recipe Index)*. The latter, which like most Creole dishes is always made with tomato, has become a standard shrimp dish in other parts of the world as well.

Perhaps the most famous marine delicacy of the Caribbean is green turtle, the world's best-tasting sea turtle. Its history is an unfortunate one, intimately linked to that of the region. The green turtle used to nest all over the islands in great numbers. When mature, it is as big as a young cow, but it is easy to catch and if turned on its back cannot move; furthermore, it stays alive for months with practically no feeding. The advantages for transatlantic voyagers were obvious, and so naval and merchant ships of both the British and Spanish fleets carried live green turtles on their journeys home. They proved to be an ideal source of food, providing fresh meat that served both to prevent scurvy and to maintain morale.

So gratifying were the soups and steaks made from the ships' turtle stores that captains began stocking enough not only to feed their crews but to sell, at the high prices imports always commanded, to rich and royal Europeans. Turtle became a dish of ceremonial stature. In England an alderman's banquet, a traditional feast held by officials of the old London guild companies, was judged inadequate if it did not begin with turtle soup. Eventually the green turtle itself came to be called "London alderman's turtle."

Popular though it may have been, the turtle meat that reached England was not, as a rule, exactly fresh. A traveler to the islands in the mid-1700s, promised that she would get so much turtle she would soon be surfeited with it, did not particularly relish the prospect since the turtle meat she had tasted in London, at great expense, had always been old and tough. But it was another story when she got to Antigua. "I have now seen Turtle almost every day," she wrote, "and though I never could eat it at home, am vastly fond of it here . . . where it is indeed a very different thing. You get nothing but old ones there, the chickens being unable to stand the voyage; even these are starved or at best fed on coarse and improper food. Here they are young, tender, fresh from the water, where they feed as delicately and are as great Epicures, as those who feed on them. They laugh at us for the racket we make to have it divided into different dishes. They never make but two, the soup and the shell. . . . The shell indeed is a noble dish, as it contains all the fine parts of the Turtle baked within its own body. . . . Could an Alderman of true taste conceive the difference between it here and in the City, he would make the Voyage on purpose, and I fancy he would make a voyage into the other world before he left the table."

Inevitably the turtle suffered for its popularity. Though well protected within its shell from most natural predators, it is an easy prey for man. Strong swimmers can catch turtles with little trouble by driving them into large nets. Furthermore, the turtle's eggs, considered as much a delicacy as its meat, are particularly vulnerable—the female lays them in a shallow nest in the sand a few yards from the water's edge, then crawls back to the sea leaving the eggs unguarded. Egg hunters can in effect eliminate a whole generation of turtles on one collecting foray.

As early as 1620 the danger to the species was recognized, and laws were passed in the islands against those "lewd and improvident persons" who would "snatch and catch up indifferentlye all kinds of Tortoyses both yonge and old, little and greate, and soe kill, carrye awaye and devoure them to the much decay of the breed. . . ." But the laws had only limited effect. Through the following centuries the turtles continued to be caught in such numbers, and their nesting grounds raided so ruthlessly, that the Caribbean green turtle has long been threatened with extinction.

Today there are only two places in the Caribbean where the turtle nests in quantity. One is the Bay of Tortuguero on the northeastern coast of Costa Rica in the western Caribbean; the other is remote Aves Island near Montserrat in the eastern Caribbean. It is fitting that Aves still provides a home to the vanishing turtle, since it is itself apparently sinking slowly under the sea. Also appropriately, it was at Aves that my favorite raconteur of the old days in the Caribbean, Père Labat, once landed in the company of pirates who rapidly equipped themselves with a full load of green turtles. The good priest, although he was keeping bad company at the time, was grateful to God for sending him to so generous albeit barren an island, and he repaid its hospitality by planting orange and lime trees on it.

Today on Aves and at Tortuguero the nesting turtles are effectively protected from modern pirates and overambitious fishermen by an international effort—called Operation Green Turtle—aimed at keeping the species from disappearing altogether. And green turtle, while still caught in proper season in Caribbean waters, is now hard to find on hotel and restaurant menus.

I was determined to have some turtle on my last trip to the islands, but the quest was disappointing. On Barbados I had a fine green turtle soup, laced with sherry and tasting rich and salty, but at a famous seafood restaurant in Ponce, Puerto Rico, the turtle steak I had made me conclude that the ability to cook turtle properly is vanishing along with the turtle itself. Although the creature on my plate had the fine, meaty flavor of turtle, it was so swathed in breading and onions and garlic that it was smothered. The chief offender was garlic, that Johnny-come-lately to the islands, which is just too potent for the subtle turtle meat.

The Caribbean offers still other fruits of the sea to be sampled. The dolphin, a fish with firm, white swordfishlike flesh, is not related to the endearing mammal known either as dolphin or porpoise, except in one characteristic—like the porpoise it is an inquisitive creature, and when the captains of fishing vessels go looking for it in the Caribbean they go out of their way to troll past any log, box or sunken wreckage where the fish might be exploring. Another local specialty is bonefish, a skinny, belligerent species that provides spectacular sport fishing on the islands' coral shallows. The islanders have an ingenious way of stretching a bonefish before cooking it in order to remove the many tiny bones from its otherwise excellent flesh.

Kingfish, grouper and Spanish mackerel are also succulent Caribbean fish, and so are other denizens of the islands' waters that are harder to identify because the names by which they are locally known are so odd. Jamaicans, in particular, are inventive namers, and you will not fail to be delighted by their skill even though you may find it difficult to figure out what you are buying at the market. Among my favorite fish names are the go-far, a turbot so called because "it could share to a lot of people"; the John Mariggle, a long tapered fish so called because it is tricky and it "jump and try to shake out hook"; the God-a-me, a small fish that hides in the mud of rivers and is named for the scared-looking expression it has when caught; and the sea Anancy, a spider crab named after the greatest folk hero in the islands, Anancy, a being half spider, half man whose shrewd legendary exploits were told and retold by the African slaves and who is still revered on all the islands today.

Not only the names of Caribbean fish but their shapes as well can be remarkable and sometimes even bizarre. There is the cofferfish, which is square-shaped like a chest of buried treasure, the moonfish, which is round and silvery, and the fish the people on Martinique call *bon-Dié manié moin*—"good God handled me"—which bears unearthly fingerprints along its sides. And among the strangest-looking of all are two creatures that provide some of the finest food from the sea to be had in the Caribbean.

One of these is the conch, called lambi on most islands. Americans know the conch less for its flesh than for its pretty rose-tinted shell, which has become almost a cliché symbol of the islands. When the conch itself comes out of its iridescent house it is a veritable sea monster, an enormous snail with big horns and a bright golden eye in the tip of each horn. It can be up to a foot long, and its muscular white flesh is almost as compact as cartilage. Before it can be cooked it must be patiently marinated and then furiously pounded with a wooden beater. "He beat him like a lambi" is a phrase that has often been heard in island courtrooms from witnesses testifying in cases of assault and battery. But when the lambi has been marinated and tenderized it can be superb. I have eaten it raw in salads and stewed in chowders on many islands, and usually marvel at how soft and chewy it can become —though I confess that when improperly prepared it can have the consistency of a rubber truncheon. I like it best the way it is done on Guadeloupe, cooked in a brown sauce flavored with nutmeg, cinnamon, thyme, peppers and lots of sweet lime juice.

Another fearsome-looking but fine-tasting delicacy is the sea egg, a kind of sea urchin and a cousin of the sinister black urchin whose sharp poisonous spines are a hazard to bathers all over the West Indies. The sea egg is white and lacks the dangerous spines of the urchin, but I still do not find it a congenial creature. After a day of nervously looking out for sea urchins and eggs under my feet while swimming off a beach at Barbados I felt quite justified, even vindictive, about eating them when they were first offered to me by a local youth who was catching them barehanded. Deftly splitting them open with a thin stone, he dispensed them with slices of fresh lime, which nicely augmented their sea-salty taste.

They were intriguing in this natural state, but even better when they were served to me in a Barbadian home, cooked in the way the islanders prefer, sautéed in butter and well blended with onions. My husband and I had been invited to try them by some friends, and I thought our hostess, a 20-year-old newlywed, had overestimated our appetites when she brought to the table a two-foot-long platter heaped with fluffy yellow sea eggs. "She's a good cook," her husband confided when he saw me staring at the platter, "but she doesn't know how much to make. She never makes enough." I looked at him incredulously, but it turned out he was right. The texture of the sea eggs was so light and airy, almost as insubstantial as cotton candy, and their flavor so compelling that I realized it would be almost impossible ever to serve enough of them. We washed them down with mauby, a local drink made from the bark of a tropical tree. Mauby's bittersweet taste was just the right accompaniment to the salty, oniony urchins. In short order the four of us had emptied the fat pitcher of mauby and devoured the pile of sea eggs.

Curiously, it is often difficult to obtain fish on the islands. Although there is a great need for protein in the Caribbean diet, relatively little fish is consumed. Sociologists and ethnologists have puzzled over this and one has even reached the stark conclusion that "Caribbean people do not like fish." The truth of the matter is that the resources of the ocean have only just begun to be properly utilized. Fish spoils rapidly in tropical heat; ice and refrigeration on fishing boats and in markets are even today not commonly available. On small islands housewives must go to the town docks or wait along the shore for the little boats to pull in, hoping to be able to buy fish. Often they are turned away because the poverty of the fishermen prevents them from owning any but the simplest and most inefficient equipment; as a result their catch is too small even for their personal needs. The most common fishing boat in the islands is still a narrow craft shaped like a dugout canoe, varying in length from 10 to 35 feet. Hooks and lines, harpoons, nets made of wire and twine, wooden traps, spears and even bows and arrows are still in common use.

Furthermore, even though the islands are washed by the waters of the Atlantic and Caribbean, many of them, such as Puerto Rico, have virtually no seafaring tradition. The slaves who were taken there came mostly from the African jungles, and then for generations were allowed to do nothing but work in the cane fields. They never did acquire the skills of the sea, and many islanders today regard the waters around them as a hostile element.

Many others, however, are as much at home afloat as ashore. On Aruba there are blue-eyed, bronze-skinned fishermen who are said to be descendants of the island's original Indian population and the early European settlers; they handle their cleavers as deftly as Chinese chefs and can slice firm shark meat to precise inch-thick fillets on clumsy chopping blocks set up along the beach. Their profession is hereditary and they are intensely vain of their skills. So are the last of the Caribs on Dominica, who still practice their ancient art of building *gommiers*, dugouts made from huge tree trunks, in which, using only oars and sails, they go out fishing every day.

Perhaps the most famous mariners in the Caribbean are the inhabitants of the tiny Cayman Islands. The Caymanians, superb seamen who have passed their profession along for generations, were especially gifted at turtling, and they sailed in search of their quarry to every strand, however remote, in the western Caribbean. They are still attached to the sea with an affection almost as strong as that which binds their close-knit families. With the gradual disappearance of turtling, they have gone on to other seafaring work; today they serve aboard the tankers and merchantmen of most of the great maritime nations of the world.

I do not believe that the islanders don't like fish. I wish the sociologists and ethnologists who say they don't could eat in some of the homes I have eaten in and enjoy some of the memorable Caribbean ways of preparing fish, or witness the intense enthusiasm among the village crowds when the fishing boats pull in. But it is true that the supply on many islands is inadequate and that only when the methods of catching and storing fish are improved will Caribbean recipes for cooking fish truly come into their own.

Keshy Yena coe Cabaron (Curaçao)
BAKED EDAM CHEESE WITH SHRIMP STUFFING

Peel the cheese and cut a 1-inch-thick slice off the top. With a spoon, scoop out the center of the cheese leaving a boatlike shell about ½ inch thick. Hollow the slice from the top in a similar fashion to make a lid for the shell. Place the lid and shell in a large pan or bowl, pour in enough cold water to cover them by at least 1 inch, and let them soak for 1 hour.

Meanwhile, grate enough of the scooped-out cheese to make 2 cups and set it aside. Shell the shrimp. Devein them by making a shallow incision down their backs with a small, sharp knife and lifting out their intestinal veins with the point of the knife. If the shrimp are small, leave them whole; if they are large, cut them into ½-inch-long pieces.

Remove the cheese shell and lid from the water and invert them on paper towels to drain.

Preheat the oven to 350°. With a pastry brush, spread the tablespoon of softened butter evenly over the bottom and sides of a round baking dish at least 5 inches deep and just large enough to hold the cheese compactly. (If the dish is too shallow or too large, the cheese will collapse and spread when it is baked.)

In a heavy 8- to 10-inch skillet, melt the remaining 2 tablespoons of butter in the vegetable oil over moderate heat. Drop in the onions and, stirring frequently, cook for about 5 minutes, until they are soft and transparent but not brown. Watch carefully for any sign of burning and regulate the heat accordingly. Add the tomato, red pepper, salt and a few grindings of black pepper and, still stirring, cook briskly until most of the liquid in the pan has evaporated and the mixture is thick enough to hold its shape almost solidly in the spoon.

With a rubber spatula, transfer the entire contents of the skillet to a deep bowl. Add the grated cheese, bread crumbs, olives, gherkin and raisins, and toss together gently but thoroughly. Taste for seasoning, then stir in the beaten egg. Spoon the shrimp mixture into the cheese shell, place the shell in the prepared dish, and top it with the cheese lid.

Bake uncovered on the middle shelf of the oven for about 30 minutes, or until the top is bubbly and delicately browned. Serve the *keshy yena* at once, directly from the baking dish.

To serve 6 to 8

A 4-pound Edam cheese
¾ pound raw shrimp
1 tablespoon butter, softened, plus 2 tablespoons butter
1 tablespoon vegetable oil
1 cup finely chopped onions
1 medium-sized firm ripe tomato, peeled, seeded and finely chopped (*see sopa de gandules, page 43*), or substitute ⅓ cup chopped drained canned tomatoes
¼ teaspoon ground hot red pepper
½ teaspoon salt
Freshly ground black pepper
¼ cup soft fresh crumbs made from homemade-type white bread, trimmed of crusts and pulverized in a blender or finely shredded with a fork
6 small pimiento-stuffed olives, drained and finely chopped
1 tablespoon finely chopped sweet gherkin
2 tablespoons seedless raisins
1 egg, well beaten

Fish Stock

Combine the fish trimmings, onion, parsley, bay leaf and salt in a 2- to 3-quart glass, enameled or stainless-steel saucepan. Pour in the water and bring to a boil over high heat. Reduce the heat to low, partially cover the pan, and simmer for 30 minutes.

Strain the stock through a fine sieve set over a deep bowl, pressing down hard on the fish trimmings with the back of a spoon to extract their juices before discarding them. Cover tightly and refrigerate until ready to use. Fish stock may be frozen and stored in the freezer for months; it may be kept in the refrigerator for about a week if brought to a boil every second day.

To make about 5 cups

2 pounds fish trimmings: bones, heads and tails from any white-fleshed fish
1 medium-sized onion, peeled and thickly sliced
4 parsley sprigs
1 bay leaf
1 teaspoon salt
6 cups water

Curaçao's *keshy yena*, a baked Edam, is shown at left with a shrimp filling.

To serve 2

2 uncooked 1½- to 2-pound Maine
lobsters, split in half lengthwise
3 tablespoons annatto oil *(page 47)*
1 cup dry white wine
2 cups *sofrito (below)*
1 teaspoon finely chopped fresh hot
chilies *(caution: see page 46)*
1 teaspoon salt

To make about 2 cups

2 ounces salt pork, finely diced
(about ½ cup)
1 teaspoon annatto oil *(page 47)*
1½ cups finely chopped onions
1 tablespoon finely chopped garlic
2 medium-sized green peppers,
seeded, deribbed and coarsely
chopped
4 ounces lean boneless ham, cut
into ½-inch dice (about 1 cup)
2 large tomatoes, peeled, seeded and
coarsely chopped *(see sopa de
gandules, page 43)*, or substitute
1½ cups chopped drained canned
tomatoes
1½ teaspoons finely chopped fresh
coriander *(see Glossary, page 197)*
½ teaspoon crumbled dried oregano
1 teaspoon salt
Freshly ground black pepper

Langosta Criolla *(Cuba)*
BRAISED LOBSTER IN CHILI SAUCE

Remove and discard the gelatinous sac in the head of each lobster and the long intestinal vein attached to it. Then scoop out and set aside the greenish brown tomalley (or liver) and the black caviarlike eggs (or coral) if any. Chop off the tail section of each lobster directly at the point where it joins the body. Twist off the claws and gash the flat underside of each large claw with a large, heavy knife. Cut off and discard the small claws and the antennae.

In a heavy 12-inch skillet, heat the oil over high heat until a light haze forms above it. Add the lobster bodies, tails and large claws and, turning them constantly with tongs, fry them for 3 or 4 minutes, until the shells begin to turn pink. Transfer the lobsters to a large plate or bowl.

Pour off all but a thin layer of oil from the skillet, add the wine, and bring to a boil over high heat. Stir in the *sofrito*, chilies and salt, and return the lobsters and any liquid accumulation around them to the skillet. Turn the pieces about in the sauce to coat them evenly, reduce the heat to moderate, and cover the skillet tightly. Cook for 8 to 10 minutes, basting the lobsters from time to time with a large spoon.

Just before serving, rub the reserved tomalley and coral through a fine sieve with the back of a spoon directly into the sauce. Simmer the sauce for a minute or so longer, stirring gently, then taste for seasoning. To serve, arrange the lobster pieces attractively in a large, deep heated platter and spoon the sauce over them.

Sofrito
SPICED TOMATO COOKING SAUCE

"Sofrito" is a basic cooking sauce that is widely used in Spain and was brought to the Caribbean centuries ago by the Spanish settlers. Although some foods require a special and freshly made "sofrito," many dishes utilize the all-purpose mixture below, which may be made ahead in large quantity and either stored in the refrigerator for a week or two or frozen.

In a heavy 10- to 12-inch skillet, fry the salt pork over moderate heat, turning the dice about frequently with a spoon until they are crisp and brown and have rendered all their fat. With a slotted spoon remove and discard the dice, and add the annatto oil to the fat remaining in the skillet.

Drop in the onions, garlic and peppers and, stirring frequently, cook for 5 to 10 minutes, until the vegetables are soft but not brown. Watch carefully for any sign of burning and regulate the heat accordingly.

Add the diced ham and stir until all the pieces glisten with oil. Then stir in the chopped tomatoes, coriander, oregano, salt and a few grindings of black pepper. Reduce the heat to low, cover tightly, and simmer for 30 minutes, stirring the mixture from time to time to prevent the vegetables from sticking to the bottom of the skillet.

Ladle the *sofrito* into a large, clean jar or bowl, cover tightly, and refrigerate until ready to use. It may be kept for one to two weeks. For longer storage, ladle the *sofrito* immediately into hot sterilized canning jars, filling them to within ⅛ inch of the top. Each jar should be sealed quickly and tightly with a sterilized ring and lid.

In the Caribbean, lobster Creole features local
langoustes, or spiny lobsters, but the big-clawed
northern lobster can be substituted successfully as
shown here. In the Spanish-speaking islands this
savory blend of seafood, wine, tomatoes, onions and
peppers is called *langosta criolla*—a lilting name that
translates as lobsters in chili or hot-pepper sauce.

Three relatives of the onion—shallots, scallions and garlic—team up to give pungency to Martinique's *court bouillon à la créole,* a classic that superbly blends the fruits of the sea and the land. It may be made either with small fish cut in half *(left)* or with big fish cut into steaks *(right).* In either case, annatto oil colors the sauce, and limes and hot peppers make functional decorations.

Blaff (*Martinique*)

POACHED MARINATED FISH IN LIME-AND-HERB BROTH

To serve 2

4 cups water
½ cup plus 1 teaspoon strained fresh lime juice
1 tablespoon salt
2 one-pound firm white-flesh fish, each scaled, cleaned and cut crosswise into halves, or 4 eight-ounce fish steaks, each cut about 1 inch thick
½ cup finely chopped onions
1 tablespoon finely chopped garlic
1 teaspoon finely chopped fresh hot chilies *(caution: see page 46)*
2 bay rum berries or leaves *(see Glossary, page 197)*
4 parsley sprigs
½ teaspoon dried thyme

Combine 2 cups of the water, ½ cup of the lime juice and 1 teaspoon of salt in a large, shallow glass or ceramic baking dish, and stir until the salt dissolves completely.

Wash the fish under cold running water and place them in the juice mixture. The liquid should cover the fish completely; add more water if necessary. Let the fish marinate at room temperature for about 1 hour, then drain off and discard the marinade.

Pour the remaining 2 cups of water into a heavy 10-inch skillet and add the onions, garlic, chilies, bay rum berries or leaves, parsley and thyme. Bring to a boil over high heat, reduce the heat to low, cover tightly and simmer for 5 minutes.

Add the fish to the skillet and bring to a boil again. Reduce the heat to the lowest possible point, cover, and simmer for 8 to 10 minutes, or until the fish feels firm when pressed lightly with a finger, or the steaks flake easily when prodded with a fork.

With a slotted spoon, transfer the fish to a deep, heated platter. Add the remaining teaspoon of lime juice to the cooking liquid, and taste for seasoning. Pour the broth over the fish and serve at once.

NOTE: Any fish with firm white flesh may be used for either the blaff *(above)* or the *court bouillon à la créole (opposite page).* In the islands, these dishes are made with the red snapper familiar to American cooks as well as with more exotic local species.

Court Bouillon à la Créole (*Martinique*)

BRAISED MARINATED FISH WITH TOMATO, SHALLOT AND GARLIC SAUCE

Combine 2 cups of the water, ½ cup of the lime juice and 1 tablespoon of salt in a large, shallow glass or ceramic baking dish and stir until the salt dissolves. Wash the fish pieces under cold running water and place them in the lime juice mixture. The liquid should cover the fish completely; add more water if necessary. Let the fish marinate for about 1 hour, then pour off the marinade.

In a heavy 10- to 12-inch skillet, heat the annatto oil over moderate heat until a light haze forms above it. Drop in the shallots, scallions, 1 tablespoon of the garlic and the chilies and, stirring frequently, cook for about 5 minutes, until they are soft but not brown. Watch carefully for any sign of burning and regulate the heat accordingly. Add the tomatoes, the bouquet, thyme and a few grindings of black pepper and simmer, stirring frequently, for about 6 to 8 minutes.

Stir in the remaining ½ cup of water, add the fish pieces and baste them with the sauce. Bring to a boil over high heat, reduce the heat to low, cover tightly and simmer for 8 to 10 minutes, or until the fish feels firm when pressed lightly with a finger, or flakes easily when prodded with a fork. Do not overcook.

With a slotted spoon, transfer the fish to a heated platter. Add the olive oil, the remaining tablespoon of lime juice and 2 teaspoons of garlic to the tomato mixture. Stirring constantly, bring the sauce to a boil over moderate heat. Taste for seasoning and pour the sauce over the fish. Serve at once.

To serve 4

2½ cups water
½ cup plus 1 tablespoon strained fresh lime juice
1 tablespoon salt
Two 1- to 1½-pound firm white-flesh fish, scaled, cleaned and cut crosswise into halves, or 4 eight-ounce fish steaks, each cut about 1 inch thick
¼ cup annatto oil *(page 47)*
1 cup peeled finely chopped shallots
½ cup finely chopped scallions
1 tablespoon plus 2 teaspoons finely chopped garlic
1 teaspoon finely chopped fresh hot chilies *(caution: see page 46)*
3 medium-sized firm ripe tomatoes, peeled, seeded and finely chopped *(see sopa de gandules, page 43)*
A bouquet of 4 parsley sprigs and 1 bay leaf tied together with string
⅛ teaspoon dried thyme
Freshly ground black pepper
2 tablespoons olive oil

147

To serve 4 to 6

POACHING LIQUID

1 large onion, peeled and cut
crosswise into thin slices
1 medium-sized garlic clove, peeled
and crushed with the flat side of
a heavy knife
½ cup finely chopped carrots
½ cup finely chopped celery,
including the leaves
2 tablespoons finely chopped fresh
parsley
1 medium-sized bay leaf, crumbled
¼ teaspoon crumbled dried thyme
¼ teaspoon crumbled dried oregano
1 tablespoon salt
5 whole black peppercorns, wrapped
in a kitchen towel and crushed
with a rolling pin
½ cup strained fresh lime juice

FISH

A 5- to 6-pound red snapper or
striped bass, cleaned and scaled
but with head and tail left on, or
substitute any other whole firm
white-fleshed fish

AVOCADO SAUCE

2 large ripe avocados
3 tablespoons strained fresh lime
juice
1 tablespoon finely grated onion
1 teaspoon salt
Freshly ground black pepper
3 tablespoons vegetable oil

Pescado con Salsa de Aguacate (Cuba)
COLD POACHED FISH WITH AVOCADO SAUCE

In a fish poacher or a large, deep roasting pan with a cover, combine the sliced onion, garlic, carrots, celery, parsley, bay leaf, thyme, oregano, 1 tablespoon salt and peppercorns. Pour in the lime juice and 3 quarts of water, and bring to a boil over high heat. Lower the heat, partially cover the pan, and simmer for 20 minutes. Then let the liquid cool to lukewarm.

Wash the fish inside and out under cold running water. Without drying it, wrap it in a long double-thick piece of cheesecloth, leaving at least 6 inches of cloth at each end.

Twist the ends of the cloth, tie them with string, then place the fish on the rack of the poacher or roasting pan and lower the rack into the poaching liquid. (If you are using a roasting pan, tie the strings at the ends of the cheesecloth to the handles of the pan.) The liquid should cover the fish by at least 1 inch; add water if necessary.

Bring almost but not quite to a boil over high heat, cover tightly, and reduce the heat to the lowest point. Simmer for 30 to 40 minutes, or until the thickest part of the fish feels firm when pressed with a finger.

Using the ends of the cheesecloth as handles, lift the fish from the pan and lay it on a large board or platter. Open the cheesecloth and skin the fish with a small, sharp knife by making a cut in the skin at the base of the tail and gently pulling off the skin in strips from tail to gill. Holding both ends of the cheesecloth, carefully lift the fish and turn it over onto a heated serving platter. Remove the skin on the upturned side.

Let the fish cool to room temperature, cover it with foil or plastic wrap, and refrigerate it for at least 4 hours, until it is thoroughly chilled.

Meanwhile, prepare the sauce. Cut the avocados in half. With the tip of a small knife, loosen the seeds and lift them out. Remove any brown fibers clinging to the flesh. Strip off the skin with your fingers, starting at the narrow or stem end. (The dark-skinned variety does not peel easily; if necessary use a knife to pull the skin away.)

Chop the avocados coarsely, then purée them through a food mill set over a bowl, or press them through a fine sieve with the back of a spoon. Add the lime juice, grated onion, salt and a few grindings of black pepper, and mix well. Then beat in the olive oil, a teaspoon or so at a time. Taste the sauce for seasoning.

The finished sauce should have the consistency of mayonnaise. To prevent it from darkening as it stands, cover the sauce with plastic wrap or foil and refrigerate until ready to use.

Just before serving, spread 1 cup of the avocado sauce evenly and thickly over the skinned body of the fish. Garnish the platter, as elaborately as you like, with tomatoes, parsley sprigs, olives or sliced lime, and serve the remaining sauce in a bowl or sauceboat.

Cut the fish into serving pieces as follows: With a sharp knife cut the top layer into individual portions without cutting through the spine. Leave the head and tail intact.

Lift out the portions with a spatula and a fork, and place them on serving plates. Then gently lift out the backbone in one piece, discard it and divide the bottom layer of the fish into individual portions as before. Spoon a little of the reserved sauce on each portion.

Cuba's elegant *pescado con salsa de aguacate* is a cold poached fish, decked out with avocado sauce, tomatoes and cucumbers.

Camarones Rellenos *(Dominican Republic)*
DEEP-FRIED SHRIMP WITH ANCHOVY STUFFING

To prepare the batter, pour 1 cup of the flour into a deep bowl, make a well in the center and add the egg yolk, beer and salt. Stir the ingredients together and gradually pour in the melted butter. Continue to stir until the batter is smooth. Do not overmix. Let the batter rest for at least 30 minutes. Then beat the egg white until stiff and fold it into the batter.

In a mixing bowl, cream the butter with a large spoon, mashing and beating it against the sides of the bowl until light and fluffy. Beat in the anchovy paste, onion, lime juice and a few grindings of pepper. When the mixture is smooth, stir in the bread crumbs, a few tablespoons at a time. Refrigerate the stuffing for at least 20 minutes, or until fairly firm.

Shell the shrimp. Make an incision about ¼ inch deep down their backs with a small, sharp knife and lift out the intestinal vein with the point of the knife. Be careful not to cut too deeply or the shrimp may split in half.

Fill a deep fryer or large saucepan with vegetable oil to a depth of 3 inches and heat the oil to a temperature of 350° on a deep-frying thermometer.

With your fingers, force about 1 teaspoon of the anchovy stuffing into the cavity of each shrimp and press the openings together to enclose the stuffing. Dip the shrimp in the remaining 1 cup of flour and lightly shake off the excess. Two at a time, place the shrimp in a slotted spoon and immerse them in the batter. Immediately drop the shrimp into the hot oil and deep-fry them for 6 or 7 minutes, turning them over occasionally until golden on all sides. As they brown, transfer them to paper towels to drain. Serve at once.

To serve 4

BATTER
1 cup flour
1 egg yolk
1 cup flat beer
1 teaspoon salt
2 tablespoons butter, melted
1 egg white

STUFFING
4 tablespoons butter, softened
4 tablespoons anchovy paste
2 tablespoons finely grated onion
2 tablespoons strained fresh lime juice
Freshly ground black pepper
1 cup fresh soft crumbs, made from homemade-type white bread, pulverized in a blender or finely shredded with a fork

SHRIMP
2 pounds large raw shrimp (12 to 15 per pound)
1 cup flour
Vegetable oil for deep frying

149

VII

Tourism: Mother of Culinary Invention

Fancy-dress desserts, as well as picture-book sunsets, add to the glamor of Caribbean hotels. At the Miramar on Barbados the desserts range from a chocolate mousse called Pitch Lake pudding *(top left)* to an island-inspired cake *(bottom right)* called corn pone *(Recipe Index)*. With them are a fruited trifle *(top right)*, a coconut pie *(center)* and a tray of candied coconut.

There are two Caribbeans—the mythical one and the real one. The mythical Caribbean is a string of island paradises that are forever fertile and free of rain, peopled by happy islanders trilling calypso songs day and night. In the myth the sea is so filled with fish and the fruit trees are so laden that a hungry man has to do little more than stretch out his arm to satisfy his needs.

The makers of this myth are travel agents, travel writers and hotel and airline representatives, and most people are all too willing to believe their story. I have some friends who, though ordinarily quite realistic, fell complete victims to it. In a travel article about picturesque Dominica they read that although there were no restaurants in the rugged interior, it was possible to hike across the island and fill oneself by eating fruit off the trees. My friends forthwith decided to vacation on Dominica and to hike across it, eating fruit.

Naturally they came smack up against the real Caribbean. There was very little fruit to be picked off the trees. Tropical fruits, like northern fruits, are seasonal; they are not ripe the year round. Moreover, tropical society, like northern society, is capitalistic. Most fruit trees grow on land that is owned by someone and thus off limits to would-be fruit pickers. My friends discovered this in time, and on their hikes sensibly took along ham sandwiches. However, although it was February and the height of the tourist season, the rain fell steadily for four days and they were forced several times to turn back. They returned to New York soggy, disappointed and untanned, having set out for the mythic Caribbean and having vacationed in the real Caribbean —which *is* beautiful, to be sure, but no help-yourself paradise.

Close to 80,000 cruise-ship passengers visit Martinique in a year, and many of them are entertained by these lively dancers, who are members of the Groupe Folklorique Martiniquais. Dressed in cheerful island costumes, they perform both at resort hotels and aboard vessels moored at Fort-de-France, diverting tourists with traditional dances.

Rather, the real Caribbean is a region of distressing poverty. On many of the islands the economy has been languishing for a hundred years. Agriculture is not only poorly organized and handicapped by old-fashioned farming and marketing techniques but it is constantly threatened by hurricanes, plant diseases and serious soil deficiencies. There isn't much fish to be had in the markets because the fishing industry is underdeveloped. Very little cattle is raised on the islands and, where it is, the meat obtained often is sold before being properly aged and invariably is badly butchered. As for calypso songs, they began as songs of protest against conditions of Caribbean life. Many islanders emigrate, when they can, to more prosperous parts of the world. And of course it does rain, even in season.

I don't want to be a mythmaker about the food of the Caribbean. The cooking at most hotels and restaurants still has a way to go before it can match the menus in other celebrated tourist centers of the world. But the process is underway, encouraged by the interaction of two groups who make odd collaborators, the tourists and the islands' political nationalists.

Getting a meal of local food in the Caribbean has been a problem for the traveler for a long time. When Anthony Trollope visited Jamaica in 1859 he complained that his hosts sneered at the local fruits and recipes he had yearned to try, and fed him on canned meats and canned potatoes. He had beefsteak and onions for breakfast, a veritable ocean of oxtail soup at midday, and imported cheeses for dessert. It was because of sheer snobbery, he concluded, that nothing was considered of value by the colonials in the islands unless it came from Europe.

When the modern age of tourism began almost a century later, hoteliers took a similar attitude. They did not serve indigenous food partly because it was difficult to obtain in reliable quantity and stable quality, but mostly because they felt that the local cooking simply was not interesting enough to serve in their dining rooms. Furthermore, they believed that the sort of tourist who came to the Caribbean, obsessed with sun and sand, indifferent to experimenting, wouldn't want to try the local cooking anyway.

There was, in fact, some truth to this. Large-scale tourism in the Caribbean is a fairly new phenomenon. The first commercial flight from the United States was made in 1928, in a three-engined Fokker airplane that carried seven passengers from Key West to Havana. Before that, and for a long while afterward as well, people visiting the islands went as Columbus had, by ship. They were likely to be older people with money and plenty of leisure time, and they also were likely to regard the region as a kind of tropical rest home. When they wanted adventure they went to Europe; when they wanted recuperation they went to the Caribbean.

Gradually travel became more popular and the planes got bigger and the fares lower. By the late 1960s there were more than 50 flights a day from New York to San Juan; and because of the volume and competition the trip had become one of the best travel bargains in the world: a round trip of 3,200 miles for just over a hundred dollars.

Jet airstrips have been built on dozens of islands, and direct flights from the United States now penetrate to the farthest corners of the Caribbean. From the bigger islands, all of which will eventually be able to accommodate the jumbo jets, a network of air routes reaches even to tiny outposts like Nevis, Montserrat, Anguilla and Little Cayman. This great recreational airlift has made tourism the Caribbean's biggest business. Between 1959 and 1968 the number of Americans traveling by air to the islands increased from 932,000 to more than two million. In the same period the cruise ship business also increased from 458,700 passengers to 813,800.

Compared to the prewar tourists, most of the new travelers are younger, less affluent and more adventurous. They want sun and sand, of course, but they want something more, too. They are bent on experiencing a way of life different from the one they know at home. Since one of the most pleasant ways to learn a new culture is literally to taste it, the tourists themselves have begun asking hotel owners why their dining rooms should serve imported pears instead of papayas, filet of sole instead of local snapper, baked potatoes instead of breadfruit.

At the same time that the tourist is seeking to experience Caribbean culture, the culture itself is changing. In the 1950s the Caribbean urge to be independent grew to epidemic proportions; more and more, the islanders took

Continued on page 156

153

How a Local Pumpkin Made Good as Cinderella's Coach

Unlike Cinderella's pumpkin, which was round and orange, the Jamaican variety is a kind of large green squash with a long neck. Despite its differences, Lucille Tyson turned it into a fairy-tale coach that won a prize in the Jamaican Culinary Arts Competition. Her first step was to prepare the pumpkin by scrubbing it clean and cutting it in half lengthwise. She chose the handsomer half for the coach, scraped out the seeds and stringy fibers to create a hollow shell, and notched the edge in a sawtooth pattern to make a decorative rim around it. Here, she rubs the cut surfaces with a piece of lime to prevent discoloration.

To fill the shell, Mrs. Tyson invented a rice, shrimp and coconut-milk mixture; here she is squeezing the milk from freshly grated coconut. Next she boiled some shrimp to use as the coachman and horses, and she marinated others for a garnish.

To precook the body of the coach, Mrs. Tyson has set the pumpkin in a large pan, immersed it in water to its neck, and is simmering it for 30 minutes. The trick is to make the pumpkin tender but keep the shell firm enough to hold the filling without collapsing. After being cooked, the pumpkin was inverted to drain.

Now Mrs. Tyson works on the filling. She has already sautéed the marinated shrimp in one pan until they turned pink. In another pan, she cooked a little of the raw pumpkin in the coconut milk, and seasoned the mixture with tomatoes, scallions and rum before adding rice. When the rice was almost tender, she stirred in fresh shrimp and some lime juice and simmered them all until done. Here, having spooned the filling into the hollow of the pumpkin, she arranges the sautéed shrimp over it. The next step is to bake the stuffed squash until it becomes tinged with gold.

Finally, Mrs. Tyson adds the finishing touches that transform the baked squash into a proper coach. Here she places a boiled shrimp at the front of the pumpkin neck to sit as Cinderella's coachman, in front of a lettuce leaf that represents the back of his seat. The remaining boiled shrimp serve as horses; they are held in place with lengths of coconut fiber as reins, and the forward pair is propped up on a tomato. Later Mrs. Tyson pinned four large slices of tomato to the sides of the pumpkin with toothpicks to simulate wheels and complete the illusion of Cinderella's coach. The complete recipe is in the Recipe Booklet.

control over their islands and their destinies. Newly conscious of their heritage, however un-European it might be, they were determined to emphasize it. The results are apparent everywhere in the Caribbean today, both on the newly independent islands and on those that retain their ties with Europe. Trinidad exposes the tourist to its life style by arranging to house visitors with Trinidadian families in Port of Spain during carnival. The French islands promote handicrafts to acquaint the traveler with the scope of local skills. On Martinique, for example, a local arts center subsidized by the island government sells visitors an impressive variety of wood carvings, paintings and pottery. Some of it is first rate, such as the cane weaving and appliquéd wall hangings, or the crèches made of hollowed-out coconut husks that house dozens of tiny hand-painted dolls of the Holy Family and attendants. Martinique's awakening to its own talents also is evidenced in an exuberant group of young dancers called the Folklorique, who perform sprightly, graceful and comic dances based on island folklore.

And everywhere, food is beginning to be seen as a great friend maker, a way to bridge the gap between mainlanders and islanders. The most singular efforts at local gastronomic excellence are being made by Jamaica, the most prosperous of the newly independent island nations. This fact is all the more notable because many Jamaicans are, for a number of reasons, ambivalent about tourism. A remark attributed to the Bishop of Jamaica probably best reflects their attitude; he is reported to have said that if the tourist industry thrived on Jamaica he hoped that the tourists would be changed by the island rather than the island by tourists. The islanders, who tend to be conservative in behavior, are troubled by the tourists' informal dress and manners, but something more basic is also involved. The big hotels and cottage developments have tended to isolate themselves from the rest of island society, and have drawn their staffs, architecture and menus from Europe or America. The island's political leaders recognize the economic advantages of the hotel business but in their newly asserted pride of race have attempted to make it function profitably for Jamaicans and not just for foreign hotel owners. Their goal is to develop hotels and hotel restaurants as an outlet for Jamaican talent and as a way of bringing the tourist and the Jamaican closer.

To this end the Jamaican government sponsors an annual Culinary Arts Competition, an event patronized by women of all ages and social classes. The purpose of the competition, "the preparation of Jamaican food and drinks in new recipes," is so important to Jamaicans that provision was made for the competition in the master five-year plan adopted when Jamaica became independent in 1962. Thus the aura that surrounds the annual competition is one of prideful nationalism. The women who take part feel that beyond winning prizes for themselves they are doing a service for their country. Not only are they reviving long-forgotten culinary traditions but, as Hugh Nash, a director of the competition, put it, they are creating "more palatable and delicious indigenous dishes to replace imports, dishes which in due course will become household words to Jamaicans and a welcome fare for visitors to our island."

I was very impressed with the contestants' spirit when I attended the July finals of a recent Culinary Arts Competition. It was held in Kingston's big Sheraton Hotel, where some 100 women presented more than 230 dishes.

Bright and bold, appliquéd tapestries with local motifs like this one have become a collector's item for visitors to Martinique. An old art on the island, tapestry making has been given new impetus through government support. Many of the hangings are sold in a state-owned crafts shop in Fort-de-France; the profits are invested in several programs to emphasize native arts.

And they were merely the finalists in a competition that had begun the previous winter and had drawn on the cooking skills of thousands of women.

The judging-day excitement started at dawn when cars, some of which had been traveling all night from towns on the other side of the island, began pulling up in front of the low, sprawling hotel. They deposited cartons of cakes and confections, huge tureens of soup and platters of parboiled seafood; husbands emerged sleepy-eyed from the cars to help their nervous wives carry their creations, along with bags stuffed with fruits and props and leafy decorations.

From 9 until 11 the Sheraton's kitchens, thrown open to the contestants for last-minute preparations, were a scene of sweltering anguish. Around each of the seven huge stoves, some for baking and some for grilling and roasting, clustered dozens of women. Like a toreador, each contestant had her band of hangers-on and helpers—the woman who invented a dish did the final arrangement of it, but her crew sautéed the onions, cut the peppers,

Continued on page 160

157

Sunday brunch at the Coral Reef Club is served buffet style on a terrace overlooking the Caribbean. Amid all the fruits and flowers and salads are a roast suckling pig and a whole red snapper.

Along Barbados' "Platinum Coast," Decorative Food Is Everyday Fare

At such luxurious establishments as the Coral Reef Club *(above)* and the Miramar Hotel *(opposite)*, pampered travelers can dine in the grand style. Both resorts are at St. James on the western coast of Barbados—locally referred to as the Platinum Coast because of the elegance of the hotels and the wealth of their patrons. In surroundings like these the menus are made up primarily of Continental dishes: jellied consommé, *coq au vin*, broiled steak, lobster salad and the like, with English-inspired trifle or French-style cold fruit soufflé for dessert. While local fruits and fish have always graced such tables, it has been only in recent years that dining rooms of the fanciest Caribbean hotels have begun to feature favorite native dishes like the unfancy *asapao* and *picadillo* pictured with recipes at the end of this chapter. The result is that at long last the tourist in any income bracket can eat his way through the islands without feeling that he never left home.

This jackfish has been poached, chilled and done up in clear aspic, but its chief virtue is that it is only a few hours out of the sea.

The lobster salad at the Miramar is presented in a giant clamshell and embellished with radish roses and hibiscus blossoms.

stirred the butter and flour. Competition at the burners and sinks was frantic and there were some tearful moments. One little nine-year-old, helping to strain a pepper pot soup, was crying so with excitement that her mother kept begging her to stop her tears lest they make the soup too salty.

Promptly at 11, all the dishes were laid on long tables in the Sheraton's ballroom, ready for the judges' critical palates. There were steaming soups, like crayfish and okra gumbo, and shrimp and pumpkin chowder; there were curries of goat and poultry and jack fruit, unusual platters of baked fish cooked in coconut sauce or combined with bananas or citrus fruits, pineapples stuffed with local delicacies like shrimp or avocado. There were antique recipes like tum tum (boiled breadfruit beaten into an elastic dough), an African dish still eaten in the home parish of a very aged contestant but unknown to most of the city women; and there were never-before-seen wonders like a cake, fully four feet by five, on which an intense lady from distant Westmoreland Parish had molded, with batter and colored icing, an entire Jamaican village, complete with cabins, outbuildings, animals, bushes and grass, bananas and even a garden of yams twisting their delicate vines of icing along an icing trellis.

While the tasting and judging were taking place I talked with many of the contestants and learned that most of them had never studied cooking. They had become interested in the contest when government representatives visited their towns and villages and stirred their desire to create. They all spoke very feelingly about their creations. One young woman, Lucille Tyson, who is a secretary for an insurance company in Kingston, told me that since the inception of the contest she had longed to compete but that until the year before she had had no idea she considered good enough. Then, one day, she was inspired while reading the story of Cinderella to her two young nephews. They were having trouble visualizing how a pumpkin could turn into a coach. Lucille, an indulgent aunt, decided to demonstrate how it could indeed resemble one: she opened a Jamaican pumpkin—we would call it a large green squash—and hitched a matched team of shrimp to the front of it. The children were delighted, and Lucille realized she had an idea worthy of the culinary competition.

She perfected it and presented it as Cinderella's coach—a baked pumpkin with wheels of tomato slices, drawn by shrimp hitched with coconut strips, and filled with sautéed shrimp and rice cooked with coconut milk, tomatoes and scallions *(pages 154-155)*. The judges' appreciation was as great as that of Lucille's nephews, and perhaps more substantial, for they awarded the creation a silver medal.

Lucille was so encouraged by her award that she immersed herself in cooking and devoted all her spare time the following year to reading cookbooks and perfecting her skills. At the competition I attended, her second, she won prizes for every dish she entered. They included a mammoth stuffed and curried lobster, a graceful two-and-a-half-foot-high swan made of a new Jamaican crop, Irish potatoes, and a spectacular drink named fire on ice, a fruit punch containing otaheite apple, garden cherry and orange juice mixed with sugar, strong green tea, rum and bitters. The drink was poured over ice cubes made of coconut water and then ignited with 151-proof rum just before it was presented.

When the competition winners were announced there were a few tears, but mostly the scene was one of hugs and kisses and joyful satisfaction. The recipes of not just the winners but of all the entrants in the finals were to be printed and circulated by the government; representatives of many of the island's hotels had seen or tasted the food, and presumably these dishes were on their way to becoming "household words to Jamaicans and a welcome fare for visitors. . . ."

The movement to explore and exploit local culinary resources is growing throughout the Caribbean. Trinidad holds a competition similar to Jamaica's, although on a less grand scale, called the Better Villages Competition. On Puerto Rico a food contest, open to hotel chefs rather than amateurs, changed its emphasis in 1968 from international to Caribbean cooking; the new rules specified that either local products *or* local themes be stressed. Since most hotel chefs are artists at heart, the contest turned up not only edible food but such creations as a lard sculpture of an Arawak woman meditating, and a detailed map of Puerto Rico executed in rice and beans.

Food and politics seem to be companions on all the islands. Fidel Castro makes a point of encouraging Cuban consumption of local foods by setting the example of eating them with gusto. An amusing tale about sharing dinner with Castro is told by Lee Lockwood, a photojournalist who spent seven days with the revolutionary leader in 1964. They were encamped in the hills,

Now well into its second century, La Mallorquina is the oldest restaurant in San Juan; within its cool white walls generations of Puerto Rico's gentry have come to eat and talk. It is a particular favorite of politicians; legend says that Luis Muñoz Rivera, the great Puerto Rican leader of the late 19th and early 20th Centuries once had so heated a political argument in the restaurant that he swung his cane and cracked one of the ornate vases that stand on pedestals in the corners of the room.

and on the table were roast pig, ham sandwiches, squashlike malanga and foo-foo. Lockwood was hesitant to try the foo-foo, which is made of mashed plantains and which, according to him, looks like "sticky balls, the size of matzoh balls"; he avoided them, and concentrated on the meats. But Castro ignored the meats and piled his plate high with malanga and foo-foo. After a while he took second helpings of these and, noticing that his visitor hadn't even tried them, ladled some foo-foo onto Lockwood's plate. Lockwood found the foo-foo "extremely bland, and its consistency like that of raw dough." Apparently Castro was disappointed, for he told his guest, "You must eat foo-foo. It is a great delicacy. Very healthy too, very full of vitamins. We practically lived on it in the sierra. For us, it was our beefsteak. Now that I live in Havana I miss foo-foo very much."

Castro, of course, likes beefsteak too, as did his predecessor, Fulgencio Batista, although Batista seems to have had no penchant for Cuban dishes. I had a long chat with his former chef, Ramón Torres, who after leaving Cuba had started a tiny Cuban restaurant called Bambu in New York; although Ramoncito spoke glowingly of the pheasant and caviar and squab that always graced his employer's table, he was hard put to think of any Cuban dish the dictator revered. "Oh yes, rice and black beans," he remembered at last, "we sometimes served that."

Most islanders, however nationalistic, will grant that the tourist cannot be expected to like all local foods, that salt-fish fritters will never drive out *sole meunière* nor okra replace green beans. But advocates of the Caribbean cuisine want not just to revive traditional dishes but to use local products in interesting new combinations; not, say, to popularize foo-foo but to find new, more appealing ways to serve plantain.

The hotels are joining in the effort to add new elements to the cuisine. Some of the small hotels are particularly hard hit by the high costs of importing frozen foods, and have developed menus centered around local ingredients such as fish and poultry, out of convenience and economic necessity. For others, like the Young Island Hotel on a tiny island just off St. Vincent, the policy of fostering local cooking and using freshly grown native ingredients is a matter of deliberate choice and philosophy. At Young Island Hotel the menu emphasizes freshly caught lobster and local fish prepared in a dozen interesting ways, including tree-tree cakes, a delectable fritter made of fresh tiny fish that are salty and taste somewhat like caviar. Within a short time of its opening in 1965, the hotel had achieved a reputation for serving one of the finest menus in the Caribbean.

According to legend, Young Island was a gift to an English planter on St. Vincent from a Carib chieftain in the 1700s. The Carib had longingly admired a white stallion that Young was riding, and Young, anxious to maintain good relations with the rebellious Indians, said, "If you like it, it is yours." Sometime later he happened to remark to the Carib chief how pretty he found the little island, just 200 yards off St. Vincent. The chieftain, according to the tale, said, "If you like it, it is yours." Eventually it passed from Young to the St. Vincent government, and recently it was leased to John Houser, a former executive of Hilton Hotels International and a long-time spokesman for the new, venturesome American tourist. Turning the entire island into an elegantly designed hotel property, Houser continued the

Opposite: Cool and uncluttered, this tiled and whitewashed kitchen, now an exhibit in the Museum of the Puerto Rican Family in Old San Juan, shows the kind of kitchens used in 19th Century Puerto Rico. The stove, equipped with a hood to trap smoke and cooking smells, was fueled with charcoal shoved through the square holes in front.

complementary exchange begun two centuries ago between outsider and islander by having local Vincentian chefs develop his menu.

St. Vincent achieved independence in 1969, and to honor the occasion the kitchen at Young Island Hotel, manned by 40 local cooks, turned out a feast for 300 eminent islanders and visitors. Every dish, from the suckling pigs and an array of almost 50 vegetable creations to the local rum drinks with floating hibiscus flowers, was prepared from island-grown ingredients.

Larger hotels in the Caribbean usually serve a good deal of meat, but most of them now carefully highlight their menus with local products. The Montego Beach Hotel on Jamaica, for example, serves a great deal of American beef prepared according to French recipes for its main courses, but offers a good selection of native fruits for breakfast and many traditional soups like pepper pot, pumpkin and red pea. The hotel's local chefs have developed excellent chewy coconut breads, fragrant banana rolls and island-inspired hors d'oeuvre ranging from fried, salted coconut chunks to spicy dough-wrapped meat patties and a baked delicacy of bacon-wrapped banana tidbits.

Frequently hotel owners develop their own recipes. The owner of the Spice Island Inn on Grenada was the inventor, so far as I have been able to track it down, of a cold breadfruit vichyssoise *(Recipe Index)* that is now served at many island hotels. The owner of the Sign Great House on Jamaica has contributed a dish called chicken patois that combines layers of sliced chicken with grapefruit, oranges, pineapple, prunes, mango chutney and green peppers. This colorful concoction somewhat resembles a traditional Jamaican dish that Sign Great House also serves: "pork downtown" (sometimes called "pork in the country," depending on where you are), which features layers of roast pork with bananas, papaya and prunes.

Actually it is becoming difficult to single out those hotels that rely on local dishes to make their menus interesting, because the movement to do so is growing by leaps and bounds. Each year sees a greater increase in the hotels' ratio of local to imported foods, recipes and chefs. It is still somewhat difficult, however, to find restaurants that serve local specialties, places away from hotels that the tourist can visit for an interesting, well-prepared meal. The Caribbean—except for a few islands—does not have a restaurant tradition. There is one old restaurant, perhaps the oldest in the Caribbean, for which I, along with many others, have a special affection: San Juan's La Mallorquina. In a city increasingly dedicated to the new and up-to-the-minute, La Mallorquina remains drowsily unself-conscious, cherishing its giant ceiling fans in defiance of air conditioning and proudly displaying its ornate vases, mirrors and carved wooden tables, once the possessions of a Spanish marquis who lived on Puerto Rico in the early 1800s.

Opened in 1848 by a Spaniard from Majorca, the restaurant is responsible for popularizing a number of Majorcan recipes on Puerto Rico, among them chewy *pan de majorca* (known in Majorca as *enseimadas),* an irresistible sweet breakfast roll baked with lard and dusted with powdery sugar. At the turn of the century, when life on Puerto Rico was more leisurely, members of prominent San Juan families customarily took a late morning breakfast of local coffee and *pan de majorca* at La Mallorquina. The restaurant no longer serves breakfast, but *pan de majorca* has become a San Juan tradition and several bakeries in the narrow streets of the old city produce the rolls daily.

As the island loosened its ties with Spain, La Mallorquina too became more Puerto Rican than Spanish. Today it still serves *gazpacho* and garlic soup and *paella*, but it emphasizes a wide selection of *asapaos*. *Asapao*, related to *paella* but with a character all its own, is truly Puerto Rican, invented right on the island. *Asapao* means soupy, but I do not know whether to define it as a stewlike soup or a soupy stew. It is made with chicken, shrimp, lobster, squid or land crab, simmered with annatto-flavored rice and combined with tomatoes, onions and other seasonings. It is an earthy dish but holds its own with more sophisticated fare on La Mallorquina's menu.

In recent years other restaurants that purport to be Spanish have opened in the narrow streets of Old San Juan with less legitimate credentials than those of La Mallorquina. Their Puerto Rican or American owners seem to assume that visitors to the island really planned a trip to Spain but ran out of plane fare. To make up for this misfortune the new restaurants serve Spanish garlic soup, *gazpacho* and *paella*, and tend to ignore true Puerto Rican dishes.

One charming exception is La Fonda del Callejon, a dark-beamed, whitewashed restaurant so determined to be Puerto Rican that it serves only traditional island dishes: salt-fish fritters *(bacalaitos)*, spicy blood sausages *(morcillas)*, crescent-shaped meat patties in a crisp dough made of green plantain and taro flour *(pasteles)*, fried plantains *(tostones de plátano)*, and many others. The restaurant is in Old San Juan in a restored colonial building that also houses the Museum of the Puerto Rican Family, furnished with antiques gathered from old estate homes on the island.

La Fonda del Callejon is assisted by a government subsidy, an arrangement also enjoyed by Devon House, a restaurant in Kingston sponsored by the Jamaican government. This impressive place too is part of a museum displaying the treasures of colonial days, a reconstructed greathouse complete with antiques, formal gardens and fountains. At Devon House you can eat traditional soups like conch or turtle, or the delightfully named coo-coo roo, a chicken chowder also called cock soup, or the thin spicy fish broth known as fish tea. The main courses at Devon House are usually skewered beef or American filet mignon. But at the meal's end you will be served one of Jamaica's finest culinary delights, a cup of Blue Mountain coffee. This rich coffee is a prized local product that grows in Jamaica's Blue Mountains at altitudes of over 3,000 feet. The mountainous area, with its cooler temperature and moderate rainfall, is superbly suited for coffeegrowing. Produced only in small quantities, Blue Mountain coffee is a connoisseur's treat and for a long time was hard to find in Jamaica itself because it was so much in demand abroad. Devon House always has it, served not only as part of a meal but also as a dessert, and some visitors come just for the coffee; it may be flavored with orange rind or cinnamon stick, allspice or ginger, or gilded with whipped cream, frozen coconut cream, dark rum, or burnt sugar flambéed with rum.

But the best place of all to find good local restaurants in the Caribbean is on the islands owned by France. The French concern with fine food and predilection for dining out have long since left their mark, happily, on Martinique and Guadeloupe. In the 1880s the American writer Lafcadio Hearn spent two years in the French West Indies and was fascinated by the food. He ate *manicou* and callaloo and *poule-épi-diri*, a chicken and rice dish

Blue Mountain coffee, grown high in the hills of Surrey County in the eastern part of Jamaica, is considered one of the world's finest varieties. Jamaicans are proud of it but find it something of a luxury since so much of the crop is exported to Japan (which pays the highest prices), England and Italy. Only small amounts reach the United States. Two stages in processing are shown above: in the bag are coffee "cherries" with their skins on; the others are "parchment," or cherries whose skins have been removed.

Overleaf: Given the shade they need by the broad leaves of banana trees, coffee trees grow lushly on the Wallingford estate in Jamaica's Blue Mountains. Coffee trees live and bear fruit for more than 20 years.

165

similar to New Orleans jambalaya. Hearn wrote that Martinicans thought *poule-épi-diri* to be such a delicacy that "an over-exacting person, or one difficult to satisfy, is reproved with the simple question, *'Ça ou lè 'ncò—poule-épi-diri?'* ['What more do you want—chicken and rice?']" Hearn's encounter with Martinican food so stimulated him that later in life he, like France's Alexandre Dumas, became that rare creature—a fiction writer turned cookbook writer. His *Creole Cooking* was published in New Orleans in 1885.

Today Martinique is a particularly good hunting ground for restaurants that feature specialties like blaff and *court bouillon* and that have always done so, tourists or no tourists. Several of the island's villages—Saint-Pierre in the north and Sainte-Anne in the south, for instance—boast small restaurants where the food is simple but splendid and where the tourist is welcome but still in the minority. Martinique also boasts an array of first-class restaurants that serve fine French food as well as local fare. Establishments have their ups and downs, of course, but the last time I was in Fort-de-France, Le Foyal and La Louisiane were particularly impressive.

Nevertheless, my favorite restaurant of all is on Guadeloupe: Le Pergola, famous throughout the Caribbean for the imagination and perfectionism of its owner, Mario Petreluzzi. His menu includes sea eggs, hearts of the local cabbage palm, conch, various local fishes, pretty desserts like banana and coconut crepes, and several notable dishes using the prevalent land crab. While I have eaten land crab in a wide variety of ways since my first encounter with it back in 1958 in Puerto Rico, nowhere was it so delicious and savory as in Le Pergola's *omelette de crabe du terre*. The omelet is made with great skill, the whites and yolks being beaten separately to form a puffy pillow that is then stuffed with the downy crab meat, enhanced with chives and parsley.

Despite his Italian name M. Petreluzzi's Guadeloupian ancestry dates back 300 years on his mother's side, and he cares passionately about the island and its food. He grows angry at the mere mention of one of the new luxury hotels that serves only Continental food. "It is a tradition in France, an unwritten law," he argues, "that a restaurant located in a region must serve the regional specialties. Show me in Michelin any restaurant which will be praised if it does not serve its own region's traditional foods and dishes."

Each year more and more hoteliers and restaurateurs agree with M. Petreluzzi. True, those who want to serve local foods still find many stumbling blocks in the way. It will be a long time before restaurants and hotels can rely on a steady and quality-controlled supply of local fruits and vegetables, meat or even fish and other seafood, because the island economies need much more developing. But at least the snobbery that Trollope encountered more than a century ago is on the wane. Nowadays everyone connected with the islands—governments, hotels, restaurants, even airlines—seems bent upon perfecting island cooking. This is reality and not myth, and the tourist can take credit for much of what is happening. It was he who brought about the change by demanding that he be allowed to experience the culture of the islands as well as their climate.

Opposite: In a bay on the west coast of Antigua, a party of tourists aboard skipper Hugh Bailey's sturdy charter yacht *Sagittarius* sip white wine before tucking into a feast of freshly caught lobster. *Sagittarius,* out of English Harbor, Antigua, is a familiar sight in the islands, where sailing—and catching dinner—are prime attractions for the visitor.

To serve 6

1 teaspoon coarsely chopped garlic
1/2 teaspoon crumbled dried oregano
1 teaspoon salt
A 2½- to 3-pound chicken, cut into
    6 to 8 serving pieces
3 tablespoons lard
1/2 cup finely chopped onions
3/4 cup finely chopped green peppers
2 ounces lean boneless ham, cut
    into 1/4-inch dice (about 1/2 cup)
4 medium-sized firm ripe tomatoes,
    peeled, seeded and finely chopped
    (*see sopa de gandules, page 43*), or
    substitute 1½ cups chopped
    drained canned tomatoes
2 cups uncooked long-grain white
    rice
6 cups chicken stock, fresh or canned
Freshly ground black pepper
1 ten-ounce package frozen peas,
    thoroughly defrosted
1/2 cup freshly grated imported
    Parmesan cheese
1/4 cup small pimiento-stuffed green
    olives
1 tablespoon capers, rinsed
1 whole canned pimiento, drained
    and cut lengthwise into 1/2-inch
    strips

To make 1 eight-inch round cake

1 tablespoon plus 1/2 pound butter,
    softened
2 cups yellow cornmeal
2 cups flour
1 cup sugar
1/2 teaspoon vanilla extract
1/4 teaspoon ground nutmeg,
    preferably freshly grated
A pinch of salt
6 eggs, lightly beaten
1 cup milk
2 tablespoons light rum
1 cup seedless raisins
1/4 cup candied cherries, coarsely
    chopped

Asapao (*Puerto Rico*)
CHICKEN-AND-RICE STEW

With a mortar and pestle or in a small bowl with the back of a spoon, mash the garlic, oregano and salt to a smooth paste. Pat the pieces of chicken completely dry with paper towels and rub them with the paste.

In a heavy 4- to 5-quart casserole, heat the lard over high heat until a drop of water flicked into it splutters instantly. Starting them skin side down, brown 3 or 4 pieces of chicken at a time. Turn the chicken with tongs and regulate the heat so that the pieces color quickly and evenly without burning. As they brown, transfer the pieces to a plate.

Add the onions and green pepper to the fat remaining in the casserole and, stirring frequently, cook for about 5 minutes, or until the vegetables are soft but not brown. Stir in the ham, then add the tomatoes and cook briskly until most of the liquid in the pan evaporates and the mixture is thick enough to hold its shape lightly in a spoon. Return the chicken to the casserole and turn the pieces about to coat the chicken with the tomato mixture. Reduce the heat to low, cover tightly, and simmer for about 30 minutes, or until the chicken is tender. Transfer the bird to a plate and, when cool enough to handle, remove the meat from the bones and cut it into 2-inch squares.

Meanwhile stir the rice, stock or stock and water, and a few grindings of pepper into the tomato mixture remaining in the casserole and bring to a boil over high heat. Reduce the heat to low, cover tightly, and simmer for about 20 minutes, or until the grains are completely tender. The mixture will be soupy (which is what *asapao* means) when the rice is cooked.

Stir in the peas, grated cheese, olives and capers. Mix well, then add the chicken and arrange the pimiento strips on top. Cover and simmer for 2 or 3 minutes longer to heat the peas and chicken through. Taste for seasoning and serve at once, directly from the casserole.

Corn Pone (*Barbados*)
CORNMEAL CAKE WITH RAISINS AND CHERRIES

Preheat the oven to 350°. With a pastry brush, spread 1 tablespoon of softened butter over the bottom and sides of an 8-inch springform cake pan.

Sift the cornmeal and flour together. In a deep bowl, cream the remaining 1/2 pound of butter, the sugar and 2 tablespoons of the cornmeal mixture together by beating and mashing them against the sides of the bowl with a large spoon until they are light and fluffy. Add the vanilla, nutmeg and salt and, beating constantly, slowly pour in the eggs in a thin stream. Beat in about 1 cup of the cornmeal mixture, then 1/4 cup of the milk, and continue adding alternately until all the cornmeal and milk have been combined.

Stir in the rum, raisins and cherries, and pour the batter into the prepared pan. Bake in the middle of the oven for about 1½ hours, or until the top of the cake is golden and a cake tester or toothpick inserted in the center comes out clean. Let the cake cool for 4 or 5 minutes before removing the sides of the springform. Then, with the aid of a large metal spatula, slide it off the bottom of the pan onto a cake rack to cool completely.

Asapao. a chicken-and-rice stew, now gives an authentic local flavor to the menus of many Puerto Rican hotels.

Concombres en Salade *(Martinique)*
CUCUMBER SALAD

With a swivel-bladed vegetable parer or a small, sharp knife, peel the cucumbers and cut them in half lengthwise. Seed them by scraping the tip of a small spoon down their centers. Then cut the cucumbers crosswise into ¼-inch-thick slices.

Place the cucumbers in a bowl, add the salt, and turn the slices about with a spoon to coat them evenly. Let the cucumbers stand at room temperature for about 30 minutes, then drain off all the liquid accumulated around them and pat them dry with paper towels.

Drop the cucumbers into a serving bowl, add the chilies, lime juice and garlic, and toss until all the ingredients are thoroughly blended. Cover the bowl tightly with foil or plastic wrap and marinate the salad at room temperature for at least 1 hour. Just before serving, remove and discard the garlic and sprinkle the top of the salad with a few grindings of pepper.

To serve 4

2 medium-sized firm fresh cucumbers
1½ teaspoons salt
2 teaspoons finely chopped fresh hot chilies *(caution: see page 46)*
2 teaspoons strained fresh lime juice
1 large garlic clove, peeled and crushed with the flat side of a large, heavy knife
Freshly ground black pepper

171

To serve 8 to 10

STUFFING

A 1-pound loaf of homemade-type
white bread, sliced
½ cup pitted green olives, finely
chopped
½ cup finely chopped fresh chives
1 teaspoon crumbled dried thyme
½ teaspoon salt
¼ teaspoon freshly ground black
pepper
3 tablespoons butter
1 cup finely chopped onions
1 tablespoon finely chopped garlic
¼ cup milk

SUCKLING PIG

A 10- to 12-pound oven-ready
suckling pig
2 tablespoons coarse salt, or
substitute 1 tablespoon regular salt
Freshly ground black pepper
¼ cup vegetable oil
1 fresh lime

To serve 4 as a main course or 6 as
a first course

MAYONNAISE

2 egg yolks
½ teaspoon white wine vinegar
⅛ teaspoon crumbled dried thyme
1 teaspoon salt
¼ teaspoon white pepper
1 cup vegetable oil
¼ cup sour cream
4 teaspoons strained fresh lime juice

LOBSTER

2 pounds freshly cooked, frozen or
canned lobster meat, drained,
picked over to remove all bits of
shell and cartilage, and cut into ½-
inch cubes (about 4 cups)
3 hard-cooked eggs, peeled and
coarsely chopped
½ cup finely diced celery
¼ cup finely diced scallions,
including 1 inch of the green tops

Roast Suckling Pig with Bread and Olive Stuffing *(Barbados)*

Preheat the oven to 300°. First prepare the stuffing in the following fashion:
With a sharp knife, trim the crusts from the bread. Arrange the slices side by
side on one or two large baking sheets and toast in the middle of the oven
for 5 minutes on each side. Remove the toast from the oven and raise the
heat to 350°. Tear the slices of toast into ½ inch pieces and drop them into
a deep bowl. Add the olives, chives, thyme, salt and pepper, and toss thoroughly together.

In a heavy 8- to 10-inch skillet, melt the butter over moderate heat. When
the foam begins to subside, add the onions and garlic and, stirring frequently, cook for about 5 minutes, until they are soft and transparent but
not brown. Watch carefully for any sign of burning and regulate the heat accordingly. Add the entire contents of the skillet to the toast mixture, stir in
the ¼ cup of milk and toss together until all the ingredients for the stuffing
are well combined. Taste for seasoning.

Wash the pig quickly under cold running water and pat it dry inside and
out with paper towels. Sprinkle the abdominal cavity and skin with salt and
liberal grindings of pepper, then fill it loosely with the stuffing mixture.
Close the opening by lacing it with skewers and kitchen cord or by sewing
it with heavy white thread.

Crumple a sheet of aluminum foil into a ball the size of the lime and insert it in the pig's mouth to keep it open as it roasts. Cover the ears with
small squares of foil to prevent them from burning. Brush the pig all over
with vegetable oil and place it on a rack set in a large shallow roasting pan.
If the head extends beyond the edge of the pan, double a strip of foil under
it to catch any drippings.

Roast the pig undisturbed in the middle of the oven for 1½ hours, then remove the foil from the ears, and continue roasting for 15 to 20 minutes longer. To test for doneness, pierce the thigh with the point of a small, sharp
knife. The juice should spurt out a clear yellow; if it is slightly pink, roast
the pig for another 5 to 10 minutes.

Transfer the roast pig to a large heated platter and replace the ball of foil
in its mouth with the whole fresh lime. Let the pig rest at room temperature
for about 10 minutes for easier carving.

Lobster Salad *(Barbados)*

First prepare the mayonnaise in the following fashion: Warm a large mixing
bowl in hot water, dry it quickly but thoroughly, and drop in the egg yolks.
With a whisk or a rotary or electric beater, beat the yolks vigorously for
about 2 minutes, until they thicken and cling to the beater. Stir in the vinegar, thyme, salt and white pepper. Beat in ½ cup of the oil, ½ teaspoon at
a time; make sure each addition is absorbed before adding more. By the
time ½ cup of oil has been beaten in, the sauce should be the consistency of
very thick cream. Pour in the remaining oil in a slow, thin stream, beating constantly. Stir in the sour cream and lemon juice, and taste for seasoning.

Just before serving, combine the lobster, eggs, celery and scallions in a
large chilled bowl and toss them together lightly but thoroughly. Then add
the mayonnaise and turn the lobster mixture about with a spoon to coat the
pieces evenly.

Christophene au Gratin *(Martinique)*
BAKED CHRISTOPHENES WITH ONION AND CHEESE FILLING

Wash the *christophenes* or other squash under cold running water, drain, and cut them lengthwise into halves. Drop the squash into enough lightly salted boiling water to cover them completely and cook briskly for about 30 minutes, or until they are tender and show only slight resistance when pierced with the point of a small, sharp knife.

Drain the squash and, when they are cool enough to handle, remove and discard the seed and hollow out each half with a small spoon to make boat-like shells about ¼ inch thick. Set the shells aside on paper towels to drain completely and chop the scooped-out pulp coarsely.

Preheat the oven to 350°. In a heavy 10- to 12-inch skillet, melt the 4 tablespoons of butter over moderate heat. When the foam begins to subside, drop in the onions and, stirring frequently, cook for about 5 minutes, until they are soft and transparent but not brown. Watch carefully for any sign of burning and regulate the heat accordingly. Add the chopped squash, ⅓ cup of the cheese, the salt and a few grindings of pepper. Still stirring, cook briskly until most of the liquid in the pan has evaporated and the mixture is thick enough to hold its shape lightly in the spoon.

Fill the 4 squash shells with the onion mixture, patting it in firmly. Arrange the shells side by side in a shallow baking dish large enough to hold them comfortably and dot the tops with the 1 tablespoon of butter bits. Sprinkle the squash with the remaining 2 tablespoons of cheese and bake in the middle of the oven for about 20 minutes, or until the tops are a delicate golden brown. Serve at once, directly from the baking dish.

To serve 4

2 large *christophenes (see Glossary, page 197)*, each about ¾ pound, or substitute two ¾-pound zucchini or other summer squash
4 tablespoons butter, plus 1 tablespoon butter cut into ¼-inch bits
1½ cups finely chopped onions
⅓ cup plus 2 tablespoons freshly grated imported Parmesan cheese
1 teaspoon salt
Freshly ground black pepper

Pitch Lake Pudding *(Barbados)*
MOCHA MOUSSE WITH ORANGE LIQUEUR

In the top of a double boiler, melt the butter over moderate heat. Set the pan over barely simmering (not boiling) water and stir the coffee into the butter. Beating constantly with a wire whisk or large spoon, sift in the cocoa, about ¼ cup at a time, and beat until the mixture becomes a smooth paste. Reduce the heat to the lowest possible point and keep the cocoa paste warm.

In a deep bowl, beat the egg yolks with an electric or rotary beater for about a minute. Beat in the sugar, ¼ cup at a time, and continue beating until the yolks become pale yellow and thick enough to fall back in a ribbon when the beater is lifted from the bowl. Beat in the cocoa paste, about ½ cup at a time, then the liqueur. Set aside.

In a separate large bowl, with a wire whisk or a rotary or electric beater, beat the egg whites and salt together until the whites are stiff enough to stand in firm, unwavering peaks when the beater is lifted from the bowl. Stir about one quarter of the whites into the cocoa-and-egg-yolk mixture, then pour it over the remaining egg whites. Gently but thoroughly fold them together, using an over-under cutting motion rather than a stirring motion.

Ladle the Pitch Lake pudding into a 1-quart soufflé dish, a large serving bowl, or eight individual dessert dishes and refrigerate for at least 3 hours, or until thoroughly chilled. Just before serving, spread the whipped cream lightly over the pudding, or, if you prefer, spoon the whipped cream into a bowl and present it separately.

To serve 8

12 tablespoons (1½ quarter-pound sticks) butter, cut into small bits
3 tablespoons instant coffee, preferably instant *espresso*, dissolved in ¾ cup boiling water
3 cups unsweetened cocoa
6 egg yolks
2 cups superfine sugar
⅓ cup Curaçao, Grand Marnier or other orange-flavored liqueur
6 egg whites
A pinch of salt
1 cup chilled heavy cream, stiffly whipped

Picadillo (*Cuba*)

SPICED BOILED BEEF WITH OLIVES AND RAISINS

Place the beef in a heavy 3- to 4-quart saucepan, add 1 teaspoon of the salt and a few grindings of pepper, and pour in enough water to cover the meat by at least 2 inches. Bring to a boil over high heat, meanwhile skimming off the foam and scum as they rise to the surface. Reduce the heat to low, partially cover the pan and simmer for about 1 hour, or until the beef is tender and shows no resistance when pierced with the point of a small, sharp knife. Drain the beef and, when cool enough to handle, chop it coarsely.

In a heavy 10- to 12-inch skillet, heat the oil over moderate heat until a light haze forms above it. Drop in the onions, garlic, pepper and chilies and, stirring frequently, cook for about 5 minutes, or until the vegetables are soft but not brown. Watch carefully for any sign of burning and regulate the heat accordingly. Add the tomatoes, cloves, the remaining 2 teaspoons of salt and a liberal grinding of black pepper. Still stirring, cook briskly until most of the liquid in the pan has evaporated and the mixture is thick enough to hold its shape almost solidly on the spoon.

Add the olives, raisins and vinegar and stir for a minute or so. Then add the chopped beef and stir until the meat is heated through. Taste the *picadillo* for seasoning and serve, mounded attractively on a heated platter or individual plates.

In Cuba each serving is traditionally topped with deep-fried eggs (*huevos estilo cubano, Recipe Index*). *Picadillo* may also be accompanied by such dishes as fried plantains, *riz et pois, guingombós cocidos (Recipe Index)*, boiled rice or *concombres en salade (Recipe Index)*.

To serve 4

2 pounds lean boneless beef, preferably chuck, trimmed of excess fat and cut into 2-inch cubes
3 teaspoons salt
Freshly ground black pepper
4 tablespoons annatto oil (*page 47*)
1 cup finely chopped onions
2 teaspoons finely chopped garlic
4 medium-sized green peppers, seeded, deribbed and finely chopped
1 tablespoon finely chopped fresh hot chilies (*caution: see page 46*)
6 medium-sized firm ripe tomatoes, peeled, seeded and finely chopped (*see sopa de gandules, page 43*), or substitute 2 cups chopped drained canned tomatoes
¼ teaspoon ground cloves
⅓ cup small pimiento-stuffed green olives
¼ cup seedless raisins
2 tablespoons white distilled vinegar

Breadfruit Vichyssoise (*Grenada*)

In a heavy 3- to 4-quart saucepan, melt the butter over moderate heat. Add the onions and garlic and, stirring frequently, cook for about 5 minutes, or until they are soft and transparent but not brown. Watch carefully for any sign of burning and regulate the heat accordingly.

Stir in the chopped breadfruit and the chicken stock, and bring to a boil over high heat. Reduce the heat to low, cover tightly, and simmer for about 20 minutes, or until the breadfruit is tender enough to be easily mashed against the sides of the pan.

Pour half the mixture into the jar of an electric blender, add ½ cup of the cream, and blend at high speed until the mixture is reduced to a smooth purée. With a rubber spatula, scrape the purée into a bowl or tureen. Then purée the remaining breadfruit mixture with the remaining cream. (To purée the soup by hand, force the breadfruit mixture through a fine sieve set over a deep bowl, pressing down hard on the vegetables with the back of a spoon. Or purée the mixture through a food mill set over a bowl. Stir the cream into the purée.)

Season the soup with salt and pepper, and refrigerate for at least 3 hours, until thoroughly chilled. Taste for seasoning, and serve the breadfruit vichyssoise from a chilled tureen or in individual soup plates. Before serving, sprinkle the soup with the chopped chives.

To serve 6

4 tablespoons butter
1 cup finely chopped onions
1 teaspoon finely chopped garlic
1½ cups peeled, cored and coarsely chopped fresh breadfruit (*see Glossary, page 197*), or 4 slices canned breadfruit, thoroughly drained and coarsely chopped
1 quart chicken stock, fresh or canned
1 cup light cream
1 teaspoon salt
¼ teaspoon freshly ground black pepper
1 tablespoon finely cut fresh chives

Picadillo, almost a national dish in Cuba, is a glorified version of beef hash, lavishly seasoned with tomato and pepper sauce, and garnished with olives and raisins. With it are a cool cucumber salad and beer.

VIII

Rum, the Elixir of the Islands

The tourist who steps out of his plane at a steamy Caribbean airport still dressed in his northern winter clothes invariably feels hot and sticky. Fortunately two reliable cures await him. The first is a swim, which for maximum effect should be taken within one hour of arrival. The second is a cooling, energy-restoring rum drink.

There is something about rum that is magical. It combats heat in the tropics and cold in northern regions. Planter's punches and hot toddies are completely different except that they both are built on rum, but that similarity is enough to make them both great restoratives. In the islands, the original home of rum, the liquor comes in endless surprising varieties. The Scotch, gin or bourbon drinker, accustomed to the subtle (and sometimes imagined) differences among various brands of his favorite spirit, is amazed to discover not only that there are hundreds of different kinds of rum—most of them never encountered in the United States—but that by and large they taste noticeably different from one another. The casual drinker quickly becomes fond of the many mixed drinks made with the islands' rums, while even the connoisseur is delighted to find rums that are so mellow and smooth that, like cognac, they can be sipped neat. Both types of imbiber, impelled perhaps by the high cost of whiskeys and gins, quickly learn in the land of rum to drink and enjoy the local specialty.

Not only does every major island have its own rums and varieties of rum, but every island has its own favored rum drinks; so, in fact, does every home, every hotel and every hotel barman. Planter's punch, a drink that people innocent in Caribbean ways often assume to be the name of a specific

Archsymbol of Caribbean hospitality, the planter's punch has almost as many versions as there are bartenders. But some kind of rum and fruit juice are basic to the punch, and it is often festooned with fresh fruit. This version, which has dark rum floating on top and a pineapple spike as garnish, is accompanied by a basket of crisp plantain chips *(Recipe Index)*.

drink, can be anything that makes use of both rum and fruit juice. Nowadays the rum can be light or dark, but the traditional rum for planter's punch is dark. And any kind of fruit juice can be used, from the exotic guava and mango to the more common pineapple and orange.

At one time, however, the name did stand for a specific drink, and you may still encounter the ancestral planter's punch if you are fortunate. The recipe for this classic punch is expressed in a venerable jingle that goes, "One of sour, two of sweet, three of strong and four of weak," or one part of fresh lime juice, two parts of sweetening (either sugar or sugar syrup), three parts of rum and four parts of water or ice. Sometimes the classic recipe calls for a fifth ingredient, powdered nutmeg, to be sprinkled sparingly on top of the drink. On Barbados there is an excellent museum with exhibits relating to early life in the islands, and one of them displays some 18th Century punch-making equipment: elegant crystal bowls and silver pocket-sized nutmeg graters. According to the museum, which, despite its palm-studded gardens, is as authoritative and musty in its way as its London counterparts, the word punch comes from a Hindustani word, *panch,* which means five. And five were the ingredients necessary in a punch: lime juice, sweetening, spirits, water and spice. What I inferred from the exhibit is that the wide-ranging British learned the word for punch in India and the method of making the spirit for it in the islands, and that thus evolved planter's punch, a felicitous example of imperial fusion.

A cousin of planter's punch is the classic Martinican drink called *petit punch,* which usually comes out sounding something like "tee-paunsh." It can be made with either light or dark aged rum but it is diluted by only two things, a bit of fresh lime juice and *sirop,* a heavy cane sugar concentrate that smells of the cane fields. The charm of the "little punch" is enhanced by the traditional, almost ceremonial way in which it is served. A tray is passed around bearing two bottles of rum, light and dark, a small bottle of *sirop,* a dish of very small wedges of lime, short glasses and a bucket of ice. Each drinker makes his own, varying the proportions as he likes, but generally pouring about two parts of rum to one of *sirop* with a few drops of lime juice. Visitors usually take ice to cut the sweetness of the drink, but most Martinicans prefer it sweet, as if to emphasize their pride in their bountiful sugar. (Not too long ago one paid only for the *sirop* when drinking rum punch in a bar. The rum itself was left indifferently on the counter and, like the water, was free.) The *petit punch* goes down very smoothly, and seems almost instantly to enhance the well-being of the group.

Very similar to *petit punch* in basic ingredients but quite different in concept is the Daiquiri, the most popular rum drink in the United States. The Daiquiri uses lime juice, sugar and rum, each in a greater amount than the last, but then it is shaken and strained through cracked ice.

The man who "invented" the Daiquiri was an American mining engineer, a man of refinement and social prestige, a friend of the American artist Frederic Remington. His name was Jennings Cox and in the 1890s he was supervisor of several copper mines in the eastern part of Cuba outside the little town of Daiquiri. His granddaughter Carmen, whom I met in the islands, told me how her grandfather invented the drink one day in 1896 when important and unexpected visitors from the States arrived in Daiquiri. Cox, a gin drinker, was out of his favorite potion. He sometimes drank the local Cuban rum but he feared that it would not be to the taste of the Americans. To disguise the rum somewhat, he picked limes from a tree in his garden, added their juice and some sugar to his rum; then he chilled and tentatively offered the result. It was an immediate success. For many years Cox derived much gratification from his fame as the Daiquiri's inventor and, although few people today know his story, his granddaughter zealously guards his memory. His monument is a big, old-fashioned scrapbook in which she has saved the yellowed photographs, letters and clippings that tell his tale and relate the praise of the great and the famous for Cox's "invention."

One clipping contains a rear admiral's account of his first encounter with it. Admiral Lucius Johnson and his men had landed on the beach at Daiquiri in June 1898 during one of the major campaigns in the short-lived Spanish-American War, the blockade of Cuba that forced Spain to relinquish the island. "That beach at Daiquiri seemed hot, desperately hot to us," the admiral recalled. But he and his officers soon got over their discomfort when a "tall well-tanned man whose urbane and genial manner is still a pleasant memory" invited them all for a drink "that he had put together to make the locally produced rum more agreeable to the foreign taste." When the war ended, the men took gallons of the rum home with them, introduced the Daiquiri to the Army and Navy Club in Washington and thus launched its successful career in America.

When Carmen showed me her grandfather's scrapbook we reflected sadly on how fleeting a celebrity's fame often turns out to be, and were touched and amused by the gentle effort of Cox's wife Isabel to immortalize his name. In 1909 she proudly presented him with a prettily decorated hand-lettered valentine with a poem of her own composition:

> *There was a gay man from a Mine*
> *Liked Life, Laughter and Wine*
> *A memory retentive*
> *His nature inventive*
> *Gave the world the "Daiquiri" fine.*

If *petit punch* and the Daiquiri are first cousins of planter's punch in its original form, the drink that is now commonly called planter's punch seems almost to be no relation at all. You cannot be sure what you will get when you order a planter's punch nowadays. Some recipes call for both light and dark rum. Some even call for three rums, light, medium and dark. Island-made liqueurs or Angostura bitters from Trinidad may be added. Grenadine, spices, coconut cream, fruit juice and raw fruit often make the punch seem more like a salad than a drink. Since rum combines well with many flavors and since in every man there is apparently a bit of the inventiveness of Jennings Cox, new rum drinks are devised by the hundreds each year. The Mai Tai, invented at the bar of a Trader Vic's Restaurant, calls for a rum specially blended by the Trader Vic company from a selection of Caribbean rums to produce the right texture and bouquet for the cocktail. In New York's Jamaica Arms Restaurant, where superb rums from all the islands can be sampled neat—some of them aged, like brandies, up to 20 years—the concocted drinks include yellow bird, in which rum and fruit juice are combined with Italy's golden syrupy Galliano liqueur, and Lady Nugent's tulip, a presumably ladylike drink which can produce unladylike aftereffects through its heady mixture of rum and brandy. In the islands themselves there are innumberable rum drinks with colorful names like white witch and brown skin gal, ginnal general, beach lamour and moonshot.

But most true rum drinkers consider it a redundancy to mix rum with other spirits, for rum is not only a delicious drink in itself, but is also notoriously potent. This fact was ascertained as early as 1651 by Richard Ligon, a pioneer traveler to Barbados, who wrote, "The chiefe fudling they make in the Island is Rumbullion, alias Kill-Devill, and this is made of suggar canes distilled, a hot, hellish and terrible liquor."

And kill-devil, alias rumbullion, alias rum, has had a hot, hellish and terrible history. Although one of Alexander the Great's generals noted during the Greek conqueror's campaign in India in 325 B.C. that there was in that country a drink made of fermented sugar cane, historians believe that the drink in question was most likely a beer, and that the first distilled sugar-cane liquor was produced on Barbados in about 1630. Its quality was questionable to say the least. So high was the alcoholic content of this formidable beverage that Ligon tells the story of a slave who lost his life just in carrying it from the still to the drinking room. "In the night, not knowing the force of the liquor he carried [he] brought the candle somewhat nearer than he ought, that he might better see how to put it into the Funnel which conveyed it into the Butt. But the Spirit being stirr'd by that motion, flew out, and got hold of the flame of the Candle, and so set all on fire, and burnt the poor Negre to death, who was an excellent servant."

Others lost their lives through drinking the fiery and usually unaged liquor, and still others in the raucous aftereffects of rum drinking. Indeed, although a few scholars suggest that the name rum came from an abbreviation of the Latin word for sugar, *saccharum*, most believe that the word is a shortening of the 17th Century English words rumbullion and rumbustion, which meant tumult, rumpus. There is no question that the liquor and its effects were held in very low esteem by many thoughtful people of the time. As an English archbishop, Thomas Tenison, put it, it was "destructive to Nature, wasting the Vitals and an enemy of Propagation."

Rum's fierce reputation was not improved by the company it kept. The famous skull and crossbones flag was sometimes supplemented on pirate ships by an even more fearful pennant, which showed a skeleton holding in one hand a dagger and in the other a glass known as a "rummer." In fact, pirates seem to have preferred brandy when they could get it, by hook or crook, but the pirates-and-rum association is a strong one. Robert Louis Stevenson strengthened it when, inspired by the name of an island in the West Indies called Dead Man's Chest, he wrote in *Treasure Island* the lines that have frightened four generations of children: "Fifteen men on the Dead Man's Chest, yo-ho-ho, and a bottle of rum! Drink and the devil had done for the rest—yo-ho-ho, and a bottle of rum."

Rum was even more nefariously associated with the slave trade. New England merchants imported West Indian molasses and manufactured their own rum from it, then shipped the rum to the west coast of Africa. There it was used as currency to purchase human cargoes, which were then sold to the West Indian planters in exchange for more molasses. This 17th and 18th Cen-

Continued on page 184

Where Rum Begins–in a Forest of Cane

For 32 gallons of rum, you need one short ton of sugar. For one short ton of sugar, about 10 tons of sugar cane. And for 10 tons of sugar cane, almost one acre of prime plantation land. That, in brief, is the equation that helps explain the green forests of spiky cane that cover so much of the West Indies. Some of the cane goes to make small boys happy; and much of it, of course, goes into sugar. But millions of acres of cane go into the ocean of rum produced each year in the Caribbean—the dry Cuban and Puerto Rican varieties; the darker Barbadian and Martinican potions; the heavy Jamaicans and Demeraras. All rum, whether distilled from cane juice or molasses, comes from cane. And connoisseurs everywhere acclaim it as the noblest of cane's contributions.

Standing in a sugar-cane field not far from where Napoleon's Empress Josephine was born, a young Martinican enjoys his version of an afternoon candy bar by sucking the sweetness from a juicy cane stalk. It is a pleasure shared by children and adults all over the Caribbean.

Overleaf: On a Barbadian hillside overlooking the sea, workmen stack newly cut cane on a truck bound for a sugar mill for processing.

181

tury practice has gone down in history as the famous—or infamous —"triangular" trade.

Many New England fortunes were built on the triangular trade, and the merchants were brazen about it. One notorious slave trader, Simeon Potter of Bristol, advised his agents on the Gold Coast of Africa to "Make yr chief Trade with the Blacks and Little or none with the white people" because slaves purchased from independent black chiefs could be bought for less than those purchased from organized companies of white traders. Potter had other instructions for his lieutenants too: "Worter yr Rum as much as possible and sell as much by the short measur as you can."

The rum made in the Caribbean islands was at first given only to slaves and servants, partly as a way of making them more content with their fate; their masters preferred imported brandy and Madeira. But eventually even the planters, as well as Englishmen and Americans in increasing numbers, began favoring the drink. Some people were scandalized by its popularity. The American Quaker John Woolman vainly urged the boycott of rum not only because he thought it so bad for people but also because it was produced "by the labor of those who are under such lamentable oppression." But most people liked the drink so well that they easily excused themselves for drinking it. The 18th Century English poet William Cowper lightheartedly expressed the general attitude of his day in these lines:

I own I am shocked at the purchase of slaves;
And fear those who buy them and sell them are knaves;
What I hear of their hardships, their tortures and groans
Is almost enough to draw pity from stones.
I pity them greatly, but I must be mum,
For how could we do without sugar and rum?

One reason for rum's popularity in Cowper's time was that the drink had gradually become associated with British valor at sea. In the previous century sailors of the Royal Navy had been allowed beer, which often went sour after a few weeks on board. Then it was discovered that rum not only kept well in casks, but that its flavor and body actually improved with age. In 1655 the Navy began to issue rum to its men. Thirty years later Samuel Pepys, as Secretary to the Navy, expressed skepticism as to whether "Rumm" was as suitable to the "Health and Satisfaction of our Seamen" as brandy, and requested that an inquiry be held into the effects of the rum issue. Despite his concern, rum continued to be issued in ever more generous amounts, until the official Navy rum ration, dispensed in equal tots twice a day—the first was taken in the morning on an empty stomach—was equivalent to six double whiskeys.

Then, in 1731, the tide turned. Admiral Edward Vernon, commander-in-chief of His Majesty's naval forces in the West Indies, decided that while rum might produce courage and contentment in some sailors, it also caused illness and severe discipline problems. Vernon, a thoughtful and brave man (George Washington was so impressed by the admiral that he named his home after him) defied the fury of his men in the interest of their health and ordered that their rum ration be diluted in the proportion of one part rum to three of water. The sailors had already nicknamed the admiral Old Grog, from his habit of coming aboard his ships wearing a distinctive cloak made of a coarse material called grogram. When he watered down their rum ration they dubbed the new drink "grog." For many years the word was widely used to mean not only rum and water but any alcoholic drink. We rarely use the noun anymore, but we still use the adjective "groggy" to describe the effects of drinking.

In America grog became a patriot's drink. Washington was elected to the Virginia House of Burgesses in 1758 not so much by political campaigning as by distributing 75 gallons of rum among the voters. Paul Revere might never have roused Massachusetts sharpshooters on the night of his famous ride had not it been for rum. Apparently, events did not happen just as Long-fellow described them in his famous poem. Revere started his ride silently, with the intent merely of warning a few patriot friends that the British might be up to something. But he was chased by two enemy horsemen. He eluded their pursuit but, upset by his near-capture, stopped in at the home of Isaac Hall, a friend and local rum manufacturer. Hall poured Revere several draughts of heavy Medford rum; Revere tossed them down and what happened after that is history.

Eventually rum became elevated to a gentleman's, even a prince's, drink. Its rise to this eminence culminated in 1892 when Spain's court physician prescribed Cuban rum for a 6-year-old royal prince suffering from a severe attack of grippe complicated by high fever and insomnia. Immediately the fever began to abate and the boy fell asleep. He soon regained his health —and subsequently became King Alphonso XIII—and the Bacardi family, manufacturer of the health-restoring rum,was granted permission to use the Spanish coat of arms on its label.

The rum we drink today differs considerably from the liquor that spurred Paul Revere. What Isaac Hall produced in his Massachusetts distillery was heavy-bodied, pungent and dark in color; since the late 19th Century, rums on the whole have been of higher proof, lighter in color and texture, and more varied. They can be generally divided into three categories, light, medium and heavy. Light rum, almost as dry in flavor as vodka, is primarily used in cocktails. The more traditional heavy rum, full-bodied, pungent in bouquet and usually dark in color, is most often used for punches, where it must compete with other flavors. In the middle is a wide spectrum of versatile light- to middle-bodied rums, ranging in color from golden to ruby to deepest mahogany; they can be used in cocktails or punches, or treated like liqueurs and drunk neat.

Because many Americans favor light-bodied drinks—as evidenced by the popularity of light beer and light Scotch—light rum is the biggest seller in the United States. However, people who prefer their rum fuller-bodied claim that drinking light rum is like drinking skimmed milk, and should be done only out of medical necessity. All this is a matter of custom, and custom is subject to change. Heavy rum was preferred in America until around the start of World War I; then came the shift to light-bodied rum. Today interest seems to be growing in the medium rums, perhaps as a result of the sophistication that travel has spread among Americans. Visitors to the Caribbean have experienced rum the way islanders prefer it, not in cocktails but in drinks in which the *taste* of rum is what is important. A mild but still flavorful rum is essential for this kind of appreciation.

Old San Juan's La Fonda del Callejon is renowned not only for its Puerto Rican food but also for its rum drinks; the specialty of the house is the *coqui,* photographed here in the restaurant's inner court. Unlike the fruity rum drinks made with lime, pineapple or banana, *coqui* is a smooth, creamy tipple concocted from two kinds of rum and enriched with fresh coconut cream *(Recipe Index).* The ingredients grouped around the glass include, from right: rum, evaporated milk, coconut, vanilla, nutmeg, egg yolk and Triple Sec, an orange-flavored liqueur.

However it varies, rum owes its distinctive taste to its origin in sugar cane. Most distilled spirits are made from various grains, some from grapes or other fruit; only rum comes from the cane plant. It is sometimes distilled directly from fresh cane juice, but more often it is a by-product of sugar production. In making sugar, the stalks of cane are crushed until they exude a sweet juice that is boiled. The sugar in the juice crystallizes, leaving various impurities that remain as a thick, sticky, dark-brown semiliquid—molasses. It is at this point that most rum making starts. Molasses that is left lying in the tropical sun will ferment readily and actively, and it is believed that rum production began in the early 1600s when a Barbadian sugar planter got the idea of carrying the process another step and distilling his naturally fermented molasses.

Today the fermentation process is begun either by the addition of dunder, a residue left from a previous distillation, or by the addition of yeast. Rum makers are close-mouthed about their procedures and particularly so when it comes to the yeasts they use. It has been said of a leading Puerto Rican rum company that it breeds its yeast in secret, like Derby runners, staking everything on the yeast's individuality. A prominent Haitian rum manufacturer grows mystical in talking about his yeast, attributing the excellence of his rum to the fact that the yeast and sugar cane he uses both grow in the same area of the island; this, he asserts, produces a natural harmony that is reflected in the taste of his rum.

Once the molasses is fermented the distillation process begins. Either a pot still or a column still may be used. Pot stills distill at a lower proof and remove fewer of the impurities that impart taste and aroma to spirits, and thus the rum that results—the traditional rum—tends to be heavier in flavor and bouquet. But however distilled, the rum that emerges can hardly be called rum. Like all spirits at this stage, it is colorless and its flavor is undeveloped. It is aging that gives most rum its ultimate characteristics. For a light rum the liquor is placed in ordinary oak casks or simply in covered tanks; for a heavier rum, charred oak casks are used. Sugar caramel is added to attain the desired color and the rum is left to age. Some rums are bottled without aging; some are barrel-aged only a few months, others for as long as 25 years; sometimes batches of various ages are blended.

Rum distilled in a column still is drawn off at a very high proof—that is, with high alcoholic content—and is eventually reduced by the addition of distilled water. Most rums are between 70 and 100 proof—between 35 and 50 per cent alcohol—but several distillers also produce an overproof rum, bottled at 151 proof, or more. This is a little scary to drink, but it is excellent for use in desserts or flambéed dishes. A curious story told about this rum is that the original demand for it came not from people in the Caribbean but from whalers and trappers in Canada's frigid Hudson Bay where, when winter sets in, ordinary rums will freeze and break their containers. Supposedly in sympathy for the northerners' frustration the tropical islanders began to manufacture the overproof rum, whose alcoholic concentration makes it as pourable as antifreeze even at the North Pole.

Light rum is usually associated with Puerto Rico and Cuba, where it was first developed in the late 19th Century, and heavy rum is often thought of as being Jamaican. Actually, all the islands produce light and heavy rums and many intermediate rums as well. Jamaica makes not only dark Myers rum but golden-colored Appleton Estates rum and amber 15-year-old Lemon Hart. Puerto Rico's most famous rum is Bacardi, a light variety that was also produced in quantity in Cuba before the revolution there in 1959. Bacardi also makes a dark-colored and richer-tasting Anejo. Many Puerto Ricans, however, prefer the slightly heavier Barralitos rum, which gets a more intriguing flavor being aged in sherry casks.

As befits the island that is the original home of rum, Barbados boasts a number of distinctive varieties—among them Gosling, Lightbourne and Mount Gay—of particularly fine rums, semilight in body and color and with a mild, almost smoky flavor. Haiti produces a rum that has long been the favorite of American connoisseurs, although recently it has become more difficult to obtain. This is Barbancourt, a medium-bodied, pleasantly flavored variety that reflects the French skill at brandy making in that it is double-distilled, as brandy is. Interestingly, while the product of the second distillation is the connoisseurs' favorite, the first distillation is sometimes bottled and sold domestically as the favorite means of propitiating the local voodoo gods. Unaged and called *clairin* because it is colorless, it is the libation poured upon the ground in voodoo ceremonies.

My own favorite rums come from Martinique, where a few distilleries make their rum not from molasses but directly from cane juice. St. James —the only brand easily available in the United States—Bally and Clément are all excellent examples of sugar-cane rum made on Martinique. The companies that produce these rums operate on a smaller scale than do most of the distilleries using molasses. Since they do not make sugar and therefore have no molasses set aside, they manufacture their rum only during the actual sugar-cane cutting season. But the rum they produce is superb; its admirers poetically claim that it has more of the sun and the fragrant earth in its bouquet than any other type.

Having enjoyed both Bally and Clément rums, I eagerly accepted the offer of a Martinican friend who knew both proprietors to take me to see their distilleries. At both the cane was being brought in on battered trucks or even wearier-looking mules. The yards outside the distilleries were littered with scraps of cane, and for miles around the air was laden with the ripe, oversweet smell of sugar being crushed. The machinery in the distilleries seemed to me like a nostalgic exhibit of old locomotives—hissing pistons, huge iron flywheels, clacking valves. The buildings themselves were wooden, with creaky steps and roofs that revealed occasional patches of the hot blue tropical sky.

My Martinican friend was embarrassed by the old machinery and said apologetically, "You as an American will probably view this as a sort of handicraft." But I explained that I found something wonderful in the very simplicity of the operation and in the way in which the relationship of the raw sugar to the finished rum was almost tangible. (There is a bit of the artisan in me as there is, I think, in anyone who likes to cook. The great resurgence of American interest in cooking seems to me almost a deliberate courting of the old ways, a defiance of the technology that gives us frozen tacos and packaged chicken pies and canned vichyssoise.) I tried to make this clear to my friend but he—as a man keenly interested in the economic development of his island—was more concerned with a future that would put modern machines at the service of his island's traditional art.

Sometime later I visited the Bacardi distillery on Puerto Rico and was impressed but oddly disappointed by the huge, 55,000-gallon molasses fermentation vats two stories high that froth like some giant child's bubble bath, and by the white-coated technicians and the computers they used to control the distilling process. But at the end of the tour I recovered my appreciation for the art of rum making when I was introduced to a shy quiet man in sloppy work clothes, a member of the Bacardi family, who was seeing to the blending of rums of various ages and proofs that produces the various Bacardi products. Like a winetaster in a vineyard cellar, he was using what in the end is the only standard of excellence—his own taste and judgment. I talked to him awhile and later wrote my Martinican friend that perhaps the making of all good rum, like all good food, is a handicraft.

Handicraft or not, the production of rum is certainly an industry at which the islanders excel. Although the United States imports rum from only seven places in the Caribbean—Puerto Rico, the Virgin Islands, Jamaica, Trinidad, Barbados, Haiti and Martinique—a great many other islands manufacture their own rums.

A number of them also manufacture excellent liqueurs from tropical flora other than sugar cane. Curaçao's orange liqueur made from that island's bitter oranges is perhaps the most famous, although Jamaica's sweet rum-based Tia Maria, flavored with Blue Mountain coffee, is fast becoming a rival. Jamaica also makes Pimento Dram, a liqueur based on the oil of the allspice berry, which is known as pimento on that island. Chococo from St. Croix is a coconut liqueur delicately flavored with chocolate. Puerto Rico uses its plentiful pineapples and bananas to make flavorful liqueurs. Haiti uses these too, and also mangoes and papayas, and even manufactures a fragrant liqueur from hibiscus flowers.

But rum is of course the triumphant alcoholic offering of the islands. Wherever your plane lands, one of the first questions you will be asked is, "Have you tasted our rum?" And whether because you are hot or excited by traveling or just responding to the questioner's enthusiasm, as soon as you do sample the local rum you discover that it tastes better than rum ever tasted at home. It is the perfect drink for the climate, heady and compelling. Your plane has physically taken you to the tropics but your mind still lingers in the north. The first rum on arrival completes your voyage by transporting you psychically. Cold and cares are forgotten. The second rum is hypnotic. Its golden color reflects the sunshine all around you, and its bouquet is redolent of graceful cane fields. Rum in hand, you find yourself at rest, ready to take joy from the mere contemplation of the island-strewn Caribbean.

Honeymooners sipping tall rum drinks (*above*) share a view and a hammock at the Caneel Bay Plantation on St. John in the United States Virgin Islands.

Overleaf: The montage of labels represents just a sample of the hundreds of rums produced in the Caribbean. Included are labels for Tia Maria (*top center*), a Jamaican coffee-flavored liqueur made with rum, and Angostura bitters (*top right*), a Trinidadian flavoring added to many rum cocktails. In the foreground is a row of rum-based drinks (*from left*): a pitcher of rum punch, a Bacardi cocktail, dark rum on the rocks with lime juice, and beside it, a frozen daiquiri made with light rum, a pony of Tia Maria, a tall rum Collins and, at top right, a banana daiquiri, a peach daiquiri and a Blue Mountain cocktail (*recipes on following pages*).

Rum Punch

To serve 2

1 ounce strained fresh lime juice
1 tablespoon superfine sugar
3 ounces light or dark rum
4 ounces (½ cup) water
3 or 4 ice cubes
2 thin orange slices

Combine the lime juice, sugar, rum, water and 3 or 4 ice cubes in a mixing glass, and place a bar shaker on top of the glass. Grasping the glass and shaker firmly together with both hands, shake them vigorously 9 or 10 times. Remove the shaker and place a strainer over the mixing glass. Pour the punch into 2 chilled highball glasses filled with ice cubes, garnish with orange slices, and serve at once.

Blue Mountain Cocktail

To make 2 cocktails

3 ounces medium-dark rum such as
   Appleton Estates or Mount Gay
1½ ounces vodka
1½ ounces Tia Maria or other coffee
   liqueur
¼ cup strained fresh orange juice
2 tablespoons strained fresh lime
   juice
3 or 4 ice cubes

Combine the rum, vodka, coffee liqueur, orange juice, lime juice and ice in a mixing glass, and place a bar shaker on top of the glass. Grasping the glass and shaker firmly together with both hands, shake them vigorously 9 or 10 times. Remove the shaker and pour the cocktail unstrained into 2 chilled 8-ounce old-fashioned glasses. Serve at once.

Planter's Punch

To serve 2

7 ounces dark rum
2 ounces strained fresh lime juice
4 tablespoons superfine sugar
A dash of Angostura bitters
1 cup crushed or finely cracked ice
Freshly grated nutmeg
GARNISH (OPTIONAL)
2 maraschino cherries and 2 fresh
   pineapple or banana strips, or 2
   thin lime or orange slices

Combine 6 ounces of the rum, the lime juice, superfine sugar, bitters and cracked ice in a mixing glass, and place a bar shaker on top of the glass. Grasping the glass and the shaker firmly together with both hands, shake them vigorously 9 or 10 times.

Remove the shaker and pour the contents of the glass, unstrained, into 2 chilled 10-ounce highball glasses.

Place a teaspoon upside down in each glass in turn and very slowly pour ½ ounce or more of the rum over the back of the spoon, letting it trickle off onto the surface of the drink so that the rum floats on top. Grate a little nutmeg over the drink and serve at once.

Planter's punch is often served garnished with some kind of fresh fruit. If you like, add a maraschino cherry and a pineapple or banana strip to each drink, or slit the lime or orange slices from peel to center and stand them on the rim of each glass.

Daiquiri

To make 2 cocktails

6 ounces light rum
1 ounce strained fresh lime juice
2 teaspoons superfine sugar
3 or 4 ice cubes

Combine the rum, lime juice, sugar and ice cubes in a mixing glass, and place a bar shaker on top of the glass. Grasping the glass and shaker firmly together with both hands, shake them vigorously 9 or 10 times. Remove the shaker, and place a strainer over the mixing glass. Pour the Daiquiri into 2 chilled 4-ounce cocktail glasses, and serve at once.

Frozen Daiquiri

To make 2 cocktails

4 ounces light rum
1 ounce strained fresh lime juice
2 teaspoons superfine sugar
2 cups finely cracked ice

Combine the rum, lime juice, sugar and cracked ice in the jar of an electric blender, and blend at medium speed for about 20 seconds. Pour the contents of the jar, unstrained, into 2 chilled 6-ounce champagne glasses and serve with short drinking straws.

Pineapple Daiquiri

Combine the pineapple juice, rum, lime juice and Cointreau in the jar of an electric blender, and blend at high speed for about 20 seconds. Taste and stir or blend in a little superfine sugar, if you find it necessary. Pour the Daiquiri into 2 chilled 8- to 10-ounce old-fashioned glasses filled with ice cubes, and serve at once.

Banana Daiquiri

Combine the banana, rum, banana liqueur, lime juice and ice in the jar of an electric blender, and blend at high speed for 20 or 30 seconds, until the banana is completely pulverized and the mixture smooth and frothy. Taste and add superfine sugar if necessary. Pour the Daiquiri into 2 chilled 8-ounce old-fashioned glasses and serve at once.

Peach Daiquiri

Combine the peach, rum, Cointreau, lime juice, sugar and ice in the jar of an electric blender, and blend at high speed for about 20 seconds, or until the peach is completely pulverized and the mixture smooth and frothy. Pour the Daiquiri into 2 chilled 6-ounce champagne glasses, and serve at once.

Cold Rum Soufflé (Jamaica)

Sprinkle the gelatin over ¼ cup of cold water and set it aside to soften. Meanwhile, with a whisk or a rotary or electric beater, beat the egg yolks and 4 tablespoons of the sugar together in a mixing bowl until the yolks are pale yellow and thick.

Pour the evaporated milk and the cornstarch mixture into a 2- to 3-quart enameled, stainless-steel or glass saucepan. Stir over low heat until the milk thickens enough to coat the spoon heavily. Remove the pan from the heat and, beating constantly, add the egg yolks and softened gelatin. Return the pan to low heat and continue to stir until the mixture is smooth and thick enough to coat the spoon heavily. Do not let the custard come near the boiling point or it will curdle; if it seems to be getting too hot, lift the pan off the stove to cool it. It must heat long enough, however, to thicken.

Strain the custard through a fine sieve into a large mixing bowl. Then warm the rum in a small pan over low heat. Off the heat, ignite the rum by touching a lighted kitchen match to it and shake the pan gently back and forth until the flame dies. Stir the rum and vanilla into the custard.

Wash and dry the whisk or beater; then, in a separate bowl, beat the egg whites until they are frothy. Add the remaining 4 tablespoons of sugar and the salt, and continue beating until the whites are stiff enough to stand in firm, unwavering peaks on the beater when it is lifted from the bowl.

Set the bowl of custard into a pot or another larger bowl filled with crushed ice or ice cubes and cold water. Stir the custard for 4 to 5 minutes, or until it is quite cold and begins to thicken. Scoop the egg whites over the custard and, with a rubber spatula, fold them together gently but thoroughly.

Ladle the soufflé into a 1-quart soufflé dish and refrigerate for at least 3 hours, or until firm and set.

To serve 2

1 cup canned pineapple juice
4 ounces light rum
½ ounce strained fresh lime juice
1 teaspoon Cointreau
Superfine sugar

To make 2 cocktails

½ medium-sized ripe banana, peeled and coarsely chopped
4 ounces light rum
½ ounce banana liqueur
½ ounce strained fresh lime juice
½ cup crushed or finely cracked ice
Superfine sugar

To serve 2

½ medium-sized firm ripe peach, peeled, seeded and cut into chunks
1½ ounces light rum
½ ounce Cointreau
1 ounce strained fresh lime juice
1 teaspoon superfine sugar
1 cup crushed or finely cracked ice

To serve 6

1 envelope unflavored gelatin
¼ cup cold water
4 egg yolks
8 tablespoons sugar
1 cup evaporated milk
1 tablespoon cornstarch combined with 2 tablespoons cold water
¼ cup dark rum
½ teaspoon vanilla extract
4 egg whites
A pinch of salt

To make 2 cocktails

4 ounces light rum
2 ounces strained fresh lime juice
2 teaspoons grenadine
1 teaspoon superfine sugar
3 or 4 ice cubes

To serve 2

5 ounces canned pineapple juice
4 ounces light rum
2 ounces bottled coconut syrup
2 ounces strained fresh lime juice
3 or 4 ice cubes

To serve 2

8 ounces medium-dark rum, such as
    Appleton Estates or Mount Gay
2 eggs, lightly beaten
2 teaspoons superfine sugar
2 dashes Angostura bitters
1 cup crushed or finely cracked ice
Freshly grated nutmeg

To serve 1

3 ounces medium-dark rum, such as
    Appleton Estates or Mount Gay
1 ounce strained fresh lime or lemon
    juice
1 teaspoon superfine sugar
2 or 3 ice cubes
6 ounces cold club soda
1 thin orange slice (optional)
1 maraschino cherry (optional)

To make about 1 quart

1 ounce fresh ginger root, in one
    piece (about 1½ inches long and
    1 inch in diameter), peeled and
    crushed with the flat side of a
    cleaver or large, heavy knife
The peel of 1 medium-sized lime
⅓ cup strained fresh lime juice
½ cup sugar
3¾ cups boiling water
1 teaspoon active dry yeast
¼ cup lukewarm water (110° to
    115°)

Bacardi

Combine the rum, lime juice, grenadine, sugar and ice cubes in a mixing glass, and place a bar shaker on top of the glass. Grasping the glass and shaker firmly together with both hands, shake them vigorously 9 or 10 times. Remove the shaker and place a strainer over the mixing glass. Pour the Bacardi into 2 chilled 4-ounce cocktail glasses, and serve at once.

Piña Colada

Combine the pineapple juice, rum, coconut syrup, lime juice and 3 or 4 ice cubes in a mixing glass, and place a bar shaker on top of the glass. Grasping the glass and shaker firmly together with both hands, shake them vigorously 9 or 10 times. Remove the shaker and place a strainer over the mixing glass. Pour the *piña colada* into 2 chilled 8-ounce highball glasses filled with ice cubes, and serve at once.

Rum Flip

Combine the rum, beaten eggs, sugar, bitters and ice in a mixing glass, and place a bar shaker on top of the glass. Grasping the glass and shaker firmly together with both hands, shake them vigorously 9 or 10 times. Remove the shaker and pour the rum flip, unstrained, into 2 chilled 10-ounce highball glasses. Grate a little nutmeg on top and serve at once.

Rum Collins

Place the rum, lime or lemon juice and sugar in a 14-ounce Tom Collins glass and stir with a bar spoon to dissolve the sugar. Add the ice cubes, fill the glass with cold soda, and stir briefly. Garnish the drink, if you like, with an orange slice and/or a cherry.

Ginger Beer (*Trinidad*)

Starting a week ahead, combine the ginger, lime peel, lime juice and sugar in a large ceramic bowl, and pour the boiling water over them. Stir until the sugar dissolves completely, then let the mixture cool to room temperature.

In a small bowl or cup, sprinkle the yeast over the lukewarm water. Let it stand for 2 or 3 minutes, then stir to dissolve the yeast completely. Set the bowl in a warm, draft-free place for about 5 minutes, or until the mixture begins to bubble and almost doubles in volume. (If no bubbles develop, discard the mixture and repeat the process with yeast from a fresh package.) Add the yeast to the ginger mixture and stir thoroughly.

Cover the bowl tightly with foil or plastic wrap, place it in a warm, draft-free place, and let the mixture ferment for a week. Stir the ginger beer every other day. After a week the mixture will be mildly carbonated.

Strain the ginger beer through a fine sieve and, using a funnel, pour the liquid into a 1-quart glass or ceramic bottle and cork it tightly. Let the beer ferment at room temperature for 3 or 4 days longer, then refrigerate until it is thoroughly chilled.

Serve the ginger beer in chilled tumblers, with or without ice cubes.

Cruzan Dawn

Combine the ice cubes, rum and vermouth in a 6-ounce old-fashioned glass and stir briefly with a bar spoon. Serve at once.

Coqui

RUM AND COCONUT CREAM DRINK

Combine the coconut cream, evaporated milk, egg yolks and vanilla in the jar of an electric blender, and blend at high speed for 30 seconds, or until the mixture is smooth. Add the dark rum, medium-dark rum and Cointreau, and blend for a few seconds longer. Refrigerate the *coqui* for 4 hours, or until it is thoroughly chilled.

To serve, pour the *coqui* into chilled parfait or punch glasses and sprinkle the top lightly with nutmeg.

Floating Island (Jamaica)

In a heavy 1- to 1½-quart saucepan, combine the egg yolks and sugar and beat with a whisk for 2 or 3 minutes, until they begin to thicken. Whisking constantly, slowly pour in the cream. Place the pan over low heat and, stirring constantly and deeply with a wooden spoon, simmer for 10 to 12 minutes, or until the custard is thick enough to coat the spoon. Do not allow the mixture to come anywhere near the boiling point or it may curdle. Let the custard cool to room temperature, then pour it into a serving dish about 8 or 9 inches in diameter, and refrigerate for at least 3 hours, or until it is completely chilled.

Just before serving, melt the guava jelly in a small skillet over low heat. Remove the pan from the stove. With a wire whisk or a rotary or electric beater, beat the egg whites until they are stiff enough to stand in unwavering peaks when the beater is lifted from the bowl. Beating constantly, pour the melted jelly slowly over the whites in a thin stream and continue to beat until the jelly and the whites are well blended.

To make the "floating islands" for which the dessert is named, scoop up about ¼ cup of the beaten egg whites in a ladle or serving spoon and drop it gently on the surface of the custard, spacing each island an inch or so from the other.

With the same beater, in a chilled bowl, beat the heavy cream until it begins to thicken. Add the confectioners' sugar and the rum, and continue beating until the cream is stiff but not buttery. Place a heaping teaspoon of the whipped cream on each of the islands and serve at once.

Caribbean Cocktail

Combine the pineapple juice, rum, lime juice, bitters and ice in a mixing jar, and place a bar shaker on top of the glass. Grasping the glass and shaker firmly together with both hands, shake them vigorously 9 or 10 times. Taste and add superfine sugar, if desired.

Remove the shaker and pour the cocktail, unstrained, into 2 chilled 8-ounce old-fashioned glasses. Add enough club soda to fill each glass to the brim. Grate a little nutmeg on top and serve at once.

To make 1 cocktail

2 or 3 ice cubes
2 ounces Cruzan Clipper rum, or substitute another medium-dark rum such as Appleton Estates or Mount Gay
1 ounce sweet vermouth

To make about 1 quart

1¼ cups coconut cream made from 1¼ cups coarsely chopped fresh coconut and 1¼ cups light cream (*see Recipe Booklet*)
¾ cup evaporated milk
2 egg yolks
1 teaspoon vanilla extract
1 cup dark rum
1 cup medium-dark rum, such as Appleton Estates or Mount Gay
2 tablespoons Cointreau or other orange-flavored liqueur
Freshly grated nutmeg

To serve 4

4 egg yolks
¼ cup sugar
2 cups light cream
⅓ cup guava jelly
2 egg whites
½ cup heavy cream
2 tablespoons confectioners' sugar
¼ cup dark rum

To serve 2

½ cup canned pineapple juice
2 ounces medium-dark rum, such as Appleton Estates or Mount Gay
1 tablespoon strained fresh lime juice
½ teaspoon Angostura bitters
1 cup crushed or finely cracked ice
Superfine sugar
Club soda
Freshly grated nutmeg

An Island Eating Guide

Here is a traveler's guide to eating in the Caribbean islands. It is not a comprehensive list of all available dishes but represents some of the local specialties, offered by specific islands, that have been enjoyed by those who worked on this book. Throughout the islands the fresh fruits, fish and shellfish are superb. The same vegetables (under many different names) grow and are prepared in various ways on most of the islands. Be sure to sample them and then ask for some of the dishes listed here. (Many of them are described in detail in the Glossary or the text; *see General Index.*)

Antigua, Montserrat, Nevis

Boija (coconut-cornmeal bread)
Funchi (cornmeal pudding)
Fish soup
Pepper pot soup
Stuffed crab back
Pumpkin soup
Salt fish with avocado or eggplant

Aruba and Curaçao

Keshy yena (stuffed Edam cheese)
Sopito (chowder)
Calas (bean fritters)
Tripe soup
Stobá (lamb or goat stew)
Boterkoek (butter cookies)
Funchi
Pastechi (meat-stuffed turnover)
Cachapas (cornmeal pancakes)
Ayacas (leaf-wrapped meat roll)

Barbados

Flying fish
Sea eggs (sea urchins)
Conch fritters
Jug-jug (cornmeal Christmas pudding)
Conkies (cornmeal dish)
Pudding and souse (blood sausage and head cheese)
Pepper pot stew
Turtle steak
Sea moss jelly

Cuba

Moros y Cristianos (beans and rice)
Black bean soup
Green plantain soup
Ajiacco (spicy meat stew)
Langosta enchilada (lobster in spicy sauce)
Picadillo (spicy ground meat)
Ropa vieja (shredded beef)

Dominica

Tannia soup (taro soup)
Mountain chicken (frogs' legs)

Dominican Republic

Carne mechada (stuffed beef roast)
Locrios (rice and meat stew)
Sopon (soupy rice casserole)
Pastelitos (meat-filled turnovers)
Mofongo (plantain balls)
Sancocho (meat stew)

Grenada and the Grenadines

Callaloo (soup with greens)
Flying fish
Carrot soup
Jacks and bluggoe soup (fish and banana soup)
West Indian plum pudding
Soursop fool
Breadfruit vichyssoise
Lambi souse (marinated conch)
Guava and nutmeg jellies
Turtle soup

Guadeloupe and Martinique

Sea eggs
Soupe de poisson (fish soup)
Land crab omelet
Acrats de morue (codfish fritters)
Blaff (fish in broth)
Court bouillon (fish in Creole sauce)
Colombo (curry)
Callaloo with crab
Hearts of palm vinaigrette
Crab stew
Pâté en pot (thick meat soup)
Boudin (blood sausage)

Haiti

Riz au djon djon (rice and black mushrooms)
Tassau de dinde (dried meat)
Griots de porc (fried pork)
Sauce Ti-Malice (tart sauce)
Codfish salad
Acrats de morue (codfish fritters)
Stuffed crab
Flambéed lobster
Crab stew

Jamaica

Pepper pot soup
Curried goat
Salmagundi (herring salad)
Salt fish and ackee
Baked black crab

Stamp and go (codfish fritters)
Brown fish stew
Duckunoo (sweet potato dessert)
Cassava cakes
Jerk pork (barbecued pig)
Matrimony (star apple and orange drink)
Akkra (pea or bean fritters)
Red pea soup
Pumpkin soup
Escovitch (marinated fish)
Mackerel run down (fritters)
Rice and peas

Puerto Rico

Land crab in the shell
Land crab pie with yucca
Baby goat fricassee
Ostiones (mangrove oysters)
Surrulitos (corn-and-cheese sticks)
Mofongo con chicharron (plantain with cracklings)
Arroz con pollo (chicken and rice)
Asapao (chicken stew)
Pasteles (leaf-wrapped meat rolls)
Piononos (meat-stuffed plantains)

St. Martin (France and the Netherlands)

Steak Creole
Soupe de poisson

St. Vincent

Stewed shark
Breadfruit sweets
Callaloo
Arrowroot sponge

Trinidad and Tobago

Rice and peas
Sancoche
Pepper pot
Pudding and souse
Pelaus (rice with meat or seafood)
Mangrove oysters
Roti (Indian bread with various fillings)
Shark meat on hops bread
Roast pork with rice and red beans

Virgin Islands

Meat patty
Callaloo
Salt fish and rice
Herring gundy (herring salad)
Fish chowder
Tannia soup
Turtle or lobster stew
Conch salad

Glossary

ACCRA (akkra, akra): Originally a West African fritter, made throughout the islands. The traditional Jamaican akkra is a fritter made of ground blackeyed peas or soybeans; the same thing is known as *cala* on the Dutch Islands. Accras are also made of a heavy batter into which a variety of ingredients are mixed, salt cod being the most popular. This combination is called stamp and go in Jamaica, *acrat de morue* in the French islands and *bacalaitos* in Puerto Rico.

ACHIOTE: *See* ANNATTO.

AKEE (ackee): Oblong or egg-shaped fruit of an evergreen tree widely cultivated in Jamaica. The scarlet pod encloses cream-colored flesh whose bland texture and taste is often compared to scrambled eggs. It is traditionally served in Jamaica with salt fish. Available canned in some Latin American markets.

ALLSPICE (pimento): Dark-brown berries of an evergreen tree native to the West Indies. The berries resemble smooth oversized peppercorns and their aroma and flavor suggest a blend of cloves, cinnamon and nutmeg. The world's largest producer of allspice is Jamaica, where it is called pimento, not to be confused with pimiento, which is a kind of *Capsicum* pepper.

ALLSPICE OIL: Oil extracted from the leaves of the allspice tree and used in making a Jamaican liqueur called Pimento Dram.

ANNATTO (*achiote*): Rusty-red dried seed of a tropical American tree. It is used primarily to color cooking oil or lard a bright orange yellow, but also lends a delicate flavor. Available in Latin American and some Oriental markets.

APIO (*arracacha*): Root of a tropical plant popular in the Caribbean, used as a starchy vegetable and as an ingredient in SANCOCHO. Available in some Latin American markets.

ARROWROOT: Starch obtained from the roots of a plant native to tropical America. Finely ground to the consistency of cornstarch, it is used as a flavorless thickening agent in light sauces and glazes.

ASAPAO: The word literally means "soupy" in Spanish and is used to describe a thin stew made with rice and with chicken, meat or fish; a traditional Puerto Rican dish.

BACALAO: Spanish for salt cod.

BAKES: Fried baking-powder biscuits, a specialty of Trinidad.

BAY RUM: Evergreen tree related to myrtle and allspice, native to the West Indies. The spirit distilled from its leaves is used in cosmetics. The small dark berries, also called malagueta pepper, are used in a way similar to ALLSPICE.

BEANS: Islanders use the term peas (or *pois*) for both beans and peas of various kinds. For instance, the Haitian *riz et pois* is a dish of rice and red kidney beans. The beans used in the recipes in this book are dried and available in most groceries. *See* GANDULES, HABICHUELAS, FRIJOL NEGRO.

BLAFF: Fresh fish poached in a clear stock seasoned with hot peppers. Traditional in the French islands.

BREADFRUIT: Round or oblong fruit with a tough, yellowish-green and bumpy or prickly skin. It may measure up to 8 inches in diameter and weigh as much as 10 pounds. The flesh is cream-colored and has a flavor and texture that is often compared to grainy bread. It is eaten like a starchy vegetable, boiled, roasted or fried. Available in some Latin American markets.

CALABAZA (West Indian pumpkin, green pumpkin): Pumpkins belong to the squash family, and in most parts of the Caribbean the term calabaza, or pumpkin, is used to mean a squash. Sizes, shapes and skin coloring vary, but calabazas usually have firm yellow flesh and a delicate flavor somewhat like that of Hubbard or butternut squash. Available in some Latin American markets. *(See picture, page 50.)*

CALLALOO: Caribbean-wide soup made with callaloo greens and crab meat. The word may also be used to mean CALLALOO GREENS.

CALLALOO GREENS: The term is used both for the young leaves of the DASHEEN or TARO plant and for the Oriental potherbs known as Chinese spinach. Available in some Latin American markets.

CAPSICUM: *See* PEPPERS.

CARAMBOLA: A tropical fruit, yellow green in color and star-shaped in cross section; it is about 4 inches long. It has a thin, waxy rind and a juicy, mild-tasting flesh with smooth brown seeds. Best eaten raw or used in iced drinks.

CASHEW: Evergreen tree and shrub native to the West Indies. It bears a tart, reddish, pear-shaped cashew apple, from the bottom of which grows the kidney-shaped nut, edible only when roasted.

CASSAREEP: Juice squeezed from fresh grated cassava root, which is boiled down and used as a thickening agent and a bitter-sweet flavoring in Trinidadian PEPPER POT.

CASSAVA (manioc, yuca, mandioca): Long, irregularly shaped root at least 2 inches in diameter with a dark-brown rough barklike skin and hard white starchy flesh. The bitter variety is poisonous until cooked. It is the base for tapioca and manioc meal, but in the Caribbean is chiefly used to make starch. The root used in the recipes in this book is the sweet variety, which is available year round in most Latin American and Puerto Rican groceries. *(See picture, page 50.)* Refrigerated, the root will keep safely for 2 or 3 weeks.

CHAYOTE: *See* CHRISTOPHENE.

CHERIMOYA: Fruit of a small tree native to the West Indies. Varieties differ widely; most are about the size of a grapefruit, but some weigh as much as 15 or 16 pounds. The skin is soft, greenish brown and bumpy; the flesh is white, juicy and sweet. Available in the United States in summer in fancy groceries and Latin American markets.

CHICHARRONES: Fried pork cracklings available packaged in most Latin American markets.

CHILIES: *See* PEPPERS.

CHOCHO: *See* CHRISTOPHENE.

CHORIZO (Spanish sausage): Lightly smoked sausage of coarsely chopped pork, seasoned with garlic, sweet red pepper and hot paprika. Available in 4-inch links or canned (packed in lard) at Latin American or Spanish groceries. The link variety will keep for several weeks in the refrigerator, but should not be frozen.

CHRISTOPHENE (*chayote*, chocho): Tropical squash, round or pear-shaped, ranging from white to dark green; 3 to 8 inches long. It may be smooth or corrugated and is sometimes covered with soft spines. The firm, crisp flesh is more delicate in flavor than summer squash. Available in some Latin American markets the year round. Keeps for about a week in the refrigerator. *(See*

picture, page 50.)

CILANTRO: *See* CORIANDER.

COCIDO: Spanish word for stew.

CONCH (lambi): A large edible mollusk with a beautiful spiral shell found throughout the islands; its firm flesh is generally tenderized by pounding before being served in salads or chowders. Usually pronounced "conk" in the Caribbean.

CONKIES: Cornmeal mixed with chopped meat, raisins, coconut and spices, wrapped and cooked in envelopes of banana leaves. A traditional Barbadian specialty.

CORIANDER (*cilantro, culantro*, Chinese parsley): Aromatic herb that resembles flat-leaf parsley in appearance, but has a much more pungent flavor. It is sold fresh by the bunch in Latin American stores and Chinese markets. Do not wash the leaves or remove the roots before storing; it will keep for about a week if refrigerated in a plastic bag.

COURT BOUILLON: In the French islands of the Caribbean, the term describes a traditional recipe for poached fish. Not to be confused with the classic court bouillon of French cooking: the liquid in which fish or other food is poached.

CRAPAUD: French for the large frog found on Dominica and Montserrat, where it is also called mountain chicken and considered a delicacy.

CUMIN SEED: Yellowish-brown seed of a plant of the parsley family. Shaped like a miniature corn kernel, it is aromatic and reminiscent of caraway. Often used in curries. Available whole or ground.

CURAÇAO: Liqueur produced in the Dutch islands from the peel of bitter oranges.

DASHEEN: *See* TARO.

DJON DJON: Tiny Haitian mushrooms with caps considerably smaller than a dime. When cooked, they give off a dark brownish-black liquid and color. Dried European mushrooms can be substituted.

ESCABECHE: The word literally means "pickled" and is used to describe a Spanish and Portuguese method of preparing fish, seafood, poultry or game birds. Recipes vary, but typically the food is cooked and then pickled in a vinegar marinade.

ESCOVITCH: The Jamaican version

of ESCABECHE, made with fish that is browned in oil, then immersed in a vinegar marinade.

FARINE: On the French islands, a shortened form of *farine de manioc,* or cassava meal.

FLOATS: Fried yeast buns, a specialty of Trinidad. Traditionally served with codfish ACCRAS.

FRIJOL NEGRO (black bean, turtle bean): Small, flat charcoal-colored bean no more than ½ inch long. It is a native of the Americas and related to the common navy and kidney bean. Available dried in most groceries. *See* BEANS.

FRUTA BOMBA: Cuban name for PAPAYA.

FUNCHI (fungee): Cornmeal pudding, like Italian *polenta.*

GANDULES: Spanish name for PIGEON PEAS. *See* BEANS.

GINGER ROOT: Gnarled brown root with a moist firm yellow flesh. It is about 3 inches long with a more pungent flavor than dried ginger. Available in Latin American and Chinese markets year round. Wrapped in a plastic bag and refrigerated, the fresh root will keep for 2 or 3 weeks.

GUAVA: Oval or somewhat pear-shaped fruit of an evergreen tree native to tropical America. Guavas are usually from 2 to 5 inches in diameter, and their skin is thin and a pale yellow. The flesh varies from white through shades of salmon to deep pink, according to type; inside is a mass of small hard seeds. Guavas taste sweet and are eaten raw or stewed. They are also made into jams, jellies and guava paste, a rich preserve. These are often eaten in the islands with cream cheese. Canned guava shells, guava paste and guava jelly are available in most Latin American markets and some better groceries.

GUAVA JELLY: Clear, very firm jelly made from ripe guavas. At its best it is a deep red wine color and retains the characteristic musky sweetness of the fruit.

HABICHUELAS: Spanish name for red kidney beans. *See* BEANS.

JACK FRUIT (*jaquier, jaca*): Oblong fruit with green, lumpy skin, closely related to the breadfruit but enormous—it sometimes weighs as much as 70

pounds. Though the fruit is malodorous, its soft flaky yellowish pulp is sweet, and can be eaten raw or cooked; it is especially popular in curries. The large white seeds inside taste somewhat like chestnuts when roasted. Available occasionally in Latin American markets.

KACHOURI: Deep-fried fritter of Indian origin made with chick-pea meal and chopped scallions.

KESHY YENA: The term, from the Spanish, means, literally, "stuffed cheese." A specialty of the Dutch islands, it is made with Edam cheese and various mixtures of meat, poultry, fish or seafood. Traditionally the cheese is hollowed out, stuffed and baked.

LANGOSTA (*langouste*): Spiny lobster, native to Caribbean waters, highly prized for the meat of its tail. It lacks the large claws of the northern lobster.

LECHOSA: Spanish word for PAPAYA.

LOQUAT: Small yellow-orange pitted fruit the size of an apricot with the flavor of a peach. Available canned in Latin American markets and Oriental stores.

MACE: *See* NUTMEG.

MALAGUETA PEPPER: Name given to the small dark berry of the bay rum tree used in such dishes as BLAFF. *See* BAY RUM.

MALANGA: Member of the TARO family.

MAMEY APPLE: Large tropical fruit, related to the mango, with thick brown skin and orange-red sweet pulp that can be eaten raw or cooked.

MANGO: Fruit of an evergreen tree taken from India to the West Indies about 200 years ago. Mangoes range from plum-sized varieties to those weighing 2 or 3 pounds. Usually oval in shape. The skin is smooth and yellow or yellowish green, often with a splotch of scarlet; the stone inside is long and flat. When ripe, the yellow flesh is sweet and juicy. Available in better fruit stores and Latin American markets between April and September. (*See page 116.*)

MANIOC: *See* CASSAVA.

MOFONGO: Dish of the Spanish-speaking islands made from highly seasoned boiled, mashed half-ripened plantains.

NASEBERRY (sapodilla): Tropical fruit about 3 inches in diameter with a brown rough skin and a sweet brownish-purple pulp. Available in better fruit stores and Latin American markets in summer.

NUTMEG: Brown oval seed of the fruit of the nutmeg tree, which flourishes on Grenada. When ripe, the nutmeg is covered with a thin black shell surrounded by a red lacy network, or aril, which is mace. Covering both is a thick fleshy pericarp that can be used to make jelly or ice cream. Both nutmeg and mace are fragrant and slightly bitter, but mace has a more pronounced aroma and flavor. Mace is generally available ground; nutmeg is available whole or ground.

OTAHEITE APPLE: *See* POMERAC.

PALM HEARTS: Tender ivory-colored hearts or shoots of palm obtained from the core at the crown or top of the palm tree. Used as a vegetable or salad ingredient. Available canned in Latin American markets and most better groceries.

PAPAYA (pawpaw, *lechosa, fruta bomba*): Large cylindrical melonlike fruit of a tree native to the West Indies. Papayas range from 3 to 20 inches in length and may weigh as much as 10 pounds. The skin is thin and smooth and, when the fruit is ripe, both skin and flesh are orange yellow to deep orange; inside is a mass of small blackish seeds. Papaya flesh is rather sweet, with a slight musky taste, and is eaten raw or used in cooking. When green, the fruit is made into chutney. Available ripe and green in fine fruit stores, Latin American markets and better supermarkets. (*See page 116.*)

PASTELES (*ayacas*): Puerto Rican specialty made of a stuffing of meats with raisins, olives, capers, almonds in cornmeal or mashed plantain wrapped in a plantain leaf and steamed. Found in all Spanish-speaking islands.

PASTELITOS (*pastelillos, pastechi,* patty): Small meat-filled turnovers baked in a pastry crust.

PÂTÉ EN POT: Traditional dish of the French islands; a very thick soup made of finely chopped lamb and innards and vegetables.

PAWPAW: Name for PAPAYA on English-speaking islands.

PELAU (pilaf, pilau): An Indian dish consisting of rice cooked with

meat, fowl, fish or seafood.

PEPPER POT: In Trinidad, a highly seasoned stew made with meat, game or fowl, and thickened and flavored with CASSAREEP. In Jamaica, a spicy soup made with meat or fowl and vegetables.

PEPPERS: Every podded pepper —sweet, pungent or hot—is a member of the *Capsicum* family and a native of the New World. Hot peppers, or chilies, vary enormously in shape, color, size and degree of hotness. Most ripen from green through orange yellow to red; color does not indicate pungency, but fully ripened ones may have a more pronounced flavor. Chilies lose their flavor quickly and must be stored in the refrigerator. They are available in Latin American markets and often in other groceries. (*Caution: see page 46.*)

PICADILLO: Highly seasoned hashlike meat dish made with raw ground beef or cooked beef. The Cuban version, with olives and raisins, is especially famous.

PICKAPEPPA: Brand name of two Jamaican sauces: Pickapeppa sauce, a sweet mango sauce, and Pickapeppa hot pepper sauce, a hot chili sauce resembling Tabasco.

PIGEON PEAS (*gandules,* goongoo or gunga peas): Round seeds the size of a small garden pea. Young pigeon peas may be eaten green, but the seed is usually used mature and dry, when it is brownish in color with flecks of gray. Canned green pigeon peas are sometimes available in Latin American markets; the dried variety is generally available. *See* BEANS.

PIMENTO: *See* ALLSPICE.

PIONONOS: Puerto Rico's deep-fried plantain rings filled with spiced ground beef.

PLANTAIN (*plátano*): Fruit of the banana family and similar in shape, but larger and not so sweet; must be cooked before eating. Available all year in Latin American markets in all degrees of ripeness from green to yellow to dark brown. Plantains ripen at room temperature, but may be kept at a desired stage for 2 or 3 days if refrigerated.

POLOURI: Small fritter of Indian origin made with split-pea meal.

POMELO: *See* SHADDOCK.

POMERAC (Otaheite apple): pear-shaped red fruit about 3 to 4 inches long with white flesh, eaten raw or cooked and made into jams.

ROSELLE (*rosella*): See SORREL.
ROTI: Flat round unleavened bread of Indian origin.

SAHINA: Deep-fried fritter of Indian origin made from TARO leaves and split-pea meal.
SANCOCHO (*sancoche*): Stew of the Spanish-speaking islands made with a variety of meats and vegetables.
SAPODILLO: See NASEBERRY.
SEA EGG: Island name for a white sea urchin, the ovaries of which are considered a delicacy.
SHADDOCK (pomelo): Thick-skinned citrus fruit, from which the grapefruit was developed, with sharp-tasting, reddish flesh; introduced into the islands in the 17th Century.
SHROB (shrub): Liqueur made on the French islands from rum and the peel of bitter oranges.
SOFRITO: The term literally means lightly fried and describes a basic sauce used in Spanish and island cooking. Always made with either onions or garlic and often with both, a *sofrito* usually contains tomatoes, peppers, herbs, spices and ham. Its ingredients are chopped, then cooked in oil.
SOPITO: A creamy fish chowder made with coconut milk; a specialty of the Dutch islands.
SORREL (roselle, *rosella, flor de Jamaica*): Tropical flower grown throughout the islands. Its fleshy sepal (the leaflike calyx or cup beneath the blossom) has a faintly acid taste and is used in making drinks, jams, jellies and sauces. Available dried in Latin American markets.
SOURSOP: Large dark-green heart-shaped fruit with spiny skin. Its pithy flesh has black seeds and is slightly acid. Often made into a drink or ice cream.
STAMP AND GO: Jamaican fried codfish cakes; made of a heavy batter flavored with annatto, onions and chilies.
SURULLITOS: Puerto Rican fried cornmeal-and-cheese sticks.
SWEET POTATO (*boniatos*): Tuberous vegetable native to the Americas. Its skin color ranges from nearly white to brown, pink, magenta and even purple. The flesh may be white, yellow, orange or purple. Yellow- and orange-fleshed varieties are popular in the United States and are available in most groceries; white sweet potatoes may be found in Latin American markets. Often confused with YAM.

TAMARIND: Brown pulp of the seed pod of a tree cultivated throughout the tropics; used for flavoring. The pod is brittle, cinnamon-colored and shaped somewhat like a pea pod, but is up to 8 inches long. The pulp has a somewhat acid taste.
TANGELO: Hybrid fruit created in the 1890s by crossing a tangerine with grapefruit. It can be round or pear-shaped, with rough or smooth orange-colored skin. The flesh of some is rather acid tasting; others are sweeter. Available in better fruit stores and Latin American markets in the fall and early winter.
TARO (dasheen, tannia, malanga, elephant's ear, *yautía*): Tuberous edible plant root, about the size of a large baking potato with dark-brown barklike skin (*see picture, page 50*). Taro's firm flesh can be white, green, gray or violet and has a somewhat nutty taste. The word taro can also refer to the leaves of the plant. These, also known as CALLALOO and elephant's ears, are green, somewhat heart-shaped, and may be as much as 3 feet long; their flavor is faintly bitter and reminiscent of spinach. Leaves and roots are available year round in Latin American and Oriental markets and in some groceries, especially in the Southeastern United States.

UGLI: A thick-skinned hybrid citrus fruit that was developed on Jamaica. A cross of grapefruit, orange and tangerine, it is called ugli because of its lumpy appearance.

WEST INDIAN PUMPKIN: See CALABAZA.

YAM: Large tropical tuberous vegetable that occasionally may weigh as much as 100 pounds. It has a thick, somewhat hairy skin (*see picture, page 50*). The flesh may be white, yellow or red and is starchy and slightly sweet. Available in Latin American markets. (In the United States the terms yam and Louisiana yam are often erroneously applied to the soft orange-colored SWEET POTATO; they do not belong to the same botanical family.)

Mail-Order Sources

The following stores, grouped by region, accept mail orders for canned and dried Caribbean ingredients. Because policies differ and managements change, check with the store nearest you to determine what it has in stock, the current prices, and how best to buy the items you are interested in. Some stores require a minimum of $5.00 on mail orders.

East

Pena's Spanish Store
1636 17th St., N.W.
Washington, D.C. 20009

Cardullo's Gourmet Shop
6 Brattle St.
Cambridge, Mass. 02138

Casa Moneo Spanish Imports
210 W. 14th St.
New York, N.Y. 10011

Heintzelman's
1128 Northway Mall
Pittsburgh, Pa. 15237

Midwest

La Preferida Inc.
177-181 W. South Water Market
Chicago, Ill. 60608

Marshall Field & Co.
111 N. State St.
Chicago, Ill. 60690

El-Nopal Food Market
544 N. Highland Ave.
Indianapolis, Ind. 46202

Swiss Colony
Lindale Plaza
Cedar Rapids, Iowa 53402

Continental Gourmet Shop
210 S. Woodward Ave.
Birmingham, Mich. 48010

Delmar & Co.
501 Monroe Ave.
Detroit, Mich. 48226

La Paloma—Tenorio & Co.
2620 Bagley Ave.
Detroit, Mich. 48216

The Market Basket
3205 W. McNichols Rd.
Detroit, Mich. 48221

Heidi's Around the World Food Shop
1149 S. Brentwood Blvd.
St. Louis. Mo. 63117

Spanish & American Food Market
7001 Wade Park Ave.
Cleveland, Ohio 44103

South

The Delicatessen, Burdine's
Dadeland Shopping Center
Miami, Fla. 33156

Imperial Supermarket
5175 S.W. Eighth St.
Miami, Fla. 33134

Epicure Markets
1656 Alton Rd.
Miami Beach, Fla. 33139

Central Grocery
923 Decatur St.
New Orleans, La. 70116

Progress Grocery
915 Decatur St.
New Orleans, La. 70116

Morris Zager
230 Fourth Ave. N.
Nashville, Tenn. 37219

Antone's Import Company
Box 3352
Houston, Tex. 77001

Jim Jamail and Son
3114 Kirby Dr.
Houston, Tex. 77006

Pier L Imports
5403 South Rice Ave.
Houston, Tex. 77006

West

Del Rey Spanish Foods
Central Market, Stall A-7
317 S. Broadway
Los Angeles, Calif. 90013

Jurgenson's
1071 Glendon Ave.
Los Angeles, Calif. 90024

Casa Lucas Market
2934 24th St.
San Francisco, Calif. 94110

Mi Rancho Market
3365 20th St.
San Francisco, Calif. 94110

American Tea, Coffee & Spice Co.
1511 Champa St.
Denver, Colo. 80202

Canada

Woodward's
Chinook Center
Calgary 9, Alberta

S. Enkin Incorporated
1201 St. Lawrence St.
Montreal 129, Quebec

Pirri's Dixieland Market
1108 Pharmacy Ave.
Scarborough 731, Ontario

Recipe Index: English NOTE: An R preceding a page refers to the Recipe Booklet.

Recipe Index: Caribbean

General Index

Numerals in italics indicate a photograph or drawing of the subject mentioned.

Credits and Acknowledgments

The sources for the illustrations in this book are given below. Credits for the pictures from left to right are separated by commas, from top to bottom by dashes. All photographs are by Richard Meek except: page 4—top right Salvatore Fragliossi for SPORTS ILLUSTRATED —Charles Phillips, Phillip Dowell. 12,13—Map by Mary Sherman. 14,15—Michael Rougier. 36—Drawing by John Frederick. 38,39—Drawings by Robert Geissman. 50 —Manuel Millan. 55—Drawing by Robert Geissman. 86,87—Derek Bayes courtesy the Trustees of the British Museum. 106—Richard Meek courtesy Hart Preston Collection. 119—Drawings by Robert Geissman. 158 —Michael Rougier. 189—Michael Rougier.

For their help in the production of this book, the editors wish to thank the following: on *Antigua:* William DeCoudres, The Hawksbill; Gwendolyn Tongue, Government Supervisor of Home Economics; on *Barbados:* Clenell Bynoe, Barbados Tourist Board; *in California:* Louise Hartmann, Dole Pineapple Co., San Jose; John Scelsa, Calpac Corp., Santa Ana; on *Curaçao:* Sarita Brandão; Edsel Jesurun, Curaçao Tourist Board; Delia Maduro; Olga and Alfred Morón; Bep Newton; *in Detroit:* Sister Karen Kennelly; on *Dominica:* Phyllis and Robert Allfrey; *in the Dominican Republic:* Armando D'Alessandro; Adria de Manón; on *Grenada:* Lloyd Charles; Raymond Harford, Grenada Nutmeg Assn.; Alan Krassner; Gertrude Protain, Grenada Tourist Board; on *Guadeloupe:* Robert Chéenne, Roger Fortuné, Guadeloupe Tourist Board; Jeanette Reignard; *in Ithaca, New York:* Dr. Robert Smock, Cornell University; on *Jamaica:* Doreen Kirakadie and Desmond Henry, Jamaica Festival Office; Myrtha Swire, Jamaica Tourist Board; *in Litchfield, Conn.:* the White Flower Farm; on *Martinique:* Jacques Alexandre, Association of Sugar Cane Planters and Manufacturers; Robert S. Barrett IV, U.S. Consul; Denise and Max Elizé; *in New York City:* The American Sugar Assn.; Sam Aaron, Sherry Lehmann Inc.; Alexis Bespaloff; Dorothy Bowes; British Overseas Airways; Dennis Brown, The Bronx Botanical Gardens; Bessie Byam; Pearl Cameron, Trinidad and Tobago Tourist Board; Byron Clement, French Government Tourist Office; Norman Cooper, Rums of Puerto Rico; Peter Davis, Jamaica Arms Restaurant; Frank Doherty, Ross Associates; Eastern Airlines; Pierre Edugene; Charles Elliott; Andrew Geller, Raymond Loewy-William Snaith Inc.; Georg Jensen; Mary George; Hammacher Schlemmer; Joseph Hidalgo, U.S. Dept. of Agriculture; Macy's; Vincent Manchusi; Dorothy Newman; Pan American Airways; Mme. de la Pine, French Government Cultural Service; Plummer McCutcheon; Lewis Politi, New York Botanical Gardens; The Pottery Barn; RMH International; Frederick Ruoff, Jamaica Tourist Office; Nicole Scott; Lyonelle Singer; Dr. C. Lavitt Smith, The Museum of Natural History; John Squire, The Rock Corporation; Mirtha Stengel; Lillian Stuckey, Bernard Lewis Agency; Carmen and Luis Valldejuli; Hendriena van Hoboken, Curaçao Tourist Board; Robert C. Warner, Robert F. Warner Inc.; José Wilson; *on Puerto Rico:* Ellen Hawes; Roberto Huyke and Dr. Jesús Vélez-Fortuño, The University of Puerto Rico; *on St. Croix:* Walter Lewisohn, The St. Croix Landmarks Society; *on Trinidad and Tobago:* Sylvia Hunte; Dr. Joan Kazim; Therese Mills; Naomi Osborne, U.N. Information Center; Derek Walcott; *in Washington, D.C.:* The Distilled Spirits Institute; Norbert D. Roche, U.S. Treasury Department; William Roland, The United Fresh Fruit and Vegetable Assn.; Gordon Webb, U.S. Department of Agriculture.

Sources consulted in the production of this book include: *The Making of the West Indies* by Augier, Hall, Gordon and Reckford; Longmans, London. *Sources of West Indian History* by Augier and Gordon; Longmans, London. *The Story of Sugar* by Aykroyd; Quadrangle Books, Chicago. *History of the British West Indies* by Burns; Allen and Unwin, London. *Jamaica Talk* by Cassidy; Macmillan, New York. *West Indian Cookery* by Clark; Nelson, Edinburgh. *The Memoirs of Père Labat* tr. by Eaden; Constable, London. *The Traveller's Tree* by Fermor; Harper and Row, New York. *The World of Vegetable Cookery* by Hawkes; Simon and Schuster, New York. *Two Years in the French West Indies* by Hearn; Harper and Row, New York. *The Barbados Book* by Lynch; Toplinger, New York. *The West Indian Scene* by Percy; Van Nostrand, New York. *The Caribbean* by Rodman; Hawthorn, New York. *Cooking the Caribbean Way* by Slater; Paul Hamlyn, London. *Caribbean Cook Book* by Springer; Evans, New York. *Rum, Romance and Rebellion* by Taussig; Minton Balch, New York. *Caribbean Here and Now* by Ullman and Dinhofer; Macmillan, New York. *The Art of Caribbean Cookery* by Valldejuli; Doubleday, New York. *Journal of a Lady of Quality, 1774-1776* ed. by Walker; Yale University Press, New Haven. *Documents of West Indian History* by Williams; PNM Publishing, Trinidad.

x

PRODUCTION STAFF FOR TIME INCORPORATED

John L. Hallenbeck (Vice President and Director of Production), Robert E. Foy and Caroline Ferri. Text photocomposed under the direction of Albert J. Dunn